Great
Directors
at Work

GREAT DIRECTORS AT WORK,
STANISLAVSKY, BRECHT, KAZAN, BROOK

David Richard Jones

UNIVERSITY OF CALIFORNIA PRESS

Berkeley   Los Angeles   London

University of California Press
Berkeley and Los Angeles, California

University of California Press, Ltd.
London, England

© 1986 by
The Regents of the University of California

Library of Congress Cataloging in Publication Data

Jones, David Richard.
   Great directors at work.

   Includes index.
   1. Theater—Production and direction.   2. Theatrical
producers and directors—Biography.   3. Stanislavsky,
Konstantin, 1863–1938.   4. Brecht, Bertolt, 1898–1956—
Knowledge—Performing arts.   5. Kazan, Elia.   6. Brook,
Peter.   7. Chekhov, Anton Pavlovich, 1860–1904. Chaika.
8. Brecht, Bertolt, 1898–1956. Mutter Courage und ihre
Kinder.   9. Williams, Tennessee, 1911–1983. A Streetcar
Named Desire.   10. Weiss, Peter, 1916–1982. Die Verfolgung
und Ermordung Jean Paul Marats.   I.   Title.
PN2053.J62   1985   792'.0233'0922   [B]   84-16171
ISBN 0-520-04601-3

Printed in the United States of America

1   2   3   4   5   6   7   8   9

For Susan Jones

" . . . whose youth and freshness
Wrinkles Apollo's, and makes pale the morning."

Contents

Acknowledgments

A number of individuals helped me in realizing this book, and I acknowledge them here with the greatest pleasure. Gus Blaisdell provided a conversational ground remarkably fertile considering his sometime antitheatrical prejudice. William C. Dowling gave a push when I needed it. Robert Holzapfel checked me on German. Natalie Chrohn Schmitt read a chapter, and both her enthusiasm and her skepticism were bracing. James Linnell helped at several turns, particularly with his unpublished thesis on Brecht's early productions. Long before I began planning this book, Robert Hartung gave me the chance to direct *Mother Courage and Her Children*. William Melnitz read an earlier version of this book with such enthusiasm that he changed its fate. Ellen Dowling and William Weldon gave food and shelter along the research route and let me look in on their work with *A Streetcar Named Desire*. Luckily for me, Doris Kretschmer at the University of California Press followed her hunch and saw my work through to publication. Mary Lamprech and Lydia Duncan improved the prose and the thought. Susan Jones, Mort Jones, and Sam Jones gave me the encouragement that writers and directors need most from the ones they love most.

For permission to reproduce photographs, I must thank Barbara Brecht-Schall and Morris Newcombe. The photograph from Konstantin Stanislavsky's *The Seagull Produced by Stanislavsky* is reproduced with the permission of the publisher, Theatre Arts Books, 153 Waverly Place, New York, N.Y. 10014. The photograph of *Streetcar* was taken by Eileen Darby for Graphic House.

Finally, thanks to the actors and directors who either worked with me on productions of these plays or allowed me to view their productions. The full list of these true companions is too lengthy for inclusion here, but it is headed by Joy Bell Tauber, Marilyn K. Pittman, Stuart Dyson, Doris Drucker Duhigg, and Bryan Burdick.

Introduction

My subject is theatre directing in four internationally famous instances. The four directors—Konstantin Stanislavsky, Bertolt Brecht, Elia Kazan, and Peter Brook—all were monarchs of the profession in their time. Without their work, theatre in the twentieth century—so often called "the century of the director"—would have a radically different shape and meaning. The four men are also among the dozen or so modern directors whose theatrical achievements have become culture phenomena. In histories, theories, hagiographies, and polemics, these directors are conferred classic stature, as are the four plays on which they worked. Chekhov's *The Seagull,* Brecht's *Mother Courage and Her Children,* and Williams's *A Streetcar Named Desire* have long been recognized, in the theatre and in the study, as masterpieces. They are anthologized, quoted, taught, parodied, read, and produced constantly and globally. The culturally conservative might question the presence of *Marat/Sade* in such august company, but Peter Weiss's play stands every chance of figuring in Western repertories, classroom study, and theatrical histories until well into the twenty-first century. In their quite different ways, these are all classics of that Western drama which is part of our immediate heritage.

The intersections of these men with these plays are historical highlights of our modern theatre. In 1898 *The Seagull* confirmed the artistic seriousness of the Moscow Art Theatre's tentative first season, began the celebrated Stanislavsky–Chekhov collaboration, and was an early, revolutionary example of realistic style. Just as historic was the *Mother Courage* that Brecht developed over 1948–1951. First as his decisive move to dominate post–Nazi German theatre, then as the keystone of the Berlin Ensemble repertory, this *Courage* prophesied that Brecht would be the teacher and Brechtism the teaching to dominate the theatre of the third quarter of the twentieth century. Kazan's *Streetcar* (1947) is another multifaceted chapter. This production established the stardom of Jessica Tandy and Marlon Brando, endorsed the greatness of Tennessee Williams, elevated Kazan to the apex of American directing, and spurred the general recognition—reinforced fourteen months later by Kazan's direction of Arthur Miller's *Death of a Salesman*—that American theatre had reached a remarkable new maturity of psychological realism. And *Marat/Sade?* What would the theatre of the 1960s have been without this German play written by a Swedish resident about the French Revolution and transformed by a British director into a work that reached fruition in America? What would the era's theatre have been without the paired influences of Brecht and Artaud so popularized by *Marat/Sade* and by Peter Brook's other work?

These four directors are vital to modern directing history because they are all intellectual figures, artists full of ideas about work and art and culture. All of them have contributed mightily, even when inadvertently, to the progressive intellectualization of theatre and directing that is a marked feature of our time. Because his ideas are sometimes derivative, often mystical, and always debatable, Brook's reputation as a theatre intellectual is wobbly. Nonetheless, it is an international reputation, won by virtue of his unceasingly radical approach to whatever ideas he argues. Particularly in print, Elia Kazan appears the least theoretical or philosophically inclined of the four, but as one of America's foremost Stanislavskians during the 1940s and 1950s, he influenced thousands of contemporaries through theatre, film, and the Actors Studio he helped found. As I write this, he is at work on a book about directing that may enable us to admire his capacities in yet another field. About Brecht's intellectual standing there is little doubt. For decades his strong analytical-critical faculties almost overshadowed his literary-poetic and theatrical abilities, to the detriment of his broader reputation. But Brecht the director proposes the same program as Brecht the theorist: a theatre of point of view, with thinking actors, interpretive directors, and audiences awakened to their stake in life. On either side of the Brechtian half-curtain, using the mind should be both a necessity and a pleasure. Finally, Stanislavsky pioneered the role of modern theatre-intellectual —a researcher-experimenter-theorizer trying to rationalize the theatre's irregular, highly unconscious practices to the scientific age. By analogy, he is the theatre's Freud, its Mendel. These four are also a good study in style. So aggressive was each in this aspect of directing that each was sometimes called "only" a stylist, "merely" a stylist, as if such reviews were a countersign on the director's passport to fame. Their careers show not only stylistic force but stylistic contradiction and variety. Stanislavsky is known as the father of modern realistic theatre and appears in that guise here, but during his lifetime he had a wider and longer reputation as a sensationalist, having gained as much fame from Maeterlinck's *The Blue Bird* as from Gorki's *The Lower Depths*. By contrast, Brecht was an antirealist who derived the great virtues of his theatre—clarity and density of meaning—from realist motives, especially the motive to examine human behavior in its social and socialized dimension. Kazan is famous for his "intensity"—for brawny, male physicality and for set-smashing—but his aggressive control over tone and rhythm also worked to create light, scherzo scenes, delicately evanescent emotion, and a gallery of great female performances. Brook began as a fantasist of the Anouilh-and-visual-opulence school and then developed both an attractive, somewhat Oriental plain style and that modernist temperament which provokes us to analyze his art even as we enjoy it. Such command of differing styles may not be indispensable to directors—good and great ones have a narrow range—but such diversity is notable in other modern masters, for instance, Max Reinhardt.

My four chapters present directors engaged in highly various kinds of work, at various stages, in various postures, under various contracts. An exemplary posture is the director alone with the script, the dreamer alone with the text and his imagination. Virtually all directors go through such a phase in preparing any production, but Stanislavsky's solitary study of *The Seagull* is a canonical example of that phase. Thus, in Chapter 1, I largely ignore the final production in order to concentrate on a written document, the play's *mise-en-scène* or proposed staging. I explain how a director directs for what I call a "paper stage," an artificial testing ground where the imagination becomes creatively engaged with a challenging script. Many directors prefer this earliest of production phases precisely because their imaginations are freer and more poetical then, less compromised and executive. In this crucial stage of work on *The Seagull,* Stanislavsky's imagination wandering unrestrainedly through the script yielded an artistic proposition about realism and mood that profoundly influenced subsequent Western theatre.

In Chapter 2, "Bertolt Brecht and *Couragemodell 1949,*" I present Brecht as pedagogue explaining the rationale, methods, and effects of his own directing, always with a special moral: pay relentless attention to detail. *Couragemodell 1949,* the German-language "modelbook" or workbook assembled from three separate stagings of *Mother Courage and Her Children,* is an excellent study for several reasons. First, there is its sheer eminence, for the play is a masterpiece, the productions were world-famous, and this modelbook is probably his most instructive. Second, the model illustrates Brecht's mature theatrical ideas, the "dialectical" theories earlier articulated in *A Short Organum for the Theatre* that were the basis for his career's splendid final flowering. Finally, in *Couragemodell 1949* he is always concrete in his approach, translating the particular experiences of his own work into specific aids to future productions. Thus the modelbook serves as a useful reminder to the directing guild and its members who are too often jacks-of-all-trades and maids-of-all-work, too often purveyors of helpless generalizations. If you want to mean, Brecht tells us, mean particularly. Make your point in detail.

Elia Kazan's experience with *A Streetcar Named Desire* is an essential study in the complexity of high-wire directing in the high-pressure commercial zone. Here, working within a vast network of what Gatsby's friend Meyer Wolfsheim called "gonnegtions," the artist must attend to acting methods, union rules, social philosophy, knowledge of the author's heart, casting decisions, and other technologies of money and spirit. This complexity is especially evident with regard to *Streetcar* because Kazan was the only one of my subjects to direct a true premiere and because he was employed on Broadway at a time when Broadway could be believed in, when its manifold nature and intense commercial pressure were sometimes centered by the claim of art. So Kazan had to cast and create new characters, had to develop Williams's script for the stage, had to produce a hit (he was both ambitious and financially involved), and finally had to meet his constant requirement—a production that pleased Elia Kazan. In this case, the results established his mastery over serious American drama, a mastery virtually unchallenged for most of two decades, until Kazan decided to abdicate and left the theatre.

Peter Brook's version of *Marat/Sade* gives us a picture of the contemporary director, the director-*auteur* whose productions originate in his workshop. In the summer of 1963, Brook assembled a Royal Shakespeare Company "workshop," that is, a group without a production plan but with an intention, in this case to investigate the ideas of Antonin Artaud. Over the next twelve months, Brook used this "Theatre of Cruelty" group to try exotic experiments both in private and in public, then enlarged its number to stage Jean Genet's *The Screens,* and finally used workshop personnel and ideas in his production of *Marat/Sade,* a hot new German property about Freud and Marx in the age of Robespierre. The Brook story epitomizes much of recent theatre history because theatre experiment since 1960 has been dominated by productions generated from within workshops, originating to some serious extent with the interests and explorations of their directors.

The four chapters about such various activities have several aims in common. First and foremost, I want to treat these artistic incidents appreciatively and critically, thereby offering them as models. Unlike many other art works, these theatre productions are not visible, audible, or otherwise reproducible, so a certain percentage of my time is inevitably spent in describing them, re-creating the real or imagined theatrical experience as best I can. But like any other art works, these productions offer themselves for criticism. This opportunity leads me to discuss individual directors' careers and philosophies, to analyze their other works, to recount production anecdotes, and to focus on specific solutions to very particular problems. (The reader will want to have these four plays close at hand or freshly in mind.) And, because critical treatment can reveal their great strengths, these productions frequently become models—I mean, of course, models of their times, of historical styles, and of particular directors' methods. In addition—though I hasten to assert that my book is not meant to be a how-to manual—the works of Stanislavsky, Brecht, et al. reveal specific, practical ways of solving problems, using the imagination, and expressing the self.

My second intention is to raise interesting questions about directing itself. As Brecht suggests in the *Couragemodell,* "In studying what follows—a number of explanations and discoveries emerging from the rehearsal of a play—one should, above all, be led by the solutions of certain problems to consider the problems themselves."[1] In the plainest words, I think we have little intelligent criticism or intellectual understanding of directing. This becomes particularly obvious when we compare the success of our efforts with the gyrating critical complexities that have so long surrounded arts like poetry and painting. We disagree in a muddled way about whether directing is an art, about what the art consists of, about what its kinds or "isms" might be, about its vocabulary, and about much more that is equally important to a sophisticated treatment of the subject. My four studies are offered neither as a systematic progression nor as illustrations of a particular performance theory, but as specifics moving toward, not from, a body of thought.

For example, depicting directors in what I earlier called various phases or postures gives an adequate overall image of how inherently unsystematized and fluid "directing" is and has been. But why and how is the task so unsystematized, so changeable from case to case? First, the position of "director" is no older than a century and its job description has only progressively been codified. Historical examples are very inconsistent in terms of which activities were expected of individual artists. Second, theatre is notoriously collaborative, with actors, designers, producers, and lawyers trying to influence a production's growth and style. Most often, directors are supposed to coordinate these collaborations to achieve unity and sense, but from example to example the interplay of power, art, and chance so typical of theatre creates tremendously various situations. Third, whether particular directors are temperamentally dictators or hired hands, the collaborative structure and its many media make their work a complex operation, with many voices, many parts, and an unpredictably interactive set of means and tools. Finally, directing is a process accomplished over considerable time, not a momentary lyric flash of inspiration-creation. Weeks, months, and sometimes years elapse between the initial doodling or dreaming and the final technical rehearsals with their split-second electronic calibrations. During this span of time, all ideas are influenced by changing circumstances and deadline pressures. Because of the compounding of all these factors, the director's world is confusing to casual observers and resistant to coherent intellectual or critical treatment.

Criticism of directing would benefit from more quarreling over its canon. What do we know of an art without a body of great, authoritative instances? What does "sublime" mean in visual art without Michelangelo, in music without Beethoven, in drama without Sophocles? Will other artistic qualities make sense unless we can compare examples, Arnoldian touchstones, and *locus classicus* incarnations? What can we understand about great achievement or innovative aesthetic attack without a great productions list resembling T. S. Eliot's ideal "tradition," particularly in its open-endedness and constant revision from the present? Although not the only critical strategy, this is a useful and educational one. As my title clearly suggests, I would propose these four productions for immediate, charter membership in such a canon. Others by the same directors are candidates as well. And a few dozen additional productions come quickly to mind—famous shows like Reinhardt's *The Miracle,* Vsevolod Meyerhold's *The Inspector General,* the Living Theatre's *Frankenstein,* Orson Welles's *Macbeth,* and Robert Wilson's *Einstein on the Beach.* When we have a body of analysis for such works that is as developed as Laurence Senelick's *Gordon Craig's Moscow Hamlet: A Reconstruction,* we may know something significant about theatre directing.

Discussion of directing, whether it takes place in the shop or in the classroom, is normally enveloped in a terminological miasma. A simple example is the word "style." For many critics and directors, style is that bright idea or production concept that distinguishes a particular show from all others: John Gielgud's *Hamlet* in rehearsal, Brook's *Dream* on trapezes, A. J. Anton's *Much Ado About Nothing* in the style and period of Booth Tarkington. For others, style is a term always accompanied by a qualifying adjective like "realistic," "nonrealistic," "expressionist," or "postmodernist," and thus it describes a basic aesthetic, approach, or premise. For still others, style is always individual, the director's signature. W. B. Yeats often quoted the French critic Sainte-Beuve's assertion that "there is nothing immortal in literature except style"; that is, what does not dissolve in time is how we put our thoughts.[2] More technically, I see style as the shaping of theatrical image or experience: shaping by controlling its visual and aural tempo, texture, mood, pace, atmosphere, sharpness of meaning (thematic thrust), and other relevant qualities; shaping and controlling on a momentary, juxtapositional, and overall basis; classically (though not always), shaping by releasing values implicit in a play's text; and classically (though not always), shaping in order to manipulate audience reaction.

Another example is the word "image," surely one of the most common terms in contemporary theatrical vulgate. ("The Theatre of Images" is gaining great currency as a label for contemporary experimental drama, particularly for our postmodernist attacks on narrative form.) But what, more specifically, is an image? The basic modern definition comes from Ezra Pound and other "imagists" of the World War I period, who defined an image as "a radiant node or cluster," a bounded but explosive patterning of energy (like a bomb), "which presents an intellectual and emotional complex in an instant of time." These fragments suggest three important qualities of the image, whether poetic or theatrical: (1) it begins as a visual impression just as theatre began as "a place for seeing," but then transcends its exclusively visual nature; (2) it can bridge not just our senses (sight and sound) but our faculties (senses, emotions, intellect), thus evoking a larger, wholer human response; (3) it is characterized by its quality of epiphany, or sudden clarity and discovery ("in an instant of time"). As T. E. Hulme said about verse images, far from being "mere decoration" or ornamentation, they are "the very essence of an intuitive language."[3] Like a line or a shot in other arts, the image is a primary unit of signification.

More terminological confusion surrounds one of theatre's simplest, most obvious facts: the basis of theatre is the presence of the human actor. However complex the theatrical style or imagery, however complicated the turn of thought, directing frequently reduces to the kind of human presence that is elicited from actors—how it is stimulated, how it connects to collective or individual audience psyches. But what is this mysterious X factor? Brecht and Bernhardt both called it "charm." Stanislavsky called it "the human spirit." Walter Benjamin called it "aura." Like most other English-speakers in the profession, I call it "presence," meaning something considerably richer than any individual actor's ego. I mean both *presentness* (now-ness) and *presence* (here-ness), a present tense in both space and time. Presence, I think, is the binder of theatrical imagery, and nowhere is this more obvious than in the contemporary theatre of absence and estrangement. Presence, the anthropological view argues, is also the origin of theatre, a god or spirit appearing here, now, because a ritual has evoked it. Thus a successful *Hamlet* should be a visitation, not an understanding.

These three examples of the profession's need for a new lexicon are all complicated by a more general problem, which Andrew Sarris describes in writing about film: "In addition to its own jargon, the director's craft often pulls in the related jargons of music, painting, sculpture, dance, literature, theatre, architecture, all in a generally futile attempt to describe the indescribable."[4] The use of these same vocabularies in theatre criticism is not made any more palatable by the late-twentieth-century belief that analogies between arts are critical barbarisms. However, unless we can be content with social-scientific jargon or French phrases, we may have to accept for now that directing does have a painterly aspect after all, that thrust or round theatres bring out a sculptorly function, that musical comparisons are usually illuminating, and so on. Words like "color," "tempo," "composition," and "theme" will be appropriate so long as they are useful, and so will the many terms we borrow to describe the small units of directing, its elements or pieces: "moment," which implies that directors arrange pieces of time; "picture" (or "image"), which stresses visually separable units; "detail," which emphasizes relations of part and whole; and "beat," which is used to parse action and anatomize motive.

But these terminological difficulties pale beside the intellectual confusion over a simple, fundamental problem: is directing truly an art at all? How can a director be said to create if the assignment is merely to stage someone else's play? That is not creating to a very meaningful degree, is it? This argument usually includes a distinction between creation and interpretation, and the introduction of an interpretive category within the arts has led to frequent comparisons between directing and orchestral conducting, both of which came to be regarded as professions in the same period. However useful, particularly to the spread of culture over time and space, both professions seem to be some aesthetic distance from the picture of the Romantic poet dream-creating his pleasure dome, eyes aflash and hair afloat in the inspirational breeze. Coleridge comes to mind here because it is his aesthetic that is in question: art is imaginative product, and since human imagination, in Romantic theory, echoes the Universal Imagination of Creation Itself (the source of galaxy and proton), poetic imagination can (should?) create like the Deity *from nothing*, imagining into existence new entities, things never known before. To the Coleridgeans, which means to most Anglo-American intellectuals of the twentieth century, theatre directing might best be called the exercise of "fancy" —shuffling the counters of memory and association, rearranging the fixities and definites of another's creative vision (the director as museum curator).

There are two lines of disagreement with this familiar argument. First, Coleridgean aesthetics are founded on an idea of Creation that few intellectuals now accept. Consequently, the Coleridgean position is continually undermined by the contemporary awareness that Shakespeare did not "make up" his stories, that Michelangelo invented neither the marble of his statue nor the iconography of his fresco, and that Virgil had no hand in creating the epic form that determined so much of his poem's nature and success. And what was the name of that genius who designed Chartres? "Originality," "organic art," and "the artist-god" are critical notions that fit nicely into the particular phase of bourgeois individualism from which they come, but they are not ideas sufficient for every day. If we live under the shadows of Flaubert and Beckett (watching fingernail clippings decompose on the floor of an empty room), we are also contemporary with John Cage and with Julian Beck and Judith Malina—with collective creation and creative chance. There is more to art than its inventiveness quotient.

Second, directors do create in the Coleridgean sense, making a new entity—if not from nothing, an original nevertheless. They create theatre productions, which never existed before 8:00 P.M. and turn into vapor after midnight. Directors make actual in one world (the theatrical) something only projected or imagined in another (the literary). Thus the frequent literary objection that literature is compromised in the theatre is countered by the theatrical certainty that dramatic literature is once and for all realized there. David Cole makes this point in his book, *The Theatrical Event:* "Theatre . . . provides an opportunity of experiencing imaginative truth as present truth."[5] Meyerhold is more doctrinaire: "Words in the theatre are only a design on the canvas of motion."[6] Staging a script is so different from conducting a musical score (for instance, compare the precision of musical and script notation) that the analogy is worth very little. Playwrights have been and can be the creative figures in theatre, but almost always have played an ancillary role. Note how recent and tentative the idea of "textual authority" is, even for classical drama, and how even more recent and tentative is the idea of granting living plays and playwrights any literary value and stature whatsoever. (Intellectual reviews and university English departments still treat drama as the poor, lame sister—or the disreputable one—among the genres.)

Surely directors do create works of art, sometimes using plays as playwrights sometimes use stories and as storytellers sometimes use experiences from life. What do we frequently say about our best classic revivals? "It was the play as I had never understood or imagined it before." "It was a new work." And sometimes, particularly since 1960, directors do not use plays at all. Here is a very typical example of how we define directing today, from J. Robert Wills's *The Director in a Changing Theatre* (1976): "Directing for the theatre may be described as the process of transforming personal vision into public performance. . . . The director must first develop a capacity for creating vision, an ability to fuel his imagination from many sources; he must then be able to transform his vision into a theatrical reality, using his mastery of many theatrical crafts."[7] The alert reader will already be commenting that the words "script" and "play" appear nowhere in this definition. Yet this is a valuable formulation precisely because Wills defines the job as that job now exists, as an activity that no longer depends on preexistent literature.

Directing admittedly involves a tension between the primary-imaginative creation *ex nihilo* and a secondary-imaginative interpretation or intermediation. But instead of using that tension to demonstrate that directing is not an art, I prefer to see it as central to an understanding of how directing is and has become an art. Creative-interpretive tension is fundamental to many directing landmarks and many individual careers, as shown by Kazan's move from writer's director to writer and Brook's transition from daring interpreter to independent maker of texts. If we can hold onto the dialectic truth of that tension (film critics call it *metteur en scène* v. *auteur*), we can understand why some of directing's great choices were made, and why and how directors become independent artists. We can even understand the historical aspect of Harold Clurman's genial and accurate definition of directing: "a job, a craft, a profession, and at best, an art."[8]

The belief that directing is an art has stimulated one of the most publicized controversies of mid-twentieth-century theatre—the argument over "directorial authority." Surely contemporary theatre's single most remarkable feature is the powerful control exercised by its directors. This new "directors' theatre" has given us Jerzy Grotowski, Joan Littlewood, the Living Theatre, *A Chorus Line,* and Patrice Chereau, but it has also created alarm, particularly among critics and playwrights. On any Sunday you might hear the lament that directors, in seizing so much power so quickly, have driven theatre off its historical rails. These now-independent theatre "artists" were not long ago stage managers, straw bosses to the stars, ink-stained wretches recording and reviving the blocking plan that always had the actor-manager up center and everyone else artistically dispersed. "A baby in the theatre," Stella Adler calls the director, noting that "there had been a lot of very good theatre before he came along."[9] Who granted these myrmidons the power to write—for that is what it comes to, as in the *auteur* controversy of film criticism—and whence all this talk about the "art" of directing?

Such reactionary criticism ignores two obvious points: playwrights too have earned considerably more power than they had a century ago, and directors everywhere still serve at the mercy of the money changers. But most important, the lamenters try to unwrite history, and in favor of what better model is seldom clear. I am inclined to accept the historical fact that directors have become central to modern theatre and then to consider a corollary, that modern theatre is no doubt more sophisticated and more artistic for that change. When we need a new system, we will certainly create it. For now I think we should attempt to understand the one we have.

How do we explain the historical change to a directors' theatre? Prior to the late nineteenth century, aesthetic decisions were handled mainly by actor-managers, men and women who controlled everything in their theatres from corporate finance to costume material to starring roles. A product of the rebirth of European theatre around 1600, this sturdy system eventually faced unprecedented challenges. As theatres relentlessly grew in size throughout the nineteenth century, the actor-managers became committed to large auditoriums, sizable profits, star casting, and spectacular proscenium staging. Mechanically, this meant that theatrical means were now so materially huge and so aesthetically complex that they no longer fit easily in the hands of a leading actor. Specialization set in, as it did in many other lines of production. By the end of the century, the artistic challenge to the old system was even more formidable. Revolutions were taking place in theatrical taste—about what could be discussed or shown on stage, about the critical relation of theatre to society, about the importance of ensemble performance and unified production, about realism and abstractionism, and about the shape, size, and function of theatre buildings past, present, and future. Modern productions suddenly faced questions that had been avoided for centuries. Which kind of theatrical arrangement best suits this production? Which kind of scenic aesthetic fits this particular play? This kinetic, confusing period, with its new information, questions, and theories, was the setting for a revolutionary idea, generated by predecessors, derived from examples and myth: some figure who was neither writer nor actor could control what a piece of theatre might be like.

Inherent in the idea was the implication of inevitable artistic control. In 1905, when the conception of directing was still very young, Gordon Craig enunciated the basic logic: if theatre is an art, then there must be "an artist of the theatre," and if this artist is granted the customary courtesies accorded an artistic position—jurisdiction over meaning, form, and style, and the freedom to use his or her own material—then we are talking about as full an imaginative license as need be.[10] Today's personally expressive, independently creative directors testify to the historic reality of this drive for imaginative freedom, that is, to the most self-consciously artistic impulses within the ranks. Another testimony to the urge for control is the large number of directors, from Charles Kean to Charles Marowitz, who have experimented with theatrical form by reworking classic texts, for dead authors simply have less power than living ones. A final testimony is the new power directors take in developing scripts by contemporary playwrights—power used in readings, workshops, rewrites, and showcases. At least in the United States, it seems that the director has moved a desk into the playwright's workroom, the better to channel inspiration from the beginning.

So "directorial authority" comes down to independence and power. The independence I describe is not only from script or collaboration, but just as importantly from dead traditions and bad habits, from rotten clichés, stale thoughts, and poor assumptions about what theatrical art can or cannot be. That is why good actors need and want good directors, why aggressive theatres hire them, why we all—no matter how we are disposed on other matters—yearn for productions that are well directed, that enliven contemporary works, peel the old wallpaper off the classics, and show action, word, and character in all their presentness. The fact that directors have powerfully influenced modern theatre because they have taken and been given the power to do so is poorly understood in theatre writing and in the theatre generally. Of course, whatever we think about theatrical power situations will be influenced by our own politics. An autocratic aesthetic will come easily to a court theatre like the Meininger or to an heir of the actor-manager tradition like Craig. A romantic-collectivist like Grotowski may be expected to counter his strongly creative behavior with a critique of the diplomacy, manipulation, and "tactical *savoir faire*" demanded in directing.[11] In the chapters that follow, I hardly touch on the ramifications of the power of the four directors, for I want to emphasize aesthetic results. But until we have a directing history or a theatre history that anatomizes certain questions (Where did creative control reside in earlier theatres? How and why did directors gain it in Europe at the end of the nineteenth century? What are the systematic, aesthetic, and moral dimensions of this change?), we will not understand well enough what we are discussing.

Finally, let us return to the corollary stated earlier, that because directors have gained control over stylistic and interpretive questions, theatre in the twentieth century has become more sophisticated, more artistic. Does this Macaulayesque claim of progress seem extravagant? Not when we consider that (1) 1880–1980 is the third great age of Western drama, an era comparable or superior to the eras of Sophocles and Shakespeare in such respects as duration, number of productions, cultural reverberation, and artistic achievement; and (2) the same century has been the century of the director. Directors have rescued, championed, and protected scores of new and unusual dramatic visions that would unquestionably have been relegated to the closet in earlier ages. They have been the primary cause of acting's modern sophistication, especially its extension throughout an ensemble. And they have created in vast numbers what the actor-managers could manage only occasionally—productions that are well thought-out, unified, and satisfactorily artistic.

Believing this, I naturally take pleasure in introducing four such productions by four of the geniuses of the business.

1

Konstantin Stanislavsky and *The Seagull:*
The Paper Stage

Given Circumstances

D URING THE late Russian summer of 1898, Konstantin Sergeyevich Stanislavsky spent a month and a half alone in a tower in the Ukraine, devising a *mise-en-scène* for Chekhov's *The Seagull.* The tower's window opened onto the grainfields sprawling away from his brother's estate in Kharkov. His mind's view stretched hundreds of versts farther north, to Pushkin, where the members of the Moscow Art Theatre were in a barn putting together a repertory for their critical first season. Weeks later, as he was finishing, the company returned to Moscow to rehearse at the Hunt Club and to occupy the dilapidated Hermitage Theatre. But between August 12 and September 20, the director sat at his desk and struggled in isolation, trying to decipher the puzzle that was Chekhov's difficult and unusual play—to discover what it meant, and how a theatre production might convey that meaning.

What did he do in those weeks? Specifically, he took a copy of the play and cued in scores of diagrams plus 500 notes on everything from love to barking dogs. Taken together, these represent a speculative version of the play, a ground plan for its production. Of course, a mise-en-scène is no more an evening at the theatre than a ground plan is an office building, and, seen in relation to the whole process of directing a play, Stanislavsky's work was only one step. But even as a step in a sequence, the making of his mise was an artistic event with its own integrity, an imaginative act that raised issues for analysis and comment.

Typically, directors in this position or at this stage are devising stage arrangements for a play they have picked and will direct—that is, they are participating in a process they have begun and will complete. This case is different, for this production of *The Seagull* was primarily the enthusiasm of Stanislavsky's partner, Vladimir Nemirovich-Danchenko. Nemirovich, a vocal literary champion of Chekhov, had taken a strong initiative with this particular play. Early in 1898, trying to compose his inaugural repertory, he had badgered Chekhov with letters pleading for the rights to *The Seagull,* arguing repeatedly that he would be responsible—he was a literary man, someone who understood. Stanislavsky's name went unmentioned. On August 21, when rehearsals began, Nemirovich told Chekhov, "I shall look upon the 'rehabilitation' of this play as one of my greatest services to the cause of drama."[1] In general, Nemirovich acted the missionary, defending and shepherding the piece, giving a four-hour lecture to introduce the company to the first two acts, sending Stanislavsky off to the Ukraine with his marching orders, and working the written mise into rehearsal as the pages arrived in the mail, one act after another. Of the play's twenty-six rehearsals, Nemirovich directed fifteen, and although both men received (and deserved) directing credit in the program, to a significant extent Stanislavsky had created a production for Nemirovich, drawing upon his inspiration and creating with his approval. Such collaboration may strike the contemporary reader as unusual, but at the Moscow Art Theatre it was frequent, congenial, and a wise use of the leadership structure.

But perhaps Stanislavsky and Nemirovich needed each other to combat the atmosphere of doubt and concern surrounding *The Seagull* in late 1898. However well established he was as a literary man, Chekhov was mortally afraid of risking a Moscow failure with this play that had already failed, embarrassingly, in an underrehearsed and uncomprehending production two years earlier at the Alexandrinsky

Theatre of St. Petersburg. That debacle had sent the author out into the night, swearing off theatre forever. Stanislavsky and Nemirovich were even more perilously situated. Each had interrupted a successful career to spend a year and a half planning this theatre project. Their opening production, Alexei Tolstoy's *Czar Fyodor Ioannovich* (October 1898), was an auspicious success, but they failed to mount another hit for two months. Needing a success and caring greatly for the fate of Chekhov's strange drama, they must have known moments in which *The Seagull* seemed a chilling proposition.

"Chilling"? "Strange"? *The Seagull* today is at the heart of the world dramatic repertory, its evident charms, splendid parts, and intellectual coherence recommending it to commercial and noncommercial managements alike. But for its first audiences, the play was touched with horror. Its dialogue often seemed inartistic or pointless. To its most sympathetic supporter, Nemirovich, the play described "workaday realities," a "drab existence," the "coarseness" and "inertia" of personal and social lives.[2] If the piece had comic bits, their relevance to the dominant tones and actions was drastically unclear. In short, the meaning of *The Seagull* was about as difficult to grasp in 1898 as that of *Waiting for Godot* was in the mid-1950s. If that comparison seems far-fetched (and it should not), consider what Stanislavsky wrote to his wife while working in the tower:

> All this is not serious. It is certainly not worthwhile devoting one's life to this sort of thing. Can it be that I am doing the same? This thought worries me very much. I thought the stage was a serious occupation, but it seems to be nothing but nonsense. I am beginning to wonder whether not only my life but the life of other people is being wasted. Again I could not help thinking that I ought perhaps to be doing something different.[3]

The Seagull and its burden had induced an existential crisis, a crisis of absurdity.

His first reading of the play was depressing. "Monotonous," "boresome," and "strange" were his reactions.[4] According to Nemirovich, Stanislavsky found the characters "half human," their words "too simple," and their actions groundless; the play lacked stageworthy scenes or images.[5] "Are you sure it can be performed at all?" he asked his partner, "I just can't make head or tail of it!"[6] Nemirovich answered with a two-day lecture about "the depths of

things" and "lyric qualities," but these generalities faded as
Stanislavsky crossed Russia and looked out at the grainfields, which
were just as endlessly monotonous as the play's rhythms, he thought.
By most estimations, Stanislavsky was poorly equipped for the
job at hand. His experience was extensive: ten years of producing
amateur theatre followed by another decade of producing under the
Society of Art and Literature banner. He was respected as an actor
and organizer and was gaining a reputation for directing, having
begun in earnest only eight years earlier, when his mentor Alexander Fedotov left the society. But what did those years show? That he
had a talent for handling "vaudeville," the short comic form exemplified by Chekhov's *The Bear,* which Stanislavsky directed in 1895.
And that he tended to fail critically with Shakespeare, to succeed
with Gerhart Hauptmann, and to create sensations with melodramas like *Uriel Acosta* and *The Bells.* He was known for stunning
production techniques and extraordinary abilities as a colorist, fantasist, historicist, and melodramatist. Given a large scene with
sweeping rhythms and striking effects, Konstantin Stanislavsky
was the Hal Prince of Moscow.

Stanislavsky's reputation as an elderly teacher is so widespread,
his tone so soberly philosophic, that we often forget he was a classic
showman. What words did he want to inscribe on all the world's theatres? "Simpler, easier, higher, gayer."[7] Nemirovich described the
instinct: "If the original hats were high, he must make them excessively high." So it was with long sleeves or a low door or a deep
bow—always longer, lower, deeper. There was always a shade of the
"curious," something in the mise that was "brilliant and astonishing."[8] Flair, dash, and bravura—these were Stanislavsky's talents
and loves, and the source of his respect.

But they were not sufficient to prepare him for *The Seagull.* Dramatic Illyrias—long ago and far away—were his specialty, but this
was a realistic play about a contemporary provincial gentry that he
barely knew. He was accustomed to building productions around
himself in a leading part that could be played with towering, mustachioed brilliance. In *The Seagull* there were four leading characters
(Konstantin, Nina, Arkadina, Trigorin), all of whom dominate the
story by turns and in combination. In his early directing, Stanislavsky
had repeatedly used crowd scenes, panoramas, special effects, and
startling images to cover poor character development and weak acting. But *The Seagull* is nothing but acting. It has ten realized charac-

ters, not one of them faceless or undefined, each with at least one moment of passion when those in the audience and on stage are caught up by that character's problem or condition. Today we realize that these features of *The Seagull* explain much of Chekhov's continuing popularity within the theatre: actors love to act the parts, and they love the ensemble nature of the work. But in 1898, it was the wrong play for Stanislavsky, and it was a revolutionary dramatic structure by any standards then prevailing in Europe.

Alone in the tower, Stanislavsky was thus working in doubt and against his nature. Only when he began to receive positive responses from the North—from the cast, from Nemirovich, and indirectly from Chekhov himself—did Stanislavsky gain any confidence in the notes he was making for this mise-en-scène. *The Seagull* was only a first step in a transformation of theatre and director that would not be completed for another decade, but even in this first essay, Stanislavsky was already on the path toward becoming "Chekhov's director" and the leading modern spokesman for theatrical realism.

What is (a) mise-en-scène? The term normally translates into English as a combination of what we mean by staging and setting. The French noun *mise* has active, participial meanings (laying, placing, putting), and there are many similar idioms (*mise à l'eau,* launching a ship; *mise en train,* starting). It is used often in the fields of fashion and interior decoration, and by extension, to make a *mise* of a *scène* is to lay it out, to give it style, to display it and state its mode or fashion. Mise-en-scène also describes directing as the placing of a script into the scene, onto a stage—staging or translating or realizing it, speaking theatrically. (Speaking cinematically, mise-en-scène is a common French term for film directing. Irrelevant here is the special cinematic usage of mise-en-scène that originated with André Bazin: directing within the shot by moving camera, actors, and focus, as opposed to directing by cutting film, called montage.)

In practice, whether one is discussing a production generally or a production plan like Stanislavsky's, mise-en-scène means, first, all the visual aspects of production. The *Seagull* notebook is full of stage designs, descriptions of settings, diagrams of movement and grouping, plus hundreds of notes on blocking, picturization, and visual rhythms. Second, it means the auditory aspects, which Stanislavsky illustrated in many notes about vocal rhythms, tempi, timbres, phrasings, sound effects, pauses, and that visual and auditory complex we call (particularly in Chekhov) "atmosphere." Third, in his mise Stanislavsky typically considered character questions the implicit source of those sensory stimuli which the director orchestrates. Finally, mise-en-scène in its broadest definition means *meaning* itself—the director makes a script mean what he thinks it means (what today we call "concept"). About this Stanislavsky was groping, but he became more certain as he proceeded with his work.

The mise exemplifies the "paper stage" that most directors encounter early in production. This is the stage in the process where a director is surrounded by paper: script, notebook, reference books, drawings, cardboard figures moved speculatively about. From the paper littering the desk, a director tries to create a stage in the imagination. For the moment, a theatrical artist is alone with a play and searching for a vision of it—contemplating, imagining. Getting the job and choosing the play are no longer considerations. Still to come are working ideas out, arguing them into existence, balancing profit and loss, anticipating raves and pans.

I began with a description of Stanislavsky in the tower because it so perfectly symbolizes the director's physical position at the paper stage. Withdrawal, sequestration—the pattern is followed again and again, whether a director is in a summer home on a deserted coastline or in a metropolitan hotel room. The instinct is understandable in a class of artists who inevitably mount their works in a noisy, distracting atmosphere. But as the history of romanticism reminds us, the tower is both close to heaven and removed from the earth, and the danger of the director's isolation lies in his removal from reality. Stanislavsky was among the first to realize that sequestering a director invited solipsism and dictatorship while denying the creative contributions of many other theatrical artists. Some years later, he completely changed his working methods in order to avoid these very problems (see the section on "Truth in Directing" later in this chapter).

And yet directors still seek towers because they need an imaginative isolation with a script if they are to "direct" it in any sense of that term. In the typical and traditional case, some vision of a play (based on some instinct for it, some predilection for it) precedes rehearsal, and that vision almost always comes from a personal experience of a drama. At the stage of the production process I am describing, it does not matter whether directing is judged secondary-imaginative (interpretation, intermediation) or primary-imaginative (the creation of a theoretically

new work). What does matter is that this stage is unavoidably imaginative; it can only take place in a director's imagination.

The vision in Stanislavsky's mind as he contemplated the Kharkov
wheat fields yielded a document that is a classic among written mises-
en-scène. *The Seagull Produced by Stanislavsky,* edited and introduced by S. D. Balukhaty, first appeared in Leningrad (1938) with
facing-page format for text and notes plus long essays on Chekhov,
the Moscow Art Theatre, and the early *Seagull* failure, as well as a
great deal of information on the 1898 production. An English version, with translation and notes by David Magarshack, at that time
Stanislavsky's leading interpreter in the English-speaking academic
world, was published in 1952 and is apparently the only translation
into another language. This book—not the production it helped create—is my text, my focus in the remainder of this chapter.[9]

As I have mentioned, the mise is a classic, partly for external-
historical reasons: its importance to the careers of both Stanislavsky
and Chekhov, its pivotal position in Moscow Art Theatre history, and
its place in the pioneer days of modern drama and "the age of the
director" alike. I shall also argue that it is internally successful, artistically cogent, a true version of Chekhov's play. The mise-en-scène
shows us fundamental things about directing, about its art and history,
about the imaginative and intellectual activities that define directing.

So what happened on the stage of Stanislavsky's imagination, on
this paper stage? What in fact did he "make of" *The Seagull?* As the
five-year-old said, while watching the Moscow Art Theatre production, "Mother! Let's go into the garden there for a walk!"[10]

Act 1

First, Stanislavsky created a picture and an atmosphere. In
his mise, the park on Sorin's estate was crowded, deep, and dimly lit.
Nearest the audience, running right across the stage, were two rows
of seats including benches, stumps for sitting, a long bench that
sprang up and down, and a garden seat built around a tree trunk,
down right. Back through the trees at stage right ran an avenue that
crossed a bridge over a small stream. At the left were hothouses,
more trees and shrubs, and another path running upstage. At center,
bushes and sunflowers were spread upstage from the seats to the
stream, and up center stood the stage that Konstantin had built.

When that stage's curtain opened midway through act 1, the audience saw beyond it a lake and trees, moonlit and beautiful. At the opening of the act, however, the park was a dense maze, the dark summer evening lit by a faint lantern atop a post (down right) and occasional lightning, the air filled with sounds of frogs and dogs and birds and bells and singing drunks and distant thunder.

The audience could absorb something of this atmosphere because Stanislavsky began with a ten-second pause, then allowed a few more seconds for the sound of a nail being hammered into the stage (up center). While the unseen workman hummed and puttered, Medvyedenko and Masha strolled in from stage left; he smoked, she cracked nuts. He asked, "Why do you always go about in black?" and she replied, "Because I'm in mourning for my life." In three subsequent speeches they elaborated on the subject of happiness and continued to meander across the cluttered stage. With his summary ("What a life!"), they reached stage right and vanished.

During another ten-second pause, the audience could hear more stage-hammering and environmental noises. Several indistinct figures could be seen entering far upstage.

When that pause ended and Masha and Medvyedenko reentered from the right, they noticed the activity upstage. Their conversation ran from Konstantin's play to his love for Nina to Medvyedenko's love for Masha to their mutually depressing situations. These two were, and would remain, an analogue of Konstantin and Nina. Now, they were stalled: she would not return his love, he would not accept her snuff. Stanislavsky stopped them at center stage so that Medvyedenko could light a cigarette and Masha could crack some nuts, then sent them off to the left, the direction from which they first entered, with Masha belittling Medvyedenko's fear of poverty compared to her fear of . . . "However, I can hardly expect you to understand that." Exeunt.

Konstantin and Sorin pushed through the upstage brush to one of the downstage benches, exchanging several speeches en route. Masha and Medvyedenko then returned from the left, only to be immediately ejected by the nervous Konstantin. Medvyedenko dutifully departed, but Masha stayed in place, lost in thought, talking abstractedly about her father and the dog until she came back to reality with a start, and left. In Konstantin's presence, her behavior was inexplicably changed.

The lighting of cigarettes, the cracking of nuts, Medvyedenko swinging the small club he carried, starting and stopping, entering and exiting, walking around obstructions—all these Stanislavsky added. To such a short scene, he gave busy hands and feet. Was he merely putting in "business," decorating the words with casual or momentary physical activity? He added a huge amount of such business throughout the mise. (In the next scene, Konstantin spent much time manipulating a bundle holding Nina's costume and Sorin responded by smoking and brandishing his cane, later using it to pick up his hat from the ground.) Here, however, Stanislavsky accomplished two more important tasks: phrasing the material and making a behavioral paradigm of the play.

By "phrasing the material" I mean that he gave it a rhythmic and experiential shape, parsing it into units of meaning and then sculpting those units around physical movements. A snatch of conversation while Masha and Medvyedenko walked in one direction was sealed off by a momentary exit and pause. A second piece of conversation, on a different topic, led them back the other way and then off again. A third turn was interrupted. This was theatricalizing the play's beat structure. But a glance at Chekhov's play reveals that Stanislavsky was in fact rephrasing the material, giving it a shape different from the author's. Chekhov's characters enter talking, then sit and stay seated until their exit. When they sit, it is in the middle of the first conversational topic, the first beat. Stanislavsky instead organized the characters' movements to emphasize the topic divisions. By removing the couple from the stage a second time, he avoided a double-focus blur when Konstantin and Sorin entered. And he gave the opening scene a very deliberate pace. His dark and crowded setting ensured slow and careful movement by the actors. He built the scene around pauses, which were long—ten seconds is a long time to listen to church bells and land rails.

Stanislavsky even changed the basic situation of the scene, and hence its meaning, by having Masha and Medvyedenko walk rather than sit. Chekhov's scene shows a couple returning from a stroll and sitting down to rest and chat. Stanislavsky's version had the two strolling in postprandial fashion and talking about their lives. Brecht would phrase this action inside quotation marks: "The country people stroll and philosophize." Stanislavsky thus created a first image for the audience, made an introductory statement. He was within the spirit of the play, for Chekhov tactfully delays exposition and begins with a philosophic, if comic, exchange. Such an image is quintessential in Chekhov's world, where people always indulge in bemused philosophizing rather than take action or make decisions. Arkadina describes that in act 2: "Oh, what can be more boring than this delightful country boredom! Quiet, hot, nobody does anything, everybody's philosophizing." Here, Stanislavsky found the boredom less delightful than sadly monotonous, but the Masha-Medvyedenko paradigm of life on the estate would apply until the end of the play.

The opening imagery was sharply focused by physical behavior, especially the release of plausibly implicit physical activity as an articulation of a scene's parts. This also describes Stanislavsky's treatment of Chekhov's second scene, the extended, expository conversation between Konstantin and Sorin staged on the long bench (down center) that bounces up and down. After entering, Sorin moved to sit there, facing upstage. Taking longer to settle, Konstantin came down to the bench and turned up to survey his stage from different angles and perspectives. He jumped onto the bench and cried, "Now there's a theatre for you!" Finishing that speech, he reached down for Sorin's cigarette so as to light his own, stood back up, jumped down (each move nearly dislodged Sorin), and attacked his uncle's beard and clothes. At the scene's end, hearing Nina approach, he leaped about still more, but he was always restricted to the immediate area of the bench.

Stanislavsky further restricted Konstantin's excitement in the middle of the scene. When Sorin had finished complaining about his ragged appearance, his nephew lit a cigarette and reclined on the bench, facing the audience with his head propped on his hand. Sorin asked: "Why's your mother in such a bad temper?" Konstantin's answer, which led to his long speeches about mother and theatre, began with him recumbent, fiddling with cigarettes and matches, reaching down for a flower and plucking off its petals. He sat up and swung his leg over the bench to face his uncle sideways, then stood and paced, sat back down, jumped up again, lit another cigarette, and delivered a long speech with prominent cigarette byplay. At last he lay down again by his uncle only to jump back up at the sound of Nina's approach. This is an extraordinary sequence with a rationale in character analysis. In the mise, Stanislavsky explained: "The performance of his play is to him an event that is of decisive importance to his future career. It is not for nothing that he is in such a nervous state after its failure. The more jumpy and agitated he is now, the stronger will his mood of despair be after the failure of his play." The description of Konstantin's first scene contains physical images crucial to the play's line. In the rest of act 1, Stanislavsky consistently emphasized Konstantin's high energy, making him an ardent lover of Nina, a nervously fussy director on first night, an explosively angry son when his mother interrupted the play, and a hysterically active man in despair. By the end of the act he was forcefully pushing Masha out of his way and "waving his arms in great agitation." The actor's score began on such an energetic note so that he might slowly, carefully descend into almost catatonic shock by the end of the play. The character's life thus curved gradually but inexorably toward silence, immobility, and despair. Stanislavsky recapitulated this overall pattern in the climactic interview between Konstantin and Nina in act 4. Throughout, the director's interpretation was strongly phrased in the physical.

So was Stanislavsky's illustration of a central aspect of Konstantin's character. At the beginning of this first conversation with Sorin, the young rebel poet has just finished condemning modern bourgeois theatre:

SORIN: But you can't do without the theatre, my boy.
KONST: What we want is new forms, uncle. New forms. We must have new forms. If we can't get them, I'd much rather have nothing at all.

Ignore for a moment the aesthetic argument (Stanislavsky and others have supported it; Konstantin himself later rejects it) and concentrate on the tone: insistent, repetitive, passionate. The last sentence looks ahead to the moment when Konstantin will stop his play because its reception is less than ideal, then to his later attempts to stop his imperfect life. Prior to this line, Stanislavsky moved Konstantin around on the bench—lying, picking petals, sitting—but as he said, "If we can't get them, I'd much rather have nothing at all," the young man swung his leg over the bench and left it for the first time since the scene began, pacing agitatedly up and down the stage for five silent seconds until he calmed down, regained the bench, and said, "I love my mother. I love her very much," then tore into a castigation of her "silly sort of life." The subjects of theatre and mother that overwhelm Konstantin's mind were thus linked, as they are throughout

Chekhov's scene, and this particular juxtaposition might suggest how dangerous is the tension between art and love. Also, if Konstantin cannot have the relationship he wants with his mother, would he "much rather have nothing at all?" What if he cannot have Nina? I have heard the opinion expressed that Stanislavsky's mise contains "nothing but" physical behavior, mere blocking and business. Not only is that not true, but it trivializes the issue, which is how physical activity can express character, indicate phrasing of material, and point to crucial moments. It is true that Stanislavsky's emphasis on the visual and the physical oversimplified certain minor characters, a few of whom were merely tagged with "colorful character traits." Medvyedenko, for instance, smoked constantly, and that is all he did. And Stanislavsky seemed surprisingly uninterested in Sorin, an entertaining, complex minor character. Sorin has only a few speeches early in the play, but they strongly accent his life's unsatisfactory qualities: the annoyances of country life, his undistinguished appearance, and his unfulfilled aspirations. Stanislavsky ignored these considerations and saw the character as a man holding props (blanket, cigarette, cane, hat) and having a tag trait—a laugh that was "rather startling and unexpected."

On the other hand, Stanislavsky was fairly brilliant in his analysis of Masha, making her a multifaceted minor character. Recall his addition of that strange moment when she talked abstractedly with Konstantin in the opening. Stanislavsky gave her another such moment after Konstantin's play in act 1, and several in act 4. Finally he used her odd, monotonous voice calling out the lotto numbers as a ground tone for the play's ending. In addition to her fey, dreamy nature, he deliberately emphasized two other sides of her character: emotionalism, as revealed by her heartsickness over losing Konstantin, and an earthy, comic quality. She was weepier in the mise than in the script, but she showed her provincialism too, especially when she noisily slurped her tea. He even gave her a non-Chekhovian moment of maternal concern in act 4 by directing her to ad-lib instructions about her child while showing out Medvyedenko, who was still smarting from her stinging dismissal. This was a small moment of genuine and ironic counterpoise in Stanislavsky's treatment, and a typical one. Masha may be silly when she says that she is "in mourning for my life," but the remark is also intriguing, and Stanislavsky was sufficiently intrigued by Masha to increase her range and depth.

In the middle of act 1, with the assembly for Konstantin's play, the directing changed. *The Seagull* is organized into two basic scene styles: dialogue scenes (two characters) and scenes with five or more people interacting and talking together. In Chekhov's last two plays, *The Three Sisters* and *The Cherry Orchard,* the dramaturgic balance fell very heavily toward group scenes. In fact, the central discovery of mature Chekhovian drama was how to manage a full stage artfully while still manipulating and advancing stories, both individual and group stories. But in the 1890s, when he wrote *The Seagull* and the original of *Uncle Vanya,* Chekhov wrote more actual *dia*logue, giving these works a more balanced interplay between the tête-à-tête (intimate, emotional, psychological in focus) and the larger, more emotionally diffuse pictures of provincial society in operation. Act 1 of *The Seagull,* for instance, begins with four dialogue scenes (Masha-Medvyedenko, Konstantin-Sorin, Konstantin-Nina, Pauline-Dorn), continues with the enlarged grouping of the play scene, and ends with Dorn solo, then Konstantin-Dorn, then Masha-Dorn.

In the play scene of act 1, Stanislavsky's work was almost entirely pictorial. The most famous element was the picture's upstage focus: since Konstantin's stage was up and the stage audience watched from down, the members of that audience arranged themselves with their backs to the paying audience, à la André Antoine. Stanislavsky created more pictures during Konstantin's stage preparations, throwing moonlight and shadows downstage onto the curtain, dimming the footlights almost imperceptibly so that when the curtain parted, the stage audience was thrown into silhouette against bright moon and beautiful stage.

At the point where the group's babble subsides and Nina performs Konstantin's play, Stanislavsky found his visual climax for act 1. Later, in his memoirs, he would call Nina "the cause of the failure of Treplev's talented play," emphasizing her inadequacy as an actress.[11] In the mise of 1898, however, he was not evaluating her art but using her to make an enchanting visual impression:

> On the stage is a table, on it a chair or a stool, all covered with some
> dark material—and moss. Nina is sitting on the top of it; she is draped
> in a white sheet, her hair hangs loosely down her back, the sheet, as it
> falls down her arms, forms something that resembles a pair of wings,
> through which Nina's bust and arms are faintly outlined. Her face is
> not visible, as the light is behind her. Only the contours of her figure

can be seen, and this lends it a certain transparency. This picture is supplemented by the silhouettes of the figures sitting in the foreground. The lantern, which is alight in front of the stage, will to some extent interfere with the audience's view of Nina, and that, too, should heighten the dramatic effect of the scene. Nina's soliloquy proceeds to the accompaniment of the croaking of frogs and the crake of the landrail.

There was a beautiful stage to watch, wonderful light and shadow, will-o'-the-wisps and devil's eyes, an evocative church bell striking in the distance during Nina's second long speech, which wandered on as if poetically. Like the onstage audience when the scene-within-the-scene is first revealed, the audience was probably supposed to gasp, "Ah-h!"

But the onstage audience does not remain docile, so the play ends with confusion and Konstantin's flight. Stanislavsky provided an active image in the aftermath, letting Arkadina hide her discomfort by "taking stage," pacing upstage of the rocking bench on which most of the spectators still sat. While she addressed her audience thus, the eye was free to notice the characters in more detail: Trigorin gazing off at the lake, Dr. Dorn drawing thoughtfully on the ground with his stick, and Medvyedenko finding no reception for his thoughts on spirit and matter.

Nina's introduction to the crowd is next, and Stanislavsky stressed how Nina used her budding friendship with Arkadina to develop her own fascination with Trigorin. Stanislavsky envisioned a first exit sequence for Nina before the line, "If you knew how I hate to have to go": "Nina holds out her hand to Trigorin, shyly, tenderly, reverently, is overcome with embarrassment, then runs up again, quickly, ecstatically, to Miss Arkadina and kisses her a second time." After her good-byes to Sorin and the others, Nina passed Trigorin yet again, and the novelist looked "very intently at her," probably to extract an image for his notebook. The mise continues: "she gives him her hand a second time rather significantly, is covered with confusion and runs off, Trigorin following her with his eyes." Arkadina obviously noticed this interaction, and so would any audience, for it was the most remarkable behavior Nina had exhibited since her first appearance.

Once the crowd was gone, Dorn was left alone at center stage, sitting motionless and humming. Fifteen seconds passed, and when the doctor spoke, the audience understood why he had maintained such a pensive silence since the play's interruption. He had been powerfully affected by it, by Nina's lines about loneliness, and by the devil's eyes. "Fresh, naive," he calls it. Next came his difficult conversation with Konstantin, difficult because Dorn was forced to keep up with the anxious boy who was running all over the stage, and also because he wanted to tell Konstantin how much he liked the play, although Konstantin could not bear to think of that—he only wanted Nina. Dorn then comforted Masha, who was heartsick as a result of Konstantin's continual rejection of her advances. They sat on the garden seat around the tree (down right), Masha sobbing on Dorn's knee. He repeated a judgment he had earlier made of Konstantin: "How overwrought they all are! How overwrought! And so much love, too. . . . Oh, that spell-binding lake!" Fifteen seconds passed, filled by sounds: a waltz on the breeze, the distant church bell, peasants singing, frogs, land rails, and still other nocturnal effects. Dorn stroked Masha's head: "But what can I do, my dear child? What? . . . What? . . . " Curtain.

In Stanislavsky's mise-en-scène, the overriding feature of these final scenes was their spareness. The director no longer concentrated on picture-making or on having large physical images dominate and articulate the dialogue. He was doing less, contriving his scenes less. Actors used fewer props. Movements—Konstantin, for example, had many wild ones—now were motivated from need rather than from idleness or the director's desire to color. Sound and pause and idea and action were gathering and were building conclusions. The audience was allowed to let the events of act 1 settle in the mind. This unassertive direction followed a decrease in emotional intensity after the play scene. Konstantin and Masha were still frenzied at the end, but their agitation was now seen in the context of Dr. Dorn's mood, which dominated the ending as Konstantin's energetic mood dominated the act's first half. Dorn was avuncular and wondering, distanced yet compassionate, never beyond the facetious or the serious, almost (but not quite) the *raissoneur.* "Dear me, how overwrought you are!" —that is Dorn's note.

Stated another way, Stanislavsky saw how emotional the play's final moments are and gave clear expression to emotions in the final images of Act 1. *The Seagull,* I wish to point out, is a play about drastic emotions eliciting an array of emotional responses. Its first scenes show love, love, and more love (Masha and Medvyedenko, Konstantin and Arkadina, Konstantin and Nina, Pauline and Dorn), and all the love is blocked, failing. The four characters who constitute the play's inner group (mother and son, novelist and girl next door) form a four-pointed network of attraction and neurosis around which the play's plot and minor characters are organized. The paired and triangulated confrontations of these four tell most of the story. (Put simply, each man loves both women, each woman loves both men, and the intragender relationships involving jealousy and competition are not given much play.) As Chekhov told his colleague, Alexey Suvorin, while writing the play, it has "four acts; a landscape (view of a lake); lots of literary talk, little action; a ton of love."[12]

Unlike Chekhov's later works, *The Seagull* is not conspicuously about the society in which it is set. It includes no local events, no characters having connections with contemporary Russian politics. Discussions do not dwell on nation, land, class, mankind, or the future, but on happiness. Characters do not look far beyond their feelings. And when they do, they talk about art, which has led critical modernizers to claim that *The Seagull* is a play about art. This claim finds support in the contrast between Konstantin's symbolism and his mother's bourgeois realism, in his early and late speeches about literary principles, in Trigorin's long account of his life as a writer, in Nina's life as an actress, and in the fact that all four leading characters are artists. Yet Chekhov was neither Pirandello nor Richard Foreman, and the "literary talk" he mentioned to Suvorin is just that— "talk, little action." Even if we grant that *The Seagull* is a play about artists, we should note that these artists are seen to be on vacation and that they are constantly absorbed by their emotional lives. (The major exception to these remarks, of course, is Konstantin, which is why postmodern revisions of the work—on stage and in criticism— end by making it his story.)

These characters are right to be absorbed, we might say, because their emotions prove dangerous, destructive, even fatal. Konstantin's suicidal streak is observed early, then demonstrated twice. Nina returns in act 4 in a seriously disturbed state. Trigorin's memory lapse regarding the seagull (act 4) is evidence of his emotional deadness, which seems to increase with the play's events. If we think too of Masha, Medvyedenko, Pauline, Sorin, even Dorn, we realize how difficult it is to survive this world intact, let alone happy. Arkadina may seem to stand as the exception here, but her turn is about to come when the final curtain falls. These people are damaged by their emotional involvements, and on this point the play is resolutely uncomic.

❖

Postscript, act 1. "But what can I do, my dear child? What? . . . What?" On December 17, 1898, when *The Seagull* opened at the Moscow Art Theatre, the aftermath to this curtain line was astounding. During the act, the audience had been quiet and the actors had been nervous. On stage as Trigorin during the middle of the act, Stanislavsky noted that the stage smelled of valerian drops, the popular sedative mentioned in the play. He also found his leg shaking convulsively. Now he stood in the wings of the partly filled theatre, watching the curtain fall on act 1 and waiting for a reaction. There was none. Were they going to fail as the well-known actors had in St. Petersburg two years earlier? During the silence, the actors looked down, shuffled about, looked at each other, and waited. Olga Knipper, sick with a high fever, appeared to faint. What matter now that Nemirovich had thought the act 1 mise "bold and very dynamic" or that Lilina (Stanislavsky's wife) had wrung sharp sobs of pain from Masha's final agony?[13]

Suddenly, a wave of applause crashed in on them. Stanislavsky recalled "a roar in the auditorium, and a shriek of joy or fright on the stage. The curtain was lifted, fell, was lifted again, showing the whole auditorium our amazed and astounded immovability. It fell again, it rose; it fell, it rose, and we could not even gather sense enough to bow."[14] Pandemonium followed: embraces, tears, ovations for Lilina, and Stanislavsky dancing a victory dance. The triumph continued throughout the evening. After act 3, the audience called Chekhov and then insisted, on discovering his absence, that a telegram be sent expressing the general enthusiasm. More congratulations and applause came after the final curtain. One sellout followed another that winter. People spent the night in the street outside the theatre, reading by lantern and dancing around fires, in order to buy tickets for *The Seagull.* Chekhov's reputation as a dramatist was not salvaged but made on that December 17, and the Moscow Art Theatre achieved the success with a contemporary work that most modern theatres need in their first seasons. Three years later, when the theatre's new home opened, its new green curtain parted in the middle, and near the part on each half was a seagull.

Writing to Chekhov after that tumultuous premiere, Nemirovich said that the production of act 1 would have made its author gasp.

Why did the wave of audience acclaim break over the Moscow Art Theatre stage at this point, the end of act 1? It was not like the end of act 3, where the virtuoso crowd scene was followed by a long, sweet kiss. No gunshots or other dramatic coups sustained the close of act 1; there was nothing novel beyond some unusual sound effects. The scene showed emotional suffering and a helpless response to that suffering. A logical guess is that the members of the December 17 audience found this scene to have been acted with emotional truth and that the scene made sense in terms of what they had seen of the play so far.

Truth in Directing

Stanislavsky made truth the fundamental essence and quality not of an individual artist or actor, but of *the theatre as a whole*.
—Alexander Tairov in *Konstantin Stanislavsky, 1863–1963*

Icy irony and modernist anxiety were not part of Stanislavsky's style as an intellectual or experimenter. He was instead one of the last nineteenth-century intellectuals who earnestly pursued serious, capitalized goals: "Nature," "The Human Spirit," and "Truth." In Stanislavsky's half-century career, the earnestness came from applying his prodigious energies and multiple talents—director, actor, organizer, teacher, thinker—to a search for theatre work with meaning and authenticity. His teaching of acting attempted to methodize the finding of truth. "Truth" was his ultimate test of theatre, as it was Plato's and Hamlet's.

What is "truth" in directing? Following the lines of basic philosophical discussion, there are three definitions: correspondence, coherence, and the spiritual meaning of life.

1. *Correspondence.* Truth is a quality of a proposition or a statement, and if a statement corresponds to our observation of the world, we verify the statement, or say it is true. ("The wall is white." Look, the wall *is* white.) In theatre, the act of stating translates into such acts as acting, designing, and realizing, but the question of correspondence is still relevant. We check theatrical propositions against reality every time we buy a seat, and though many of us quite understand why theatre does not always correspond totally to the world, it

is still true, as it was in the nineteenth century, that most Western seat-buyers madly enjoy theatre that does correspond. The most literal meaning of truth of correspondence is verisimilitude—truth to appearances or to the world we know. Verisimilitude has been considered unfashionable and irrelevant by many advanced circles during most of the twentieth century, particularly in theatre, where it is sometimes confused with *trompe l'oeil,* which is a confusion of motive. Many Victorian Shakespeare productions, including several of Stanislavsky's, have led critics to giggle about the verisimilitude of rabbits hopping across the floor of Oberon's magical forest. But we should not confuse tastelessness with aesthetic choice. Verisimilitude is a value in genius-level artworks, a stylistic option with its own angles of play and instruction, and an act of good faith on the part of the artist. In the late nineteenth century, verisimilitude was a (the?) cutting-edge question in novel, theatre, photography, painting, and (the latest nineteenth-century art) film.

Verisimilitude was thus a fundamental issue in and of realism, which is basically a way of imitating the world with the highest degree of fidelity to the appearance of things as they are or were. Various motives may attach themselves to such imitation, including "naturalism," which is the motive to analyze socialized humanity experimentally, using realism as an experimental tool. But realism is also the rubric under which to place the nineteenth century theatre's archeological enthusiasm. From mid-century on, Western theatre produced history piece after history piece based on new research from the field, particularly the Mediterranean. As visual design and mise-en-scène became affected by the archeologists' findings, audiences in this first great age of the illustrated magazine endorsed the value of showing the (historical) "real thing."

Stanislavsky specialized in such productions. In preparing modern Russian plays, he displayed a penchant for field trips, taking his troupe to the Khitrov Market *(The Lower Depths)* or to Tula *(The Power of Darkness)* in order to bring truth value to his art. For historical subjects, he favored research-oriented vacations. When directing *Othello* in 1896, his design and mise were enriched by images remembered from Venetian archives and from Venice itself. His acting of the Moor also came from life, from an evening's assiduous study of an Arab in a Parisian restaurant.

Two examples from this *Othello* show the problems and possibilities of verisimilitude. The Senate scene (act 1, scene 3) was characterized by the traditional magnificence, including opulent costuming, but it had a special feature: "all who were present at the meeting were in black masks."[15] This was based on some piece of Venetian history, and it was visually sensational, but it made no particular sense, especially in light of Othello's black face. The second example, the play's opening, shows Stanislavsky at his most floridly verisimilitudinous. Some sounds were heard (a tower bell, the distant splash of oars) and a realistic gondola slid up a Venetian canal, then stopped at a darkened street. A huge chain thundered onto the dock, and two men (Iago and Roderigo) followed, stopping in conversation before the colonnade of a dark house that resembled the Doges' Palace. When these men roused the owner (Brabantio) and convinced him that his daughter had been abducted by a black man, the house came alive. Windows were thrown open, servants wandered sleepily out of doors, calls were heard, and lights could be seen within. Men putting on armor ran out and crossed the bridge over the canal, but one had to return immediately for a forgotten armament. More men crowded out and into boats to take off down the canal. The streets were filled with noise and movement and agitation over the crime of miscegenation. This sounds like a scene from Franco Zeffirelli, a similarity that, in itself, reminds us of how, at its best, truth of correspondence—directing based on detailed truth to life—can vivify and can also make sense.

2. *Coherence.* A second philosophical definition of truth, largely post-Kantian, endows a system (logically or teleologically or however) with the quality of truth and then assesses the truth of propositions by measuring their coherence within the system. Something is true insofar as it is a necessary constituent of a systematically coherent whole. In aesthetics, such truth is associated with qualities like harmony, unity, and composition, as well as with the relationship between principles (declared or apparent) and achieved results. Stanislavsky tested for truth of coherence in the smallest theatrical details. A theatrical particular (such as a snuffbox) might need to correspond to some reality (an eighteenth-century snuffbox), but the crucial test was its truth within the organic, fictional world (did the snuffbox look right?). Concerning behavior, he asked:

> What does it really mean to be truthful on the stage? . . . Does it mean that you conduct yourself as you do in ordinary life? Not at all. Truthfulness in those terms would be sheer triviality. There is the same difference between artistic and inartistic truth [we might say "between

true and false verisimilitude"] as exists between a painting and a photograph: the latter reproduces everything, the former only what is essential.[16]

The point about painting and photography is a dated and discredited one, but not so troublesome as to blur Stanislavsky's demand for the "essential." One of his most famous injunctions about acting, passed on from the great actor Mikhail Shchepkin, reads, "You may play well or you may play badly; the important thing is that you should play truly." Stanislavsky glossed "truly" as meaning "to be right, logical, coherent, to think, strive, feel and act in unison with your role."[17]

Truth in acting, defined as coherence within the role, leads us to Stanislavsky's linking of truth and belief. "Truth cannot be separated from belief, nor belief from truth" may seem dangerous advice to give for dealing with a treacherous world, but "in the part" or "on the stage" (as he always added or implied), this is curiously the case.[18] He defined the terms in circular fashion ("On the stage truth is that in which the actor sincerely believes," and "one can believe only in the truth") because he described what is often a circular or feedback process: the truer something is, the more one believes it; the more one believes something, the truer it becomes.[19] Belief was a vital component in Stanislavsky's acting system and the subject of the longest chapter in *An Actor Prepares*. It was also the objective of the "magic if" that allows actors to pretend their way to truth and the point of his oft-told tale about Tommaso Salvini preparing three hours to play Othello. Stanislavsky was notorious at the Art Theatre for calling from the auditorium during rehearsals, "I don't believe it." As a Soviet writer has said, "no one ever thought of insisting on the contrary. If Stanislavsky did not believe it, it was obviously untrue."[20]

The importance Stanislavsky attached to belief was revealed by his behavior when the Moscow Art Theatre re-created some scenes from *A Month in the Country* in a Kiev palace park. The park, by the banks of the Dnieper, perfectly resembled the setting of their production's second act, and having just finished a tour with this work, they decided to experiment by playing some scenes there. In the second of these scenes, Stanislavsky and Olga Knipper-Chekhova spoke their dialogue walking through an alley of trees toward a bench on which they sat, just as they had on stage. But Stanislavsky stopped suddenly, unable to continue his "false and theatrical pose."[21] The acting in the 1909 production, Stanislavsky's first public experiment with his acting system, had received acclaim for its fidelity to life. But now the acting was not realistic but phony and theatrical. The natural setting—beautiful, fitting, the world itself—was inconsistent with the production and vice versa. When Stanislavsky's belief snapped, he stopped because the situation was false, that is, incoherent.

Coherence was his goal when, in the late 1920s, Stanislavsky came again to direct *Othello*. The first time, in 1896, he had relied on stunning production numbers to carry the early acts (rousing Brabantio, the Senate scene, the landing in Cyprus, the brawl), but when the play started to be about Othello, Iago, and Desdemona (act 3 and beyond), his production fell apart. Neither of the latter two leads was adequate, and Stanislavsky's own Othello was frankly insufficient to the task. In particular, he suffered from muscular and vocal strain because he relied on "voltage," sheer enthusiasm, rather than on a logical progression of parts. So, when planning the later production with Leonid Leonidov as the Moor, Stanislavsky retained and improved the brilliant staging coups of his earlier mise-en-scène but now put his emphasis on character, particularly on how to make the part of Othello both emotionally and physically coherent. The answer was in subdivision and adjustment of parts.

Stanislavsky's return to *Othello* in his last years is only one measure of his fascination with the play. This was the single Shakespearean tragedy that he took a leading part in producing, and he did so twice. His three books on acting (two volumes in Russian) all use *Othello* as a prominent example. Arguably the greatest Shakespearean performance he ever saw —perhaps the greatest acting of any kind that he saw and unquestionably the source of his fascination— was the Moor of Salvini, the short, mustachioed fury of the Italian and later the world stages. From Salvini Stanislavsky learned that the part demanded not voltage but strict control of its momentary emotional progression. Salvini treated scenes lightly at first, establishing audience control in the Senate scene but saving magnetism and power for the play's second half, where he articulated the steps of Othello's torment: "Salvini molded with such clearness, with such merciless logic and such irresistible persuasiveness that the spectator saw all the detailed curves of the suffering soul of Othello."[22] The actor's personal imagery also changed from minute to minute: first he was a Romeo, then a dignified middle-aged man, a tiger, and, at the end, a lost boy staring bewilderedly into the face of death.

Salvini's example, Stanislavsky's failure, and several decades of research all combined to make his later *Othello* an exercise in breaking scenes down into their units or beats and bringing these units into organic harmony. He cut the Senate scene into six large sections and advised the actors: "Let these pieces be clearly, maturely presented. . . . follow them up instead of clinging to petty tasks.[23] Stanislavsky's general advice regarding the title part was as follows: "No human passion or experience progresses steadily and unswervingly. Human feelings make an advance, then somewhat retreat, and then advance again. By such steps jealousy grows in Othello's heart." Specifically, consider act 3, scene 3—over 400 lines that show Iago rousing Othello with "Ha! I like not that" and leading him to his murderous vow and "Now art thou my lieutenant." Stanislavsky broke this long scene into three separate scenes staged for three different settings on the revolving stage. As a result, the audience would quite literally see Othello's jealousy grow in separate stages. More specifically still, Stanislavsky took the third of these scenes, the 150-line "Tower Scene," and broke it into ten sections, labeling each with an infinitive verb (a task for the actor) and an imagistic title (such as "What have I done? Faugh, how disgusting!"). Leonidov was coached to master the performance of these ten sections in no more than five minutes, keeping the line of beats as a life belt. Otherwise, he would rapidly increase his voltage and lose all control. At the most microscopic level of analysis, Stanislavsky took the Moor through his entrance to the scene:

(1) Try to find Desdemona as quickly as you can and take her in your arms;
(2) she is playful, she flirts with Othello; let him be playful too and invent some pleasant joke;
(3) passing by Iago, Othello, in his playful mood, jokes with him as well;
(4) Desdemona returns to pull Othello along to the divan and he follows her, playfully once more;
(5) he is made to recline—rest, give himself up to caresses, and respond likewise when possible.[24]

Five detailed actions support ten lines of text. This is only one example of the lengths to which Stanislavsky went in the service of coherence.

3. *Spiritual meaning of life.* A third kind of truth is more general, less technical. The "spiritual meaning of life" is sometimes an important insight into life, sometimes the kind that can be peddled door

to door. More frequently, it is the realization that life is spiritual, that we are spiritual, and that reality has a spiritual dimension. A symbolist believing this has a wide open field. A realist faces the task of evoking the spiritual from the material. But as recently as Joyce, the great realists claimed that their painstakingly detailed fictions were designed to reveal "the spirit of man." That is truth as the transcendental nineteenth-century value, as essence, as "the meaning of life."

Stanislavsky expressed his favorite definition of theatre as follows: "The fundamental aim of our art is the creation of this inner life of a human spirit, and its expression in an artistic form."[25] Such statements served him well, as a warning against excesses of naturalism and formalism, as a buoy in the shifting waters of Soviet art policy, and as a common language with such colleagues as Gordon Craig, Isadora Duncan, and Eleanora Duse. But most important, the "spirit of man" as the ultimate standard of theatrical truth was Stanislavsky's personal and practical belief. When he stopped into the Art Theatre and saw something that did not meet that standard, whether one detail or a whole production, he would lecture the offenders that "the human being and his inner spiritual life—these are what must be shown on the stage of our theatre."[26]

So Stanislavsky found it worrisome to be a "naturalist," which he was. As he told a visiting Polish actress in 1905, "I am a naturalist, and unable to change, though today naturalistic form is hateful to me."[27] He meant that he tirelessly studied (and advocated the study of) historical periods and particular locales. He studied social structure, ideology, morality, literature, economy, psychology, manners, habits, and decorative styles. As a mature director, he was determinedly Zolaesque. Yet like most serious contemporaneous realists, Stanislavsky deprecated the copying of externals as "ethnographical" or "photographical," as "mere" or "secondary" detail. Accuracy alone, as in his early work, was "outward and coarse." But harness the impulse to spiritual experience, and theatre became "spiritual naturalism" or "justified naturalism" or "spiritual realism," all of which he often espoused.

Stanislavsky's work was based on the conviction that human reality is a mixture or juncture of outer and inner, material and spiritual, body and soul. For him, the truth of reality was exclusively neither one nor the other. Physical and spiritual were "indivisible" because organically connected, symbiotic: "The life of the one gives life to the other."[28] From this conviction came particular procedures, such as directing early rehearsals with virtually complete settings and full props. From it too came his later, summary theory of acting, the "method of physical actions." In both of these cases, the material world required extensive attention, but primarily because it was a gateway to the spiritual.

Most important, from this conviction came Stanislavsky's learned allegiance to Chekhov, for their views were strikingly similar. Chekhov was a doctor and a writer, and he believed in both kinds of knowledge. Artistically, he synthesized naturalism and symbolism. (Who else in Europe at that time was simultaneously inspired by Zola and Maeterlinck?) His ideal was that scientifically competent poet of genius, Goethe. In stories and plays, Chekhov rendered the surface of Russian life carefully and precisely because he considered it the vesture of the human spirit. This places him squarely in that late-nineteenth-century high realist tradition to which Tolstoy, Ibsen, and George Eliot all belonged, of which *Ulysses* was the monumental synthesis, and of which Stanislavsky was the leading theatrical heir: the tradition of realism as a mediation of spiritual and material.

Stanislavsky's first experience with this playwright was a difficult one, as I have already shown. In his autobiography and elsewhere, he converted this experience into metaphors of searching out subterranean treasure: he and Nemirovich had "tunneled" from different directions toward the truth of *The Seagull; The Cherry Orchard* was a "secret treasure house"; Chekhov's moods were hidden in a "cave." In his mature view of Chekhov, body and soul lived the same life, miraculously hidden in each other. Stanislavsky wrote of Chekhov's plays, "It is impossible to separate us and everything that takes place in us from the world of inanimate things, light and sound among which we live and on which human psychology depends so much." That was a naturalist premise. The spiritual strategy dictated that naturalistic stage effects (such as crickets) were "necessary to Chekhov not for the sake of their external effects but for the revelation of the life of the human spirit."[29]

Unlike symbolist drama, Chekhov's plays have few religious, epiphanic outbursts like Sonya's at the end of *Uncle Vanya:* "We shall rest! We shall hear the angels." More often, his works express "the life of the human spirit" indirectly, by implication, in the subtext, in the pauses. Stanislavsky's interest in the famous Chekhovian "mood" or "atmosphere" came from its spiritual charge, the way in which frogs or dim lights or long pauses could evoke a world of shared consciousness that included thought and word but existed elsewhere too, "in the glances of the actors, in the emanations of their inmost feelings."[30] Even though the path through Sorin's estate is strewn with the shrubs of verisimilitude, the park experience is spiritual, being shot through with the *genius loci* and the spirits of the human beings in attendance.

Stanislavsky had periods when he veered to either side of this artistic and philosophical synthesis: his early productions were artificially dependent on the physical, and he had an unsuccessful fling with symbolism around 1905. But to a remarkable extent he steered a true course; in his best work he constantly aimed at this special sense of being true to life.

A final question about truth and directing concerns the relation between means and ends: Does a director's method, considered ethically or aesthetically, bear consequences for the truth of the final theatrical results—the production? Stanislavsky, whose methods changed with the years, later claimed that his despotism had stifled the Art Theatre's early productions:

> [At the time of *The Seagull*], while our actors were yet untrained, the despotic methods of the stage director were in full force. The stage director of necessity became almost the only creator of the play. Hiding in his study he made a detailed *mise en scène* that agreed with his emotions, his inner sight and hearing. He had no business with the inner emotions of the actor. He thought at that time that it was possible to order others to live and feel according to his despotic will. He gave orders to all and for all places of the performance, and these orders were binding for all of the actors. It was impossible to argue, and besides, there was no one to argue, for the actors were still merely pupils and could not cross weapons with the stage director.[31]

Stanislavsky and others have so often reinforced and elaborated the negative thrust of this self-criticism that I wish to accent the positive: he describes here a means of true creation, a consonant imaginative act, a realized stylistic vision, and a pedagogical transaction. If his early method was autocratic, how else was he to direct well in 1898? "I did not know how to do the director's work otherwise," he admitted. Neither did anyone else. And how else was he to meet the theatre's central necessity, the rising and falling curtain? "It was necessary to produce a performance," he wrote of his first big success, *The Fruits of Enlightenment.* "I showed what my imagination saw to the actors and they imitated me. Where I was able to feel things rightly the play came to life." Like so many directors, he faced the task of directing young, amateur, and mediocre actors. "If one is forced to give talentless actors big parts one is also forced, for the sake of performance, to hide their faults."[32] Was he an autocrat? Yes, a benevolent despot working in czarist Russia on a German model. No surprises there.

Directing strongly from a clear, confident vision of the play, Stanislavsky was following the new, revolutionary model of "the director." The year 1890 was important in his development, for that is when he took over the reins of the Society of Art and Literature from Fedotov, a man of stern control who taught Stanislavsky how to create a dynamic mise from "the inner seed of the play.[33] In the same year, Stanislavsky was first exposed to the Meininger Company, the most influential example available in Europe for a young director seeking to define his own style.

Duke George II of Saxe-Meiningen, inspired by his passion for dramatics, founded the first modern theatre company. He introduced ensemble acting as a replacement for the star system and insisted on strong directorial control over all creative and interpretive departments. Since his was a court theatre, its method was autocratic by definition. The duke's dictatorial directing style was passed on to one of his assistants, Ludwig Chronegk, who had charge of the company during its Russian tour. Stories about Chronegk's despotism in rehearsals appealed to Stanislavsky for two reasons: he was searching for a role, and he saw a strong parallel between the duke's company and his own. The Meininger productions appealed to him because of their dynamism and strength of image: "Productions that were historically true, with well-directed mob scenes, fine outer form and amazing discipline." To some eyes, all this historical verisimilitude and strong, bold handling was a compensation for the relative absence of high-quality acting, but it was the nature of the Meininger style to challenge the theatre of great stars, the theatre of actor-managers. The "director's methods" would show "the spiritual content" of "the creative works of the great poets," at least in Stanislavsky's analysis.[34]

For years, Stanislavsky emulated Chronegk's burning, dictatorial manner as a director. And for years the Meininger style—forceful composition dominating weak acting—was the style of the Society of Art and Literature and of the early Moscow Art Theatre. When an actor was unbearably bad, as the Iago was in 1896, Stanislavsky would plunge the stage into darkness, creating a sensational effect in the process. In the row in Cyprus (act 2, scene 3), Stanislavsky was not satisfied to have Iago cause a street scuffle or a barrack-room brawl in order to disturb Othello's marriage night. In 1896, Iago used Cassio's incapacity for wine to bring on a revolt, a disturbance shattering Venetian control over the whole angry island. The scene opened far down center in a Turkish coffee house, behind which streets ran into the hills, into the town. Iago was thus able to manipulate his pawns with the entire island seemingly at his back. At the peak of the action, with a bell clanging away, the Venetian soldiers drew up down center, their backs to the audience, and stood off an angry mob of Cypriots that had advanced threateningly through the streets and over the hills, with scimitars and sticks raised above their heads, their savage eyes gleaming. Into this confrontation, into "the very pit of death," came Othello "with a great sword in his hand with which he seems to cut the crowd in two." The mise thus stated something about Iago that the actor could not show. (K. S.: "Here . . . one could truly appreciate the satanic plotting of Iago."[35]) Of course it was an interpolation, but the interpolation succeeded nevertheless. It used the large, illusionistic stage of Stanislavsky's time (compare film today) to create a plausible and entertaining scene illustrating a theme central to Othello and to *Othello:* how fragile control can be, of a state or of a soul. With general intention the same point, Stanislavsky restaged this as a guardroom scene in 1929–30.

My point here is that autocrats can find truth as easily as democrats can, however squeamish we may be about autocratic methods. Also, we have learned our very squeamishness from Stanislavsky himself.

A few months after Russia's first revolution, in 1905, Stanislavsky took a Finnish holiday during which he faced some unanswered questions about the theatre and thereby initiated a revolution in his own career. In the next twenty-five years, with his attention increasingly on acting research, he revised his "idea of the director" and his practical directing methods. Gradually, he left the autocratic method to younger imitators like Tairov and Meyerhold and advocated a new notion of the director as "midwife." In the old model, the director commenced a period of artistic isolation, had a vision, and returned to the theatre to realize that vision via rehearsal. In the new model, directors emphasized not results ("act this way") but process (how to achieve the required results). Instead of preparing production plans beforehand and alone, the director now prepared "everything for the actor, but only after we have ascertained exactly what his needs are and what will appeal to him most of all."[36] The director-actor relationship thus became pedagogical rather than dictatorial, proximate rather than distant (contrast Chronegk behind his desk ringing a bell to stop and start action in rehearsals). Like the most famous midwife of them all, Socrates, the new director asked questions rather than demonstrating results for emulation. In his later years, instructing Leonidov in the role of Othello or V.O. Toporkov in Chichikov *(Dead Souls)*, Stanislavsky questioned, probed, and led actors through the many steps of growing into a part. And, as the director Vasily Sakhnovsky recalled in 1948, "As he did all this he never betrayed himself, never indicated what he was leading up to. All the time, he protected the creative intuition of the actor and watched the processes in which the desired state arose in the actor." Stanislavsky had always directed with "prodigious inventiveness" and "immense imagination," but his later, midwifely style created "productions where the actor's effort was the basic and chief element."[37]

Stanislavsky's new ideas about directing changed the nature of rehearsal and play preparation generally. Now rehearsals were imbued with the atmosphere of the "laboratory"; they became places for study, trial, "bold experiments and unexpected experiences."[38] Such exploration demanded time (the Moscow Art Theatre was first infamous, then famous for very long rehearsal periods) and showed a certain wastefulness (some experiments fail or prove to be irrelevant to production), but it assumed that all experimentation helped build general concepts and yielded a logic for particular solutions. This held a revolutionary implication for the process of devising a mise-en-scène. Now the mise came not before but after (as a result of) work with the actor; now a director's starting points were hypotheses rather than inspired insights. This reversal of work and idea created a major controversy among directors, particularly since the

1960s, when the laboratory and workshop became dominant forms of theatrical experimentation.

But in 1898, when Stanislavsky developed the mise for *The Seagull*, he was working in the only way he knew and in the best way then possible, from within his own creative imagination, searching there for a believable, that is, a true, *Seagull*.

Acts 2 and 3

As in any well-constructed play, acts 2 and 3 (the middle) of *The Seagull* develop the problems and attractions of act 1. Act 2 begins with a long sequence featuring all the characters except the two leading men. On a hot, lazy afternoon, the company relaxes idly on the lawn, but the peace is shattered by an argument over horses between Arkadina and the steward Shamrayev. Next come a short scene between Dorn and Pauline, Nina's soliloquy on fame, Konstantin's entry with the dead seagull and his short quarrel with Nina, and the long, climactic lecture and love scene in which Trigorin meditates for Nina on writing and on life. Act 3 takes place in Sorin's house (see Plate 1) and is more tightly focused; it is a string of dialogue scenes—Masha and Trigorin, Nina and Trigorin, followed by three scenes featuring Arkadina with Sorin, Konstantin, and Trigorin—capped by the departure of the actress's entourage. Over Arkadina's scenes is suspended the central plot question of act 3: will Nina and Trigorin establish a liaison?

Some things never change on the estate. Each summer day brings the same arguments about horses and health. The same minor characters sound their same notes: Sorin's life is unsatisfactory, Pauline's loveless, and Medvyedenko's pinched. Dorn, who seemed momentarily the *raisonneur* at the end of act 1, in act 2 lapses into incessant and detached humming. J. B. Priestley once observed that Dorn "seems to carry weight that he never really uses."[39] True, that is the essence of the man.

But other things do change, and seriously. In acts 2 and 3, Masha abandons her hope for Konstantin and embraces failure by marrying the schoolmaster. Konstantin despairs, grows hysterical, attempts suicide, and tries to provoke a duel. Nina decides to leave home and

1. Acts 3 and 4 of *The Seagull*, 1898. From Konstantin Stanislavsky's *The Seagull* Produced by Stanislavsky.

makes an open play for Trigorin's affections. Trigorin struggles to leave Arkadina and fails, but he secretly arranges to see Nina in Moscow anyway. Even Arkadina, whose life stays the same, is at least constantly flamboyant, emotional, and unpredictable.

In these two acts, the characters of Trigorin and Arkadina are explored seriously for the first time. Stanislavsky was critical of both. He eventually acted the role of Trigorin (and none too well, either), but the mise provides no special insights about the novelist because, in the tower during August and September, Stanislavsky planned to play Dorn. In fact, he seems to have paid intermittent attention to Trigorin, for the only extended blank space in his notes occurs in act 2, in Trigorin's long discussion with Nina, from his agreement to discuss his life until Arkadina's voice interrupts them. Balukhaty speculates that the director was initially vague about the character, and that the subsequent acting of the role of Trigorin gave Stanislavsky no reason to return to fill the notebook's gap. This may be true, but I think it is just as important to point out Stanislavsky's strategic headnote to this scene, which makes his silence seem purposeful. He advised Nemirovich that Nina and Trigorin, sitting down right, should not change positions during the entire scene—and that if Trigorin finally must move for dramatic relief or for emphasis, then Nina should not, but should hold her fixed position and rapt gaze so that they form a single seamless image. He wanted the scene tightly focused by blocking, by circles of attention, by stillness. To those working in rehearsal he posed a serious challenge; as he said to Gordon Craig in 1909: "the most difficult thing in the world is to put two actors on the stage and make them go through their dialogue without moving."[40]

Apart from this crucial scene, Stanislavsky had a single impression of Trigorin that dominated the mise-en-scène: he was unassertive and unenergetic. In act 1, he first entered as the fourth person in a group of six, walking behind Arkadina and hence automatically unnoticeable. Not until after Konstantin's play did Trigorin speak, and then he was reticent: "Everyone writes as he likes and as he can" is the whole of his first speech. Stanislavsky emphasized the writer's attention to his notebook and the fisherman's yen for the lake—thoughts unshared with the audience or with his friends. Trigorin was no more demonstrative in the final act, particularly during the lotto games. Unlike his mistresses, he showed no desire to dominate crowds.

He seemed by nature to be pensive, passive, quiet, and unassuming (which is why everyone actively assumed an attitude toward him). Stanislavsky stressed this in the end of act 2, when he resumed his notes on the Trigorin-Nina scene. After his long talk with Nina, Trigorin stretched and sighed, wrote lazily in his notebook, and squeamishly handled the dead seagull. At the beginning of act 3, he warmed up very slowly. He would like to stay longer at the estate, he said, but when Masha asked why he did not find a way to convince Arkadina to stay, he paused, scratched lazily behind his ear, and said, "No use." When Nina entered this discussion, Trigorin's approach was limited to surreptitious glances (like Nina's earlier). When Nina and Trigorin were left alone, she took all the initiatives while he remained restrained and off-balance.

Eventually, as he pleaded with Arkadina to let him go, Trigorin was roused to be "forlorn" and "rapturous." But his emotional demands lacked force. The argument in act 3 between the aging lovers begins with a summary image; Trigorin suddenly turns from Nina's locket and says to Arkadina, "Please, let's stay for just one more day!"—and she shakes her head no. Stanislavsky's version was: "Jumping to his feet, he runs to Miss Arkadina; speaks boldly, forcefully, confidently," and then, "Turning round to him, Miss Arkadina looks straight into his eyes. She has understood everything. A pause. She shakes her head. Trigorin deflates completely, says in a faltering, imploring voice, 'Let's, please!' and sits down on a chair despondently." This inflation-deflation continued throughout the scene. Trigorin addressed her one moment "with suddenly awakened energy"; a few moments later he clasped his head in despair, then suddenly rushed up to her, was embraced, vainly tried to fight free of her hold, and finally collapsed into the chair like "a dummy." In such rare assertive moments, Trigorin continued to wear out and wind down.

Both author and director rendered Arkadina without excessive admiration. She has an inhumane tendency to ignore other people except when she makes demands on them, and Stanislavsky portrayed this by having her sing in the hammock (act 2) and bully everyone when not in it. He punctuated her financial tightfistedness with her family, especially when she was seated at the dining room table (act 3) and in the departure scene. He gave her an added prop, a lorgnette, which was good for poking people's chests for emphasis and for peering through theatrically in moments of "demonstrated" interest.

Stanislavsky stressed her unpleasantness in scenes like the argument with Sorin in act 3, where she burst into tears and acted "thoroughly spoilt."

Being spoiled created two behaviors in Stanislavsky's treatment: violence and manipulation. Arkadina was violent in her "closet scene" argument with Konstantin (act 3). At first she skillfully rebandaged his wound with motherly care and consideration. But when he would not stop insulting Trigorin, she became enraged, threw the end of the bandage at him, smashed a chair onto the floor, and screamed hysterically at her son, who (it is worth recalling) had just tried to kill himself. Her manipulative skill made her triumphant in the emotional showdown with Trigorin. At first, as previously described, she needed only a look and a shake of the head. Then, when he rebounded—saying "Be my friend, set me free," entreating through two more speeches and repeating, "Set me free, please!"—she began her act. "Trembling nervously," reads the mise, "she recoils from him in horror, and drawing back a few steps, stops at the stove, leaning against it and staring at Trigorin." "Don't torment me," reads the script, "Boris . . . I'm frightened." When he advanced to convince her, she pushed him away and fluttered away to cry on the sofa. When he advanced again, she intercepted him with an embrace, knelt before him, and acted "a real tragedy, or rather melodrama." Throughout a long appeal, she spoke "in the tone and with the sort of pathos usually employed in melodrama," embraced his knees, wrestled him into a final crushing kiss, and then rose behind his chair to tousle his hair gently. In an aside, she told the audience, "Now he's mine!" (There are also three soliloquies here—vestiges, like those in *A Doll's House,* of another dramaturgical style.) Anyone could guess the source of her behavior, of her language, attitudes, and maneuvers, and Stanislavsky seems to have enjoyed showing her skill and efficiency in theatrical manipulation.

Arkadina has her charms, of course, and Stanislavsky let her gag charmingly before Konstantin's play in act 1, playing "the society lady" and snoring. She is lusty and vigorous, too. This woman has a career to guide, extravagant bills to pay, and men to manage. For Stanislavsky, her life was a noisy mixture of vanity, shy pride, manipulation, real love, and impulsive looniness. But at the end of act 3, when she swept out and on to her next stop, leaving three devastated men in her path, there was something terrible about her offensive, silly nature. Undertipping as she went, she was a bitch goddess, an insect queen. Was that what awaited Nina, should she be so lucky as to find career success?

Stanislavsky's stand or attitude with regard to Arkadina was that she was a spoiled child, whose childish charms made up for her barbaric irresponsibility less often than when she was young. The stand on Trigorin was that he was amoral, weak, and (hence?) irresistible to women. This latter view eventually landed Stanislavsky in trouble with Chekhov, but it is nonetheless an intelligent version of Trigorin. Both are conspicuously definite stands on characters—clear attitudes about them held by a strong director.

Clear and strong too is the basic directing method of acts 2 and 3, for it recalls the most obvious strategy of act 1—to demonstrate the structures of action, thought, and dialogue in *The Seagull* by organizing them around performance of physical tasks and other forms of activity. Stanislavsky did this in several ways, first by inflating. In the mise for act 3, he magnified Sorin's fainting spell. Woozy from listening to Arkadina reveal her parsimonious vanity ("Why, my dresses alone are enough to ruin me"), Sorin did not merely lean against the table but rather keeled over into her arms. Konstantin and Medvyedenko entered here, shedding coats and wiping boots in the hall as the old man was apparently dying in the front room. At this point, Chekhov has Sorin recover by taking a drink of water. Stanislavsky had Konstantin run in, take the water from Arkadina, fill his own mouth with it, squirt the water forcefully into the old man's face, fan the wet face with a handkerchief, and then use the handkerchief to dry the water off. This note follows: "This scene should be played as realistically as possible, so as to deceive the audience . . . to convince the audience that Sorin was dying. That would greatly heighten the suspense of the audience and its interest in what is taking place on the stage." (In theatrical parlance, this is sometimes stated cynically: when you do not know what else to do, keep your audience awake.)

As in the play's first scene, Stanislavsky imposed tasks that altered Chekhov's situations. The author began act 2 with the characters lounging on the lawn and conversing, and with Dorn reading aloud. Stanislavsky set the central garden table for tea, moved Masha and Arkadina about refilling cups, placed Dorn on the ground peeling and eating an apple, and made Masha slurp noisily from her cup. By the scene's end, when Shamrayev flew into a rage about the horses going to town, the focus on the tea table and on the act of taking tea had already been established. So the final argument could be "played by Shamrayev from his seat at the table, while stuffing bread into his mouth and washing it down with tea." At the climax, when Arkadina glared at him through her lorgnette, he jumped up, glared back at her for fully five seconds, and "fling [ing] the teaspoon angrily on the table (making the cups and saucers rattle)," he abruptly put on his cap and left. The scene's physical focus thus led to this appropriately furious, noisy conclusion, reinforcing the emotional progression from relaxation to comic rage.

This analogy of physical and emotional can yield ironic and revelatory results. In the next scene, Dorn and Pauline remained after the general exit. He had been inactive and bored, so he climbed onto the rocking bench down center and walked, "balancing himself, from one end to the other." Throughout the short scene, Dorn hummed, whistled, and swayed from side to side, quite intent on his exercises, "very cool and self-composed," absolutely galling Pauline, who was forced to follow him on the ground, begging for an emotional commitment. (No wonder Stanislavsky had her tear up the flowers Nina had given him! Pauline thought: he would not come down for me, but he did for her.) The words were supported by the activities, and the activities, by virtue of their seriousness, became dramatic actions. What the audience would see reinforced what it would hear—the story of an emotional failure (both of the couple and of the two individuals), which is a main theme of *The Seagull.* This image was clever and showy without being cheap. It was also plausible for Dorn and contrasted the gesture behind the gesture ("fearlessly walking the tightrope") with Dorn's actual boundedness, no matter that he played the lady's man in this district.

Stanislavsky's directing sometimes appears to be trivial, little more than constant prop management. Chekhov begins act 3 with Trigorin eating lunch while he talks to Masha. Accordingly, Stanislavsky invented for Masha a busy and complicated sequence of activity, which ended with her speaking to Trigorin while dressing in the hallway. After the Trigorin-Nina scene about the locket, Stanislavsky provided an additional luncheon, this time for Arkadina, whose appetite was so strong that the eating dominated and undercut everything she said to Sorin. In the mother-son confrontation that follows, Stanislavsky elaborated the already detailed Chekhovian directions about bandaging the head. Then he added the thrown bandage, the smashed chair, Konstantin's frantic twisting of a handkerchief as he began to fall apart. Arkadina repeated this hand-kerchief-twisting when she cried, and they both drank a glass of water after the spat was over. There was more busyness-of-hands-with-objects after Arkadina had conquered Trigorin. She recovered from the emotional storm by fleeing to her purse, inhaling smelling salts, applying perfume, working with comb and mirror. Equipment went in and out of the purse. Arkadina was herself again. She poured a glass of wine, mixed in water, and quaffed it.

Such prop business was actually seldom trivial, seldom without attendant values. In one case, the value was color. Chekhov notes that, while Masha and Trigorin are talking in act 3, "Yakov crosses the room from left to right with a suitcase." Stanislavsky expanded: "Yakov brings in a large suitcase and two travelling rugs, dragging them in with difficulty and putting them on [two upstage chairs]. Wipes his perspiring face with an elbow, and goes out the way he came to fetch something else." At its most significant, the actor's handling of a prop was freighted with insight. Late in act 2, when Nina first encounters the dead seagull, Stanislavsky did not let her simply hold it but had her thoughtfully stroke it, and by the time she repeated this gesture later with Trigorin, an observer might even guess that her sympathy for the bird, unshared by either man, would become confused empathy by act 4.

Props are only one example of Stanislavsky asserting the theatri-cality and meanings of his material. He was similarly emphatic in his handling of three important elements in acts 2 and 3: comedy, the crowd scene, and the play's tone.

Stanislavsky found comedy particularly in group scenes, like the lawn scene that begins act 2. Masha walking into the house on a leg that was falling asleep was meant as a small absurdity, and Stanislavsky increased its vigor by having her rub "unceremoni-ously" at the leg while walking. Dorn's disagreements with Sorin about life and illness are a running gag on the estate, and Stanislavsky used vocal directions to increase their snap. When the doctor re-sponds to the idea that Sorin might benefit from a spa, his first line, "Well, why not? Let him by all means," was spoken "very firmly and affirmatively." There was a considerable pause, a vocal shift, and the now unexpected, jolting, "On the other hand, he needn't, if he doesn't want to." Stanislavsky used a similar comic jolt when Masha spoke sharply to Nina about Konstantin's ill humor, then changed the tone of her voice to "sentimental, dreamy" and asked, "Won't you read us something out of his play, please?" Masha rhapsodized now, about Konstantin's wonderful reading voice, his blazing eyes, and his pale face, until "suddenly" Sorin's snoring broke in. Stanislavsky wrote that the comedy intensified by means of these vocal markings, "might provoke a smile from the audience. Well, I don't mind that." He was tentative about the idea of humor but assertive in directing it.

In 1898 Stanislavsky was already known for his energetic handling of crowds. His basic techniques of articulating background action and meshing it with dialogue spoken in the foreground came from the Meininger crowds, famous for their ensemble interplay. As the years passed, he learned still more about this special problem in directing, particularly how to increase the individualization of crowd members without destroying the scene's focus. He once staged an enormous crowd scene in a single on-set improvisation, because he had already personalized the characters played by the lowliest supers by providing them with histories, motives, tempi, and objectives. As he told Nicolai Gorchakov late in life, crowd scenes were finally reducible to a pattern: (1) arrival, (2) individual episodes involving major characters, (3) a general beat (such as dancing, games), (4) an individual episode based on dialogue, and (5) a dramatic finale. This is not quite the pattern he used at the end of act 3 when Arkadina leaves, but pattern there is nonetheless. On opening night, the scene brought down the house.

As Trigorin concluded his argument with Arkadina ("Oh dear, more railway carriages, stations"), activity stirred in two upstage areas. Through the door (up right center) came Yakov with the mistress's last two suitcases and a rug; he then walked through the front door (left) to put them in the carriage. The hall adjacent to the front door quickly came alive with noise and movement, for Shamrayev and a large group of servants stamped around outside and pressed in to see Arkadina depart. Shamrayev came forward to announce the carriage, then covered his embarrassment over the earlier fight with another rambling theatrical reminiscence ("Trapped in a caught!"). As Yakov reentered from the up right center door to get Trigorin's suitcase, a maid followed with Arkadina's hat and coat. A cook followed her and looked over the maid's shoulder at the preparations for departure. These figures were all Chekhov's creations, but Stanislavsky added: "An old nanny, with a walking stick and wearing spectacles, comes hobbling down from her upstairs room." He had still more extras stored in the back of the house.

This first assembly was capped by Arkadina's final arrangements before leaving. She put on her hat at the mirror (left) and was helped into her coat and galoshes by the maid and by Shamrayev. Pauline squeezed through the crowd of domestics in the front hall and stood there with her basket of plums and her emotions. But Arkadina wanted little of either. As their conversation ended, Medvyedenko and Sorin passed through, heading toward the left, and walked out into the hall. Arkadina (down right) was now undertipping the cook, the maid, and Yakov. (Poor Yakov was still struggling to fasten Trigorin's suitcase.)

Arkadina swept out into the hall, at which point the real chaos began. Pauline and Shamrayev were already there, along with the crowd of servants. Yakov moved in and out of the hall with baggage. Trigorin was in the hall, tipping liberally. Almost everyone was in the hall, in fact. The maid, cook, and nanny were the only people left in the dining room, and they were looking out into the hall. There "a whole farewell scene takes place" consisting of only two speeches (Shamrayev says, "Don't forget to drop us a line," and Arkadina asks, "Where's Konstantin?") spoken amid a great deal of noise and commotion. The servants talked loudly and bowed low. Arkadina bowed low in return. Servants pressed forward to kiss her hand. Yakov struggled with suitcases and shouted out to the coachman. Shamrayev busied about. Sorin came into the hall, shouting that if they did not hurry they would be late. Pauline pushed back into the dining room to retrieve the basket of plums. Arkadina shouted out to the carriage about her hatboxes and into the room about her son; she yelled over the heads of those in the crowd to tell the cook and maid about their tip. More kitchen maids came into the dining room from the door up right center, and they stood up on chairs to look out over the heads of the others at what was happening in the hall. One of these maids had a baby in her arms, and the baby began to cry. Arkadina finally exited, causing yet another mob scene as the crowd passed through the door, but the indefatigable Yakov had to push back against this flow, for he had forgotten a final suitcase. Then the stage was empty and harness bells could be heard ("the horses are shaking their heads," Stanislavsky explained in parentheses). The offstage noise framed the farewell between the disconsolate Nina and the hurried, but passionate, Trigorin:

> (A kiss of ten seconds. Voices off stage: 'Mr. Trigorin!' Trigorin runs
> off hurriedly. Nina stands on a chair, looking out of a window. Noise of
> a departing carriage, bells. Nina waves her handkerchief. Bows.)

The basic instincts for directing this crowd scene came from the script's stage directions (Desmond MacCarthy called Chekhov "the dramatist of good-byes"), and Stanislavsky's inflation of the departure business in no way interfered with its emotional meanings. His version simply and realistically provided more meaning. Consider what it said about the mistress's departure as an event below stairs.

In the mise for acts 2 and 3, Stanislavsky's third major emphasis was a reinforcement of an apparent change in the play's tone. During these acts, *The Seagull* turns from a satire of country life into a serious, even grim picture of failed lives. The tonal shift is especially remarkable as the action moves inside for the last two acts. The Moscow Art Theatre's designer and scene painter, Victor Simov, was instructed to point up "the contrast between the happy comfort of the genial and agreeable life in the first half of the play and the depressing emptiness, hollowness, and discord in the lives of the people in the play in the last two acts."[41] Apart from Arkadina's spats with Konstantin (act 1) and Shamrayev (act 2), most of the early, exterior action reflects a genial mood. But in acts 3 and 4 it does not: people are unhappy and in conflict, violence infects behavior, tears begin to flow. A lighthearted and light-minded summer dalliance starts to have consequences, and suddenly the world, once charmed, turns sordid and sour. The damage so notable toward the end is ultimately neither justifiable nor funny.

Clearly, act 3 is not very humorous. Stanislavsky set the mood by adding a clock ticking away in the background (time is running out, it said; time here is monotonous and depressing). The act begins with Masha's forced gaiety about her acceptance of Medvyedenko, revealing how grim her decision has been. Her self-characterization ("Mary, the world forgetting, and by the world forgot") may be her pose, but it is also a true farewell. Later, at the end of Trigorin's short locket scene with Nina, he recalls the lovely day a week ago (in act 2) "when you wore that summer frock. . . . We had a long talk and—

there was a white seagull lying on the seat." (Trigorin thus fixes the picture in his imagination.) Stanislavsky made Nina look up "quickly at him in alarm." After a pause, she said, "Yes, a seagull" with "a troubled face." As in act 2, where her "serious" and "overcast" reactions greeted Trigorin's story idea, the trouble written on her face pointed toward the bitter consequences of dalliance, whether with women or with images.

Act 3 is also less humorous because it is Arkadina's act. Stanislavsky intensified her remorselessness with Sorin by elaborating the fainting spell. In the next scene, she viciously attacked her son, both physically and verbally. Konstantin poured out his anguish and bewailed his "shattered" hopes, the loss of Nina, and his failure as a writer. Her response was to stroke his head and say, "Don't give up, my darling . . . Everything will come right." To climax her domination in this act, Arkadina vampirized Trigorin, draining him of his will, and exited in that flurry of luggage and servants, bellowing commands and undertipping as she went. This was a ruthless woman— and a stupid one. Her son had just tried to kill himself and, without bothering to decipher the message in that gesture, she was leaving him to be cared for by Sorin, who in fact already required Konstantin's services as a nurse.

These people are not thinking, not understanding their experiences, and (especially Trigorin and Arkadina) not even remembering very well. They reveal their habitual patterns of activity, and those habits, however laughable, are finally dangerous. The play makes us wonder why these people live this way. In act 2, Dorn watches the petty but furious quarrel between Shamrayev and Arkadina, then thinks about it and says it is "tiresome." Nina enters and thinks about it too from her much younger viewpoint, pronouncing it "strange." Stranger still is that dead bird of Konstantin's, which in turn makes Trigorin's thoughts jump from bird to girl to story idea: "a man comes along, sees her, and—just for the fun of it—destroys her, like the seagull here." Both men think they are being clever with their similes and symbols, when they are really being sentimental and tactless and stupid. In Ibsen and in the world, such behavior kills.

A moment at the climax of act 3 epitomized the dangerous moral situation. It was the end of Trigorin's argument with Arkadina. With his will claimed ("Now he's mine!"), Trigorin sat staring into space. As Arkadina inhaled her sal volatile and scented herself, the pauses lengthened. It was a sad moment, a sinking. Trigorin sat "with a lugubrious look on his face, staring in front of him. Then he stretches himself lazily, takes out his note-book, and begins to write (there is nothing else he can do now!)." In that final parenthesis, Stanislavsky was true both to his conception of Trigorin and to the novelist's self-estimation. After a moment, having jotted down a phrase he heard that morning that "may come in useful," Trigorin returned to stretching and complaining about the railway accommodations ("refreshment bars, mutton chops, talk"). Just so important was his own or anyone else's inner life. And if that was true, more people would be hurt before the play was finished.

Chekhov's Opinion

In the preceding discussion of tone, I have deliberately skated over the top of the great controversy concerning this play, Stanislavsky's mise, and the production based on it: Did Chekhov approve or disapprove of this Stanislavsky-Nemirovich *Seagull?* Did the dramatist not accuse the directors and actors of misunderstanding his play? And did he not generally disapprove of their work? No matter that this *Seagull* was almost universally applauded in 1898, that it saved the Moscow Art Theatre and made revolutionary changes in theatrical art and gave the dramatist a career as a playwright. In the eyes of many historians, Chekhov's reputed dislike of the production outweighs all these facts. So the antitheatrical prejudice sustains itself.

My intention is to show that "Chekhov's dislike of *The Seagull*" is a historical claim based on the flimsiest evidence and that his actual negative reactions were neither simple nor founded firmly in reality. The most commonly advanced arguments in support of this claim follow, in italics.

Chekhov must have been able to judge better than we can. In fact, Chekhov's critical remarks have little connection with either Stanislavsky's mise or the finished production. He visited the theatre very briefly during the early rehearsals, in September 1898, made some comments, and then left after a few days. He never saw the play performed that first season in Moscow. But in early May of 1899, after the season had ended, the productions had been stored, and the theatre was under renovation, Chekhov came to town demanding to see the show. So the dispirited and unconfident actors were called back to perform without scenery, costumes, props, or production effects in a strange and empty theatre (the Nikitsky) before an audience of ten. To this seriously reduced showing, Chekhov responded with a mixed opinion. He had a chance to see the actual production during the Crimean tour of 1900, but he left Sebastopol as *The Seagull* was opening. In Yalta, on April 23 of that year, an elaborate honorific speech was addressed to Chekhov after a *Seagull* performance, but there is no record that he either saw the show or commented on it. He did see the play near the end of 1900 in Moscow, but by this time all his recorded criticisms (some of which follow) had been uttered.

Chekhov disliked the departure scene in act 3 because of its excessive realism. He said that bringing in all the servants, even that crying baby, was like a piano top crashing down in the middle of a pianissimo passage, a violation of stage conventions, and a superficiality rather than an example of the "quintessence of life," which theatre art should reflect.[42] Or so he was quoted by Meyerhold, in a later attack on Stanislavsky's superficial realism. But Chekhov allegedly said this in September 1898, when Stanislavsky was still in Kharkov and the play was in its earliest rehearsals. And he apparently said it in a casual conversation with an actor who had given him a verbal impression of some intentions in the mise. Chekhov is never supposed to have made such a statement to the producers or about the production. And even if he had, would he have been very acute in his criticism?

Chekhov disliked the sound effects and other naturalistic devices. These effects were like a real nose poking through a hole in a realistic portrait, Chekhov said—realism at war with art. But again, this dislike was "in general." Again, it was supposedly mentioned in the casual conversation with the actor in September 1898. Chekhov did not hear the sound effects at the Nikitsky. But did he not make the same criticism of environmental sound later, at a *Cherry Orchard* rehearsal? His next play, he told Nemirovich and Stanislavsky at a rehearsal, would have a hero turn to his friend during a pause in the action and observe, "What fine quiet. . . . How wonderful! We hear no birds, no dogs, no cuckoos, no owls, no clocks, no sleigh bells, no crickets."[43] Like the directors, I take the remark as a somewhat serious joke, and a good joke, but a joke nonetheless. Most important, to think that Chekhov opposed accuracy or naturalism is to misrepresent his aesthetics. He was the one, after all, who insisted that a military acquaintance attend *Three Sisters* rehearsals as a "technical consultant" sits on a modern movie set—to watch for misrepresentation of military bearing, dress, or manners. And if Chekhov saw a distinction between realistic costume or behavior and realistic sound, that distinction lost all force in later theatre.

The remarks by Chekhov to the actor during early rehearsals are entertaining as anecdotes and useful as generalized warnings against inappropriately excessive realism. Meyerhold used them to criticize just that failing in the second *Seagull* production (1905), particularly by comparing it to the 1898 version, in which he had played Konstantin. But it does not say much merely to draw a line with regard to verisimilitude (this far, no farther), especially not for Chekhov, whose own verisimilitude had inspired Stanislavsky to formulate his inventions in the first place. And this discussion of excessive realism is clouded further by an inattention to specific results. For example, the baby does not cry in a pianissimo passage (Chekhov was presumably thinking about the final tender farewell between Nina and Trigorin?) but in a crowded, busy, noisy departure scene that Stanislavsky intensified precisely so that it might contrast with the quiet, lingering rendezvous at the end.

Chekhov demanded the replacement of the first Nina (Maria Roxanova), so bad was her acting. In May 1899, when he saw the Nikitsky Theatre version, Chekhov complained privately to Gorki that Roxanova "blubbered loudly throughout," which she seems to have done in act 4 more than anywhere else.[44] His disappointment should have been no surprise, for Nemirovich had told him after the first night that Roxanova was "the weakest of the lot."[45] All accounts agree that she was not right in the part and not then a terribly good actress. But how unremarkable such failure is, particularly in the first production of an innovative work where the playwright takes no active role.

Chekhov disapproved of Stanislavsky's Trigorin. To Stanislavsky's face, the author called his portrayal of Trigorin "wonderful" and "excellent," but different from his own interpretation.[46] Privately he complained that Stanislavsky had taken Trigorin's remark to Arkadina about having "no will of my own" so seriously that he had made the character too passive, "like a paralytic." A writer friend, Yelena Shavrova, had told Chekhov as much after the opening. After the Nikitsky performance, Chekhov wrote Gorki that such a Trigorin had been "nauseating to behold."[47] As we record this objection, it is worth noting how passive Chekhov's character is, as a lover (passive-aggressive), as a writer (observational), as a workman (driven but unenthusiastic), and as a sportsman (a fisherman). If Stanislavsky's acting failed to make this passivity coherent, his target was nonetheless a true one.

Chekhov also told Stanislavsky that the character should be played in checked trousers and torn shoes, which the director took to mean inelegantly. Reviving the part in 1905, Stanislavsky finally deciphered Chekhov's implicit point: Nina's hero worship of Trigorin needed to be undercut; an ironic visual cue was needed to make the audience notice her mistake. So he added the change in 1905. But historians and critics have challenged the appropriateness of this idea for good reasons—for one, would Arkadina consort with a writer who presented himself in this fashion?

Whereas Chekhov thought his plays were comedies, Stanislavsky interpreted them as tragedies. This is the famous crux of the argument over Chekhov's opinion. In fact, Chekhov called two of his four major works comedies (*The Seagull* and *The Cherry Orchard*), called *The Three Sisters* a "drama," meaning a serious play, and evaded the generic question by subtitling *Uncle Vanya* "Scenes from Country Life." Such labels are confusing both internally and comparatively, for *Cherry Orchard* and *Three Sisters* portray a family's fall and disintegration, *Vanya* and *Sisters* end with departures, and *Seagull* and *Sisters* conclude with death. All of these plays may now seem transparent in terms of character and theme, but genre remains their single great continuing mystery—a perpetual source of argument among directors, critics, and anyone else struggling to define the precise shadings, tones, and implications of specific events. Small wonder that it caused differences between its directors and its author, none of whom had ever seen such drama before.

A frequent side issue raised in the argument is Chekhov's protest that Stanislavsky "made my characters into cry-babies. That was not what I wanted."[48] He did later, perhaps, but not in *The Seagull.* Chekhov's script contains eight explicit directions for characters to cry (one in act 1, four in act 3, three in act 4). It also has four cues that introduce tears indirectly, as when characters enter having wept, are reported to have cried on exit, or speak in a voice "choked with tears." In his mise, Stanislavsky did nothing to elevate the indirect cues to direct ones, cut one of the direct cues, transposed another, and added two. The two tearful moments he added were both for Masha, at the end of act 1 and at the beginning of act 4, and both changed the play's substance in but a minor way. Stanislavsky did not turn these characters into crybabies. In the last two acts, Chekhov did that.

And yet Chekhov called his play a comedy. What did he mean by this label? Consider the greatest altercation over this issue, when Stanislavsky first termed *The Cherry Orchard* a melancholy tragedy and drew Chekhov's angry response that it was a comedy. How, or to what extent, is it a comedy? Has anyone ever proved that fascinating play a comedy in any convincing generic sense? Throughout the 1970s, I saw one director every two years announce the rediscovery of the play's comedy and then, with remarkable regularity, their productions failed. However many laughs *The Cherry Orchard* has, the play simply eludes the genre's traditional definition and assumptions. *The Seagull* failed the first time, in St. Petersburg, because someone took its subtitle literally and produced it as a preliminary in a benefit for a fat comic actress but without her in the cast, which upset the patrons.

Traditional definitions of genre are not much help in understanding Chekhovian drama because he wrote in a new genre. This is the greatest lesson Stanislavsky gleaned from these works, and though he did not learn it all at once, he learned more quickly than many critics who have the benefit of hindsight: not to trust singleness of genre or tone, not to discuss things "in general." Comic or tragic, which was Chekhov? Surely the answer is that he is a canonical case in the history of modern tragicomedy and that the pitch or tone of his plays is not tragically glum or anarchically hilarious, but ironic. Chekhov was one of the first great modern ironists, which is why his plays continue to seem so thoroughly contemporary as decades pass.

Chekhov had an ironic cast of mind, about the Moscow Art Theatre among other things—about its directors, productions, and actors. He chided them and kidded them equally. He doctored them and married one of the actresses, yet kept an orthodox literary distance from the world of theatre. He wrote parts for them, which implies respect for a fellow artist, but flared into towering anger when a silly actor spoke an irksome phrase during the first reading of *The Three Sisters*. Chekhov and Stanislavsky could be estranged and reconciled by art, estranged and reconciled by life. The playwright was not easy to understand then (and is hardly easier now) because he was almost always of two minds, of contradictory, ironic, critical disposition. And so with *The Seagull*. After the Nikitsky performance, when he told Gorki that Stanislavsky's Trigorin was "nauseating to behold," Chekhov added what few scholars bother to cite: "It wasn't bad on the whole though, quite gripping in fact. There were moments when I found it hard to believe I had written it."[49]

Chekhov disliked the treatment of act 4. According to Olga Knipper-Chekhova, Chekhov said at the Nikitsky, "I suggest that my play should end with the Third Act: I shall not permit you to play the Fourth Act."[50] Beyond Nina's annoying crying in act 4, to what can we attribute this remark? Since it was made, David Magarshack has repeated the judgment that the final act in the 1898 production was a "complete distortion of the ruling idea of the play," creating a "complete misinterpretation" of *The Seagull*.[51] The reader will want to see, as we proceed to act 4, in what spirit Stanislavsky interpreted its material and whether that interpretation is consonant with a coherent view of the play. After analyzing the mise-en-scène, I know this much: Stanislavsky's finale, if it was to work at all, could not conceivably have succeeded with the production in storage, as in the Nikitsky performance. His last act, like Chekhov's, was the most atmospheric and spiritual of the four, the most dependent on space, light, rhythm, sound, wind, pause, and delicacy of feeling.

Act 4

The opening of act 4 was a virtual reprise of the play's opening. Set at an angle onto the stage was Konstantin's study, a converted drawing room now doubling as Sorin's bedroom, with French windows (left) and a door to the dining room (right)—see Plate 1. Like the woods at the top of act 1, the study was at first deserted and dimly lit—a reddish light came from two stoves and a lamp. There was, again as in act 1, activity near the rear of the set, where a maid set the table in the fragmentary offstage dining room. Outside, wind and rain beat against the windows, rattling the panes and frames. A nightwatchman knocked, dogs barked and howled, and from the back of the house came voices—Masha's and Medvyedenko's they would turn out to be (another link with the opening of act 1). They called, "Konstantin!"

The last sounds of the play—pistol shot and whispers—are also traces of Konstantin. Chekhov not only sets act 4 in Konstantin's room but makes him the act's central character—the most frequent object of interest of all the characters, including himself. The two major scenes relevant to Nina—in which he narrates her story and meets her—keep him centrally in view. Chekhov focuses attention repeatedly on Konstantin's writing, loves, pride, and gloom, thus devoting a large portion of act 4 to accounting for the suicide that ends it. Throughout, Konstantin is a figure out of sentimental tragedy, having finally discovered the only great role of his life: Hamlet, as he had hoped. But Konstantin experiences Hamlet's melancholy and despair without Hamlet's saving intelligence and dialectic.

"Konstantin!" Stanislavsky changed Chekhov's stage directions so that this first human sound came from offstage. Offstage sounds played an enormously important part in this, the most heavily annotated act in Stanislavsky's mise. In the mise up to this point, he used sound to great advantage in the first act, taking Chekhov's already generous sound directions (stage construction at opening, singing over the lake, waltz music from the house) and adding more in the same spirit: a distant bell ringing during a pause in Nina's play speech; the sounds of frogs, land rails, and singing peasants during the pause after "Bravo, Silva!"; a dog barking as Dorn sits alone; and an even greater variety of "nocturnal sound effects" at the end. In act 2, he added no sound, and in act 3 he inserted only the ticking clock and the jingling harness bells at the end. By comparison, the fourth act is a blizzard of sound cues; in dozens of notes he amplified Chekhov's instructions (offstage piano, knocking nightwatchman) by adding barking dogs and tolling bells and, finally, a seriously intensified version of the storm. Stanislavsky also made extensive use of offstage voices, most dramatically during the Konstantin-Nina scene, when they heard Arkadina and Trigorin offstage.

Stanislavsky began the act by stressing physical tasks in a familiar way. While Medvyedenko begged for attention, his wife was absorbed in reading Konstantin's manuscripts. While Masha and her mother talked, they made Sorin's bed and cleaned Konstantin's desk. Stanislavsky was still insisting on investigating the consequences of realism. When Konstantin stalked out of the room, having rejected Pauline's appeal to be kinder to Masha, the director left the two women far right in a corner of the set. The mise note states: "It does not matter that the audience on the left side of the auditorium may not be able to see Masha sitting on the divan because Konstantin's writing desk will be in the way. That may even add *a certain charm* to the scene." I add the emphasis to point out realistic principles yielding poetic or nonrealistic results. The actors' turned backs in the early acts conveyed the same idea. Another instance occurs at the end of the play, when Masha calls out the lotto numbers. Like some silver-age realists in cinema and theatre today (preeminently Robert Altman), Stanislavsky understood that when realism turned into theatrical "interference" (that is, when simultaneous action or interplay between background and foreground fogged the clear-pane-of-glass manner of realism), the results could be aesthetically complex and, at their best, realistically poetic.

But realism and particularly the imposed physical image were increasingly irrelevant as Stanislavsky neared the end. He had shown this same tendency in acts 1 and 2, starting each with physically dynamic images and ending with quieter, simpler passages. The same stylistic movement can be observed in the mise as a whole. By the time the serious parts of act 4 take place, Stanislavsky's direction was tightly controlled. Now he paid close attention to parsing the action and to mood and atmosphere. That is another way of saying that in this act the audience would spend more time watching people think and feel. While Masha and Pauline made the bed and listened to Konstantin's piano offstage, Masha reacted quietly but intensely—sighing, waltzing a few steps over to the window, looking out into the darkness, and dabbing away a few tears. "A pause (the music goes on). Pauline stops making the bed and looks thoughtfully at her daughter. (She has evidently remembered her own love affair with Dorn.) Voices can be heard in the dining room. Dorn's cheerful voice dominates the others." The doctor then appeared at the door, pushing Sorin's wheelchair.

Two scenes follow before the arrival of Arkadina and Trigorin. The first is preparatory and desultory; it shows how the locals live when they lack outside stimulation. The most poignant moment—one that resonates in each of these characters—is when Sorin tells of his idea for a short story, "The Man Who Wanted To." No one quite realizes an ambition. "And so on." In Stanislavsky's treatment of these pages, Dorn paced and hummed, Sorin read, Pauline made the bed, and Masha quietly and lovingly arranged Konstantin's bookshelf.

Soon after Konstantin reenters, beginning the second of these scenes, he is asked to tell the story of Nina's life during the two years that have passed since act 3. This was one of Stanislavsky's loveliest sequences. Konstantin sat on a footstool below Sorin's chair, down right. Medvyedenko was behind and to their right, near the stove. Dorn was also sitting in that area, in a rocking chair far down right. Pauline and Masha sat separately to their left. When Konstantin agreed to narrate what happened to Nina, the visual focus tightened further, for Stanislavsky had Masha cross up center to sit next to her mother, "who puts her arm round her, strokes her head, pressing her close to herself." (Stanislavsky continued in parenthesis, "I fancy both of them understand each other and each of them suffers in her own way.")

Konstantin began Nina's story with mention of the Trigorin affair and her dead child, terming her private life a "complete mess." Here a pause was filled with sounds of the stormy night. Dorn asked about her stage career and Konstantin answered quickly, "Her stage career was even a worse failure, I believe." Stanislavsky placed another pause with sound effects here, letting the audience absorb this generality before Konstantin listed the particulars of her failure. Konstantin then described Nina's acting with "his gaze fixed steadily at one point," his head propped in his hands, elbows on his knees. He finished a longish speech about the stage and answered Dorn's query as to whether she had talent with "I don't know. It's hard to say. I suppose she must have." Another pause, more sound effects. The mood had deepened—Dorn had been rocking his chair when the story began, but his rocking gradually slowed and now stopped. Stanislavsky added: "All of them are motionless, as though frozen." Konstantin spoke briefly about his attempts to see Nina. Another pause, the only one of these dictated by Chekhov. Sorin stroked the boy's head, as if stroking a puppy or a child. Konstantin asked, "Well, what more do you want to know?" He spoke about her letters, her incoherence, her fixation with being "the seagull," and then stopped. More sound effects could be heard offstage. "She's here now," Konstantin said. He told of her movements, of Medvyedenko's meeting her in a field. Explaining this incident, Medvyedenko moved from the stove to stand behind Sorin's chair, the first movement since the story began. Sorin continued to stroke Konstantin's head. Konstantin's last speech about her included more pauses, during which the audience heard the harness bells of the approaching carriage. Chekhov's script has Konstantin cross the stage at this point, but Stanislavsky cancelled that direction and kept him still, sad, listless. The bells became louder. Konstantin said, "How awfully easy it is, doctor, to be a philosopher on paper, and how damned difficult it is to be one in life!" After yet another pause, Sorin said, "She was such a sweet girl!"

Dorn suddenly recaptured his facetious mood and chided Sorin, leading to the usual parry and thrust between them. When Arkadina, Trigorin, and Shamrayev entered the room, the stage was suddenly a center of activity—greeting and gift-giving and diagonal crosses—that continued until the meeting between Trigorin and Konstantin. Stanislavsky clearly organized all this activity, saving his first full stop for the encounter of the two writers.

Medvyedenko's embarrassed departure was followed by Stanislavsky's next set piece, the lotto game. For a scene of less than five minutes (two pages of script), the director provided thirty notes. The opening, with Stanislavsky's directions cued into Chekhov's script (which had no directions of its own), follows:

ARKADINA: *(Miss Arkadina speaks very loudly and vivaciously.)* The stake is ten copecks. Put it down for me, doctor, will you?

DORN: Certainly, madam. *(Gets up and pulls out his purse.)*

MASHA: *(In a bored voice.)* Have you all put down your stakes? I begin . . . *(Masha deals the cards. A pause. (Wind, rattling of windows.) Dorn hums. Miss Arkadina, who smokes, also hums. Shamrayev is drumming on the table. Sorin yawns contentedly.)* Twenty-two!

ARKADINA: Got it. *(Miss Arkadina in a very thin voice and—bursts out laughing at her own joke.)*

MASHA: Three! *(Shamrayev repeats "Three" in his deep bass, then he and Miss Arkadina burst out laughing.)*

DORN: Right.

MASHA: *(Masha speaks in a monotonous voice.)* Have you put three down? Eight! Eighty-one! Ten!

SHAMRAYEV: *(Shamrayev, who takes the game very seriously, fidgets, searches for the number on his card, and flies into a temper.)* Don't be in such a hurry!

ARKADINA: *(Brags to Trigorin. Smokes.)* What a wonderful reception I had in Kharkov! My goodness, my head's still swimming!

MASHA: *(In the same dead voice.)* Thirty-four!

Stanislavsky orchestrated both lotto scenes by accentuating vocal varieties, by mixing registers, moods (boredom and petty fury share the same table), and modes (yawning, humming, laughing, singing, and speaking in assumed, theatrical voices all appear in the first ten speeches). To ground this variety and to control the tone of the play's conclusion, he used two other vocal devices—multiple pauses and Masha's droning of the lotto numbers.

The pause—the distinctive mark of modern drama—distinguished Stanislavsky's directing. But notice how useful it was also to Chekhov, whose scripts have a far higher incidence of the note "Pause" than the scripts of any writer I know who preceded him. In the mid-nineteenth century, a Frenchman might have started a riot with a stage direction like Chekhov's after Nina's final exit: "During the next two minutes Konstantin tears up all his manuscripts and throws them under the desk."

For Stanislavsky, a pause was first a marker, subdividing scene or speech rather as typographical breaks or lines divide printed material. Thus pausing was parsing, just as we observed in Konstantin's narration about Nina. Also, when placed between two pieces of material, pauses held the rhythms and energies of both (the known and the yet unknown) in balance, in tension. "I have altogether a passion for pauses saturated with tempo and rhythm," Stanislavsky wrote in his *Othello* notes, and that passion matured in the mise for *The Seagull*.[52] In the medium-sized lotto scene, Stanislavsky used six conversational pauses (compared with Chekhov's one), filling each with expressive sound: the gusty and eerie weather, Konstantin's mournful piano, Sorin's snoring, Arkadina and Dorn singing in harmony. Whatever their external sound content, the many pauses gained weight and meaning as they contained and controlled mood. During the lotto game, the repeated pauses deflated the action, revealing this life as boring and these characters as absent, abstracted, or tired. Things do not fall apart in this world, they just slow down. Classical tragedy thrills an audience with apocalypse, but here the audience must endure the entropy. Analogies with Clausius's 1865 discoveries about entropy in physical systems are pertinent: these people and their class in general can no longer convert spiritual energy into lifework; they increase their entropy by exchanges of spirit; their little universe, like the big one, tends toward a maximum of entropy, toward rigidification and death.

This trend toward entropy was increased by Stanislavsky's second mood-controlling device, Masha's voice calling the lotto numbers. He was discovering again the expressive value of scrupulous realism:

N.B. I would make Masha—all during this scene (even during the speeches of the other characters) go on calling the numbers, any numbers (irrespective of what the others say); for otherwise we get a very awkward situation on the stage, an artificial situation which occurs on the stage every time during a game of cards, dominoes, etc., namely, the game stops to give the characters time to make their speeches. This is neither life-like nor true. Let Masha go on calling the numbers without paying attention to what the others are saying.

Masha's voice particularly influenced the scene's mood and rhythm. In his headnote to act 1, Stanislavsky spoke of wanting to portray the "sad, monotonous life of the characters." Here is that life quintessentially described, with the lotto game as its most expressive format or setting, its symbol. Stanislavsky's version of the scene eventually shocked the play's audiences.

From the lotto game's conclusion to the reunion of Konstantin and Nina is a short transitional step that Stanislavsky took very carefully. Yakov came out to announce dinner by whispering "respectfully" in Arkadina's ear. As the players exited to eat, there was no loud and furious activity. Only when they moved back to the dining room, forming a backdrop for Konstantin sitting at his desk (down right), did they become "animated" and clatter the dishes. The focus was still downstage on the abstracted Konstantin during "*a very long pause.*" He wrote "without bending his back." Was this an expression of resolve? Did he have any? His thoughts were of failure, particularly the failure of the heart. Suddenly there was a knock at the window nearest his desk.

Stanislavsky's notations with regard to the climactic scene between Nina and Konstantin are clearest about blocking. His version of the beginning is detailed, from the knock at the window through Konstantin's search for Nina to his placing of an armchair against the door to forestall intruders. They spoke near the stove at right, where she went after flitting about the room. When she suggested that they sit and talk, they moved down right where she sat in the rocking chair and Konstantin again took the footstool. They discussed their past two years until, according to Chekhov, "Nina quickly puts on her hat and cloak." Stanislavsky imagined her running "across the whole length of the stage to the French window" with Konstantin in pursuit and then putting on her wrap. Thus they were both stage left, at the French windows, for the beginning of her longest speech, but she soon moved to sit at the card table (up center) to deliver the bulk of her remarks about acting. Before saying "Sh-sh— I'm going!" she jumped up and came down again to the French windows, where she remained until her exit. Except for fetching her a glass of water, Konstantin remained standing, motionless, just downstage of the French windows, through which the storm blew. After her departure, he lingered there with the glass still in his hand.

Except for these directions for physical movements, Stanislavsky said comparatively little about this scene. (Did he simply not understand it? Was he intentionally leaving room for the actors and Nemirovich to supply the emotions? Was he deliberately making it simple?) However, he did address both major questions raised by the meeting of Konstantin and Nina: (1) what is the state of her mind? (2) why, at the end of the scene, is Konstantin resolved to commit suicide? Any director trying to create a successful production of *The Seagull* will need to find decisive answers to both questions.

What are we to make of Nina at the end of the story? Her position is ambivalent, for she shows the ill effects of the past two years, yet she has faith in the future. Should we emphasize the damage or her determination to continue in spite of it? Chekhov's script abundantly illustrates the damage: Nina abruptly loses her train of thought, lapses into irrelevancies, shows bewilderment at Konstantin's ardor, and breaks into tears. She repeats the phrase "I'm a seagull" but always contradicts herself immediately. Can this woman possibly have a professional future in the theatre, a personal future in the real world? She seems desperate, sick, and pathetic. One critical camp endorses Nina's endurance and makes her into a heroine, taking her belief in the stage ("What matters is knowing how to endure") as the play's climax and her recollection of Konstantin's play as her apotheosis. "Her idealism has disastrous consequences," says Harvey Pitcher, "but Nina survives, and breaks the spell of the lake and the seagull, because she is in the long run spiritually much healthier than the other three."[53] I would point out some wishful thinking here. She shows few signs of spiritual health. To reach such a conclusion, we must believe her ramblings and disbelieve Konstantin's prior and present testimonies to the contrary. How or where, I wonder, has she broken the spell of the lake and the seagull?

Stanislavsky clearly emphasized her sickness and unpredictability. He brought her in with a great gust of wind and a slamming door. He urged Konstantin, after a first good look at Nina, to find her "changed" beyond recognition. Emphasizing Nina's erratic behavior, Stanislavsky described her as entering, hiding in a corner until Konstantin secured the doors, and then running joyously about the stage. Stopping abruptly, she looked around in a frightened, disoriented manner. Later in the scene she bolted to the French windows, put on her coat, opened the windows, and stopped, collapsing against the doorjamb in tears. At another point, while discussing Trigorin, she spoke for some time "to herself, her gaze fixed on one point." Later still, Stanislavsky imagined Konstantin treating her in a manner strikingly parallel to his treatment of the invalid Sorin. Clearly, the director did not believe that the character was in control of her mind or her life.

Chekhov's most vivid demonstration of Nina's instability is her thrice-uttered fixation with being a seagull. Konstantin has already prepared us for this in his narrative, and Stanislavsky had drawn a clear line between woman and bird in the middle acts. So in the mise he cut the second of these lines, "I'm a seagull. No, that's not it. I'm an actress. Yes!" (spoken just before Nina hears Arkadina and Trigorin in the dining room). It is the most important cut he made, one that might enrage those critics who are trying to prove that Nina has survived and matured, for this is the only time she makes the reversal from seagull to actress. But Stanislavsky apparently read this line (wrongly, I think) as just another instance of her fixation and considered it one instance too many. In the two other "I'm a seagull" sequences, he inserted typical emphatic devices: offstage laughter and a posture change. Stanislavsky thus saw Nina as Chekhov's Hedvig Ekdal, a young woman destroyed by the power of a simile fed to her by an older, apparently more sophisticated, male. A theme of both *The Seagull* and *The Wild Duck* is that metaphor is destructive to the naive, that when young and impressionable people are encouraged by the metaphorical mode, they can go as far as suicide, as far as spiritual self-destruction.

Why does Konstantin kill himself? His life has had three fixed points: his mother, his writing, and Nina. He lost faith in Arkadina when she reconciled with Trigorin after his affair with Nina. Immediately before Nina's entrance in act 4, Konstantin castigates himself as a writer for "lapsing into clichés" and says his work is "dreadful!" Whatever hope he has for a new art is very fragile: "whatever one has to say should come straight from the heart!" —yes, but what heart? Now he sees Nina in a terrible state and arguably headed for a worse one. Worst of all, she leaves him. His motives for existence have ceased to exist.

As Konstantin gives Nina a drink of water, he asks, "Where are you going now?" and she replies, "To the town." Stanislavsky added: "Nina wipes her tears with a handkerchief and smothers her sobs. Konstantin stands motionless, . . . staring lifelessly at one point. This is where he really dies." From this point to her departure, Stanislavsky kept Konstantin motionless, standing with the glass in his hand and speaking with a lifeless voice. She gave him a final quick hug and ran off, and he continued to stand so. One of the French windows was blown shut, so powerfully that a pane broke, and then the other window was blown shut too. The sound of footsteps trailed off and other nocturnal noises became more intense. Konstantin stood for fifteen more seconds with the glass and then, still motionless, let it fall. (Stanislavsky knew this was a cheap trick and said so in the mise, but he used it anyway.) At this point, the two-minute sequence stipulated by Chekhov began, in which Konstantin destroyed his manuscripts and prepared to destroy himself.

This scene between the two young people began with Konstantin running all over the set, both outside and inside, excitedly finding and following Nina. It ended with him in a state of complete immobility. A similar pattern exists within the play, which begins with Konstantin extraordinarily active and excited, then portrays his loss of energy and grim, hooded silences, and ends with this image of Konstantin with the glass, frozen in place—a man who does not (cannot?) move. Is he a victim of the entropic society in which he lives? Another of its symbols?

Completing *The Seagull* in 1895, Chekhov correctly described it as beginning forte and ending pianissimo. In the mise, the seven diners returned noisily—pushing back chairs in the dining room, knocking and shouting at the barred door, laughing and dancing as they entered the room. Then they sat down to play lotto, which altered the mood. The gunshot momentarily excited them, but they were relieved by Dorn's lie that something had exploded in his medicine chest. They settled back down to play, and the earlier monotony resumed. Masha called the lotto numbers in her dull voice. Arkadina hummed gaily. Learning of the suicide from Dorn, Trigorin moved from downstage to the table, where he unsuccessfully struggled with himself to inform Arkadina. Masha continued to call the numbers. The characters were suspended in their worlds. The image was printed in the mind. Curtain.

This conclusion has the flavor of a traditional "strong" ending (a gunshot), which is rare in Chekhov's mature plays. When writing the first version (1895), the playwright had in fact aimed at traditional, conventionally effective dramaturgy. He ended one draft of act 1 with a startling revelation of parentage, which was about as conventionally dramatic as one could be in the late nineteenth century: Masha, the audience learned, was actually Dr. Dorn's daughter. When Nemirovich pointed out that Chekhov had done nothing with this in later acts and that he should either develop or cancel it, Chekhov replied metaphorically, "But the public likes seeing a loaded gun placed before it at the end of an act."[54] Nemirovich's trenchant answer—that loaded guns must eventually be fired, not simply removed during a scene change—may have stimulated Chekhov's deliberate handling of the literal gun in his final version. In act 2, Konstantin brings it on stage along with the dead seagull, and vows to "kill myself in the same way soon." In act 4, as the lotto players discuss the stuffed bird, the gun goes off behind the scenes.

As a director, Stanislavsky favored strong, decisive endings. Good openings, he said, were instant capital for directors, but endings were the final accounting. "The audience will never forgive you if the performance does not have exactly the right ending."[55] Since *The Seagull* ends with a traditional coup de théâtre with a modernist twist, Stanislavsky muffled the surprise and suspense of the offstage shot with quiet monotony—Masha's voice calling the numbers. We may read Konstantin's suicide romantically, as existential assertion against the mediocrity and failure of self, society, and world. We may simply think a pitiable, confused kid blew his brains out. What is certain is what remains at the end: members of provincial society and bourgeois artists droning on, oblivious. As in the closely analogous *Hedda Gabler,* the final image is a vanishing into insignificance — "People don't do such things!" says Judge Brack, as the audience stares at the corpse of one who did.[56] Like Nina, whose eager young soul blazes for a season among these people, only to be forgotten and ignored, Konstantin makes a brief, loud noise that will be absorbed, misunderstood, and finally lost in the bourgeois mind.

Evaluation

Was Stanislavsky's work on *The Seagull* successful? If we measure his success by popular interest in the play's eventual production, certainly it was. The first-night audience signified its approval with tumultuous applause. Eighteen performances were given in the 1898/99 season (a season's total second only to that of the popular historical piece *Czar Fyodor*), and the production was a prominent repertory item for three more seasons. A 1905 revival had new exterior settings and was marked by greater directorial insight into Chekhov and more sensitive acting. This new version played eleven times at the season's beginning, then disappeared at the end of the year. Meyerhold blamed its failure on excessive verisimilitude. Nemirovich remembered that "everything was excellent, but the old aroma was gone."[57] Perhaps the failure was simply a result of the December revolution and the Moscow Art Theatre's extended international tour, both of which disrupted their repertory. Whatever the cause, the play was dropped from production for decades. But the 1898 production lived on in the theatre's iconography—a seagull appeared not only on the curtain, but on tickets and programs—and in its mythology: Chekhov's play, Stanislavsky said, "brought us good luck and, like the Star of Bethlehem, lighted the new road we were to travel in pursuit of our art."[58]

Since my aim in this chapter is to analyze and evaluate Stanislavsky's mise rather than the production, I should rephrase my opening question as follows: Was Stanislavsky's treatment, his imagined version of the play, an artistic success?

Nemirovich thought so, and he was the pilot of this enterprise. He had worried at first, for his partner usually exaggerated so flamboyantly, whereas Chekhov's play obviously needed restraint. But in the pages that came back from Kharkov, Nemirovich found not exaggeration, not just competence, but revolutionary innovation. "Very audacious," he called the mise, "very much alive."[59] More specifically,

Nemirovich responded enthusiastically to the utterly novel handling of props, the concrete and vivid sketching of quotidian activity, the stunning long pauses, the realistic sound and lighting. After the first night, he told Chekhov: "I think you'd have gasped at the first and, especially, in my opinion, the fourth act."[60] The point of this is that Nemirovich himself was still gasping at how audacious and brilliant their production was.

Stanislavsky, often his own harshest critic, thought he had succeeded. He described two paths leading to an understanding of the play: Nemirovich's, through literature, and his own, over the "road of images."

> We seemed to be digging tunnels from two opposite sides towards one central point. Little by little we approached each other; now only a thin wall separated us; now the wall was broken and we could easily pass from the literary to the artistic and unite them for the general procession of the actors along the way we had found. Once we found that inner line of the play, which we could not define in words at that time, everything became comprehensible of itself not only to the actors and the stage directors, but to the artist and the electrician and the *costumier* and all the other co-creators of the production.[61]

My own opinion should be obvious by this time: The mise shows Stanislavsky successfully imagining the play. I have already described his creation of beautiful pictures, his realistic intensity, his mixture of emotion and comedy, his evocative directing of mood, and his strong handling of motive, character, and the play's progress (both its minute, beat-by-beat progress and its overall change in tone and meaning). I could also have emphasized certain other virtues, like Stanislavsky's self-critical skepticism about sensational "effects." In the remainder of this chapter, I return to the three notions of truth mentioned earlier to determine whether Stanislavsky's imagining of the play was successful in the sense(s) of being true.

1. *Correspondence.* The mise was true to events as they happen in the real world. That is precisely what Nemirovich first found so startling about it—its accuracy, its trueness to real life, its "naturalism." Truth to life is also what Chekhov had found missing when he sat watching the 1896 rehearsals in St. Petersburg. "They're acting too much," he exclaimed. "He's simply a 'leading actor,' not a novelist!" "Masha is overacting: my Masha is simplicity itself."[62] Stanislavsky

and his critics have habitually apologized for the verisimilitude of the mise, but I think they should have glorified the work for that. The sound of harness bells trailing off at the end of act 3 was both accurate and emotionally meaningful. Dialogues were subsumed in physical tasks as they are in our everyday existence, and such directing may force an audience to listen all the more closely for seeing so clearly. The image of a society falling into ghastly, silent entropy is familiar from real life; but it was also integral to Chekhov's world. At nearly every turn, Stanislavsky's realistic staging corresponded to the superficial behaviors and deep currents of life as lived by people such as these. He deserves his eminence in the line of great realists that begins with Ibsen and the Meininger Company.

If we ask whether the mise was true to Chekhov's play, to its world, we can find the answer in the historical evidence. E. P. Karpov, a "very good producer of the old school," had missed Chekhov's intention in St. Petersburg in 1896 and so had all but a few of his reputable actors.[63] The Moscow Art Theatre company was similarly stumped by *The Seagull* until Stanislavsky made sense of it. His notes provided a convincing realization of the play in which motive, utterance, movement, and meaning became more comprehensible when expressed so. His methodology was impure if judged by his own later standards, for he ignored what he came to call "inner work on the actor" and flaunted his later injunction never to "begin with results." But Stanislavsky, Meyerhold, and others all testified that rehearsals substantially developed the "inner work" spurred by the mise, and everyone was properly grateful for these results. Stanislavsky had sketched a believable world that, in turn, helped to define the world of the play.

2. *Coherence.* Does the mise make sense within itself, internally? I agree with Stanislavsky's claim that his work gradually gained coherence and helped the production process gain inner coherence. In his description of the two paths leading to an understanding of the play, quoted earlier, Stanislavsky explains that the "inner line of the play" was a vector of sense for the theatrical collaborators:

> Along this line of inner action, which Chekhov has in a greater degree than any other dramatist, although until this time only actors are aware of it, there was formed a natural force of gravity towards the play itself, which pulled all of us in one direction. Much was correctly guessed by the interpreter of the play, Nemirovich-Danchenko, much

by the stage directors, the mise en scène, the interpreters of the roles (with the exception of myself), the scenic artist, and the properties.[64]

This "natural force of gravity" unites the collaborators by providing a truth standard for all. Students of Stanislavsky's later work will recognize the same coherence in "through line" and "super-objective."

Another kind of coherence is evident in the mise's emphasis on ensemble acting. The nineteenth-century theatre had been distinguished by its reliance on great stars. Kean, Siddons, Talma, Macready, Coquelin, Irving, Salvini, and the divine Sarah: these people created the sublime theatre of the age, and their legacy—towering central parts—was still influential in the new realist dramaturgies of Ibsen and Shaw. But Chekhov was presenting a new model, a heroless drama about groups of ordinary individuals hardly more or less significant than each other. Stanislavsky perceived that *The Seagull* was not about Konstantin or Nina or anyone else in particular, but about the "sad, monotonous life of the characters." So he directed the play as a portrait of a fictional world where individuals were most notable for their collective and mutual experiences. And so he stumbled onto the great discovery of the "Independent Theatre Movement"—that ensemble acting could replace the brilliant performances by the stars of the old theatre.

3. *Spiritual meaning of life.* Stanislavsky attempted to discover the inner thread of coherence in Chekhov's play by analyzing the particular "spiritual truths" of the characters' lives. Theodore Komisarjevsky has described the central lesson of the Kharkov retreat as follows:

> [Stanislavsky] came to the conclusion after studying the script of the play that what mattered most in *The Seagull* from the actors' and producer's point of view was not the story and the situations and not even the lines, but the feelings beneath the lines and their rhythmical movement. He found that Chekhov intentionally *concealed* the feelings of the characters in the words they were saying and that the silences and pauses were often of much greater importance for the expression of the characters' inner lives than any of their speeches.[65]

Stanislavsky discovered a new fictional realm that Chekhov had created inside his drama. That world has come to be known as the "subtext." In the international theatre today, the term has many subtly different (and changing) meanings, so we may as well let Stanislavsky define it.

> It is the manifest, the inwardly felt expression of a human being in a part, which flows uninterruptedly beneath the words of the text, giving them life and a basis for existing. The subtext is a web of innumerable, varied inner patterns inside a play and a part, woven from "magic ifs," given circumstances, all sorts of figments of the imagination, inner movements, objects of attention, smaller and greater truths and a belief in them, adaptations, adjustments and other similar elements.

Stanislavsky also gave the term a pithier, more functional definition: "It is the subtext that makes us say the words we do in a play."[66]

Since Stanislavsky's time, "subtext" has come to mean the character's (or the play's) inner life. The subtext has also become a customary part of theatre's aesthetic experience. Rehearsals have changed markedly in method and content in order to enrich the subtextual reality of a production. Onstage, projections of internal life entertain and instruct, by themselves, for minutes at a time. Did this never happen before? Did no actor ever live an internal life in a part? Of course some did, leading Diderot to advocate instead cold craftsmanship in his *Paradoxe sur le comédien* (1773). But such historical quibbling should not obscure the degree to which modern theatre has treated the unvoiced inner life of the character as an artistic necessity and as a matter for systematic development. In contrast to the actors of earlier ages, who performed plays in which their words almost completely defined their characters, the modern realistic actor appears in works in which words have only the most glancing relation to psychology. With the vanishing of soliloquy and tirade, conscious articulation of subtextual psychology has become a sine qua non of impersonation. The written drama has never had less rhetoric of feeling, but acting has never had more. Film acting, because of the inexorable realism of its medium, has furthered this development in both the silent and the sound eras, raising modernist internality to an extraordinary pitch.

Earlier in this chapter I noted an estimation of Stanislavsky's mise as materialistic, mired in inert properties and focusing on outward behavior or business, and I said that this estimation trivializes both Stanislavsky's directing and our ideas about theatre art. Stanislavsky's discovery of the subtextual world makes clear that there is no longer such an easy dichotomy between spirit and matter. To quote Komisarjevsky again, "[Stanislavsky] found, too, that the inner life of Chekhov's characters is intimately connected with the life of things and different sounds around them, and that these things and sounds must be made to 'live' on the stage in harmony with the feelings of the players."[67]

Thus acting has undergone a revolution that has answered the anti-realist's charge that realism is the slave of materialism. Yeats gave a classic instance. In real life, a profoundly moved person will, for example, look into a fireplace for a long time. Realistic drama, in its ruthless mimesis, denies a similar onstage character the beautiful, revelatory language of great poetic theatre, denies him all verbal expression, and forces him simply to look long into the fireplace in order to register emotion. But Yeats's critique ignores the expressive power of the look. Cannot a look express the profound emotion that wells up in us at such times and show how we block it? Konstantin's dropping the glass on the floor, heedless of any consequences at last, perfectly symbolized and expressed his letting go of life. Masha mechanically called out her numbers, and the lotto counters hit the cards. The inner streams of these lives were clear. The moment's spiritual revelation was set in the physical, observable world.

The symbolists and poets can object as they will that the "outer" world—the social, physical, material world—is a screen, a form of static in the radio signal of the spirit. Since Stanislavsky's time, theatrical realists have been free to reverse the point, noting that the birds of the soul may shine and amaze as they turn in the black symbolist void, but they can be caught—and hence understood—in the nets of life.

2

Bertolt Brecht and *Couragemodell 1949*:

Meaning in Detail

The Modelbook

WHAT IS a *modelbook?* Physically described, a Brechtian model or modelbook is a play text amplified by illustrative and explanatory materials—especially notes and photographs—that interpret and particularize the play's actions, characters, settings, and ideas. A model is explicitly intended for other theatres, for copying, for use.

My subject is *Couragemodell 1949,* the published modelbook for *Mother Courage and Her Children.*[1] It is less book than package, for it consists of three separate paperbound volumes: script, production photographs, and notes. The script is not a special production version but the basic literary or published text of the play in the amended *Versuche* version. The photograph volume begins with 106 pages depicting the play's action scene by scene and beat by beat. These are followed by ten shots of Mother Courage, fifty-five photographs of "sequences," fourteen of *gests* (tableaux), three on miscellaneous stage business, five on motion, and a final forty that match variant renditions from the Berlin and Munich productions. The notes are also arranged by scenes, beginning with a parsing of the action, which is followed by short entries on specific issues or problems. Taken together, the books of the model demonstrate how and why this play might be comprehensibly and artistically staged.

Chronology. The *Couragemodell*'s incidental value is historical, for it records Brecht's directing of one great play in three productions. A skeleton outline of the development of those productions and their modelbook follows.

1935, 1937. Ruth Berlau, Brecht's co-worker, made her first experiments with model productions of *The Mother* and *Señora Carrar's Rifles*. Working from photographs of Helene Weigel's performances, Berlau created the stagings for her own Copenhagen productions starring Dagmar Andreasen.

September 27 to November 3, 1939. Brecht drafted *Mother Courage and Her Children* in Sweden. The compression of composition was typical of the period 1938–1940, for as he fled north through Scandinavia to escape the Nazis, he wrote plays at a speed he had never equaled: *Life of Galileo* in three weeks, *Mr. Puntila and His Man, Matti* in seventeen days, *The Resistible Rise of Arturo Ui* in thirty-four days, and *The Good Person of Setzuan* in bursts of creativity throughout this period.

April 19, 1941. The first performance of *Mother Courage* was held in Zurich while Brecht waited in Helsinki for the papers that would allow him and his entourage to emigrate to the United States.

July 31, 1947. *Galileo* opened in Beverly Hills, with Charles Laughton playing the title role. Of this performance, Berlau made a photographic record that would later serve as the basis of the *Galileo* model.

November 1, 1947. Brecht and Weigel returned to Europe, heading quickly to German-speaking Zurich so they could direct and act while awaiting developments in postwar Germany.

February 11, 1948. Berlau photographed the dress rehearsal of the Brecht-Weigel *Antigone* in Chur, Switzerland. Within a month, Berlau, Brecht, and Caspar Neher began work on the production's modelbook, published in 1949 and republished later by the Berlin Ensemble. Throughout his last European phase, Brecht would normally construct such models for productions, including those of *Puntila, Galileo, The Tutor, The Mother,* and *The Caucasian Chalk Circle.*

October 22, 1948. Brecht and Weigel reentered Germany through Czechoslovakia and the Marxist front door. They were returning on the strength of an agreement to mount *Mother Courage*. Within days Brecht began auditions, and Eric Engel returned to codirect.

January 11, 1949. *Mother Courage and Her Children,* in its first canonical production, opened at the Deutsches Theater in East Berlin, starring Helene Weigel.

August 1949 to April 1950. At least nine productions, expressly modeled on the Berlin *Courage,* were staged throughout the German provinces.

October 8, 1950. Brecht and Berlau directed Thérèse Giehse as Courage at the Kammerspiele in Munich (the second canonical production). "The arrangements of the model are triumphant," wrote B. B.[2]

January 12, 1951. Weigel starred again in *Mother Courage,* which was the fourth major production from the fourteen-month-old Berlin Ensemble, the company that Brecht had returned to Germany to create. At the Theater am Schiffbauerdamm and on tour, this *Mother Courage* solidified and matured the model, made the company's name, and became a milestone in Western theatrical history.

1951. As in other years, productions based on the model continued to be staged in Germany and elsewhere (for example, Ruth Berlau in Rotterdam, January 1951; Jean Vilar and Benno Besson of the Berlin Ensemble in Paris, November 1951). In June, while rerehearsing the piece, Brecht edited texts for the model's eventual publication.

1955. *Antigonemodell 1948* was republished by Henschelverlag, Berlin.

1956. *Aufbau einer Rolle* (The structure of a role), the *Galileo* model, was published.

1958. *Couragemodell 1949* was published.

Why make a modelbook? In his later European work, Brecht customarily gave two reasons for this innovation. The first was the anarchy of postwar German culture—"total moral and material collapse" in the production of material and artistic goods alike.[3] "The arts seem threatened with quick ruin, at least at times," he wrote in his *Workjournal* during 1951.[4] The *Couragemodell*'s opening words are an evocation of what Thomas Pynchon has taught us to call "the Zone":

Now, after the great war, life goes on in our ruined cities, but it is a different life, the life of different or differently composed groups, guided or thwarted by new surroundings, new because so much has been destroyed. The great heaps of rubble are piled on the city's invaluable substructure, the water and drainage pipes, the gas mains and electric cables. Even the large building that has remained intact is affected by the damage and rubble around it, and may become an obstacle to planning. Temporary structures must be built and there is always a danger of their becoming permanent. All this is reflected in art, for our way of thinking is part of our way of living.

Responding to these surroundings, Brecht adopted a system of theatrical production that allowed him to increase and control production in the economic sense of that word.

The second reason for the modelbook was to illustrate theatrical style, as Brecht pointed out in the introduction to *Antigonemodell 1948:* "As it is not so much a new school of playwriting as a new way of performance being tried out on an old play, our new adaptation cannot be handed over in the usual way to theatres to do what they like with. An obligatory model production has been worked out, which can be grasped from a collection of photographs accompanied by explanatory instructions."[5] Upon reentering Germany in 1948, Brecht found a state where a Brecht play had not been seen in seventeen years, where the "epic theatre" was a dead issue, where all his important work was light-years in the national past. If he was to revive and clarify a Brechtian production style, he needed to go beyond writing plays, issuing manifestos, and directing particular productions.

What does a modelbook do? This unexhaustive list has been taken from *Theaterarbeit,* the Ensemble's magnificent explanation-cum-promotion of 1952:[6]

1. The modelbook shows the basic gest of a play.
2. The modelbook demonstrates the scenic arrangements [i.e., blocking] related by the play's plot.
3. The modelbook shows the treatment of details.
4. The modelbook warns against mistakes in execution.
5. The modelbook facilitates the division of the plot, e.g., the precise parsing of the plot elements.
6. The modelbook gives tempo and running times for the production.

Moderation in using the model. These books come bound in basic Brechtian black, published under the imprint of a world-famous theatre, so they are persuasive as few such theatre documents were before or have been since. Brecht repeatedly warned against the persuasiveness of modelbooks: "A model is not a blueprint"; a model's ideas and images should serve only as a good place for rehearsals to begin; a director should treat a model as a pianist treats "The Well-Tempered Clavichord."[7] Several notes in the *Couragemodell* contain warnings against slavish imitation: "The model should not be used to excess"; and "The use of models is a particular kind of art, and there is a limit to what can be learned from it. The aim must be neither to copy the pattern exactly nor to break away from it too quickly."

Brecht called for a moderate approach to models because both "the construction of models" and "copying as an art" posed new aesthetic problems for western artists. "In order to be imitated a model has to be imitable," he said in a 1949 interview. Consumers of a model needed to learn to distinguish "the inimitable" from "the exemplary."[8]

> The persons available for the imitation are not the same as those of the pattern [i.e., model]; with them it would not have come into being. Anyone deserving of the name of artist is unique; he represents something universal, but in his own individual way. He can neither be perfectly imitated nor give a perfect imitation. (*Couragemodell*)

One illustration of the inimitable is a detail from scene 10 of *Mother Courage,* a very short scene where Courage and Kattrin stop their wagon before a house to listen to "The Song of Home." On starting up again, Weigel tossed her head and shook it "like a tired draft horse getting back to work." Brecht properly doubted whether that gesture could or should be imitated.

But just as Brecht warned against slavish imitation, he argued for "practical copying," the following of the exemplary, as a step toward creating original theatrical art. "You have to start somewhere," he wrote, "and it may as well be with something that has been fully thought out." Models were a response to the theoretical disputes about epic theatre, which he had found tiring even before his exile from Germany. And models conformed to his collectivist-objectivist vision of art:

What, [certain artists] will ask, is in any way creative about the use of models? The answer is that today's division of labour has transformed creation in many important spheres. The act of creation has become a collective creative process, a continuum of a dialectical sort in which the original invention, taken on its own, has lost much of its importance. (*Antigonemodell*)[9]

Used in moderation, a modelbook could have considerable pedagogical value. The introduction to the *Couragemodell* contains a statement I have already quoted in my introduction: "In studying what follows—a number of explanations and discoveries emerging from the rehearsal of a play—one should, above all, be led by the solutions of certain problems to consider the problems themselves."

Brecht as Director: Detail and Entertainment

Brecht was neither a playwright dabbling in directing nor a brilliant theoretician mired in "theatre business, management of men," to quote the weary Yeats.[10] Brecht demonstrated a will to direct throughout his career. Even before one of his plays had seen the stage, he convinced Arnolt Bronnen to let him direct *Parricide* (1922). When he was fired for screaming at the actors, Brecht remained undiscouraged, and when *Drums in the Night* went into rehearsal a few months later, he outshouted the titular director and took the show over. Then he went to Berlin and took it over, establishing the sensational *Threepenny* style and an insurgent presence that came to epitomize the place and the period. A tragic phase began in 1931, when he could not find a theatre for *St. Joan of the Stockyards:* "Already the reaction was too strong, and our audience had lost their money."[11] Then, as a result of his exile from fatherland and mother tongue (1933–1947), Brecht almost completely lost the chance to direct. During these years, he could fume and swear in an advisory capacity (*The Mother,* New York, 1935) or wail at the frustrations of Hollywood (of *The Visions of Simone Machard:* "I don't care if Shirley Temple plays it, only do it"), but he could not direct.[12] The years 1947–1949 demonstrate, however, that the exiled Brecht had lost neither ability nor desire. Even before leaving the United States, he was in negotiation with Berlin theatres, and when back in Europe he headed immediately to German-speaking Zurich and mounted *Antigone* and *Puntila* within months. He was hardly back in

East Berlin to rehearse *Mother Courage* in late 1948 when he began to negotiate with the Deutsches Theater about an experimental wing and a subsidy. And within a year, he and Weigel had established the Berlin Ensemble, cleared its operation with municipal and party machinery, and supplied it with actors, helpers, and plays. It opened in November 1949 with *Puntila*. From his return to Berlin until his death, Brecht put his best energies into directing and producing, and when we ask what he created in his last decade, the obvious answer is (1) some famous theatre productions for (2) a world-famous theatre company—one that became, after World War II, the most magnetic theatre in Europe, as the Moscow Art Theatre had been earlier in the century.

The consensus with regard to Brecht's directing during these last years was that it was world-class, excellent in a number of particular ways. After having seen the Ensemble's *Mother Courage,* Harold Clurman talked for the rest of his life about a greatness of directing comparable only to Meyerhold's *Inspector General,* which had always been at the top of Clurman's list. I wish to emphasize that the greatness under discussion was not primarily intellectual or theoretical but practical and experiential. As elderly teacher, Brecht insisted on this distinction:

> If the critics could only look at my theatre as the audience does, without starting out by stressing my theories, then they might well simply see theatre—a theatre, I hope, imbued with imagination, humour and meaning—and only when they began to analyse its effects would they be struck by certain innovations, which they could then find explained in my theoretical writings.[13]

Upon returning to Berlin, Brecht avoided the theoretical controversies about epic theatre by describing his art as "dialectical theatre" or "dialectical realism," hardly inflammatory terms in a Marxist-Leninist-Stalinist state. But, as a great believer in eating the pudding, he wanted theatre judged on the basis of experience rather than labels. Calling his work "the Theatre of Naiveté," as he did to Peter Brook, was less important than rounding up schoolchildren at his previews and quizzing them on the clarity of the story line in his production.[14]

Brecht's great talent as a director was his mastery of detail. His directing of *Mother Courage and Her Children* is an example of his mature theatrical style and a classic example of great theatre, but it is most important as an example of his manipulation of little images or fragments of a sprawling drama, for his attention to what he too called "detail." The following dozen details reveal his mind at work.

—Near the end of the first scene in *Mother Courage,* a Recruiting Officer lures away the first of Courage's children. To get the boy Eilif to leave, the soldier must quite literally take him "out of harness." In the modelbook, Brecht insisted that this business must be acted out, fully acted out, to show that the recruiter "is freeing him from his yoke." The metaphor was dependent on the literally physical.

—Having unyoked Eilif, the officer bribes him with a guilder. Brecht's image ("Holding out his fist with the guilder in it in front of him, Eilif goes off as if in a trance") emphasized the power of money.

—In scene 2, the General's cook must prepare some putrid meat for a celebration. The actor, Paul Bildt, fished "the chunk of rotten beef out of the garbage barrel with the tip of his long meat knife" and then carried it "carefully as though it were a precious object—though to be kept at a safe distance from one's nose—over to his kitchen table." The beef has a contradictory nature, as shown by Bildt's contradicted behavior.

—In the tent, the General called Eilif "a young Caesar," then magnificently handed across a wine jug, "though he has determined first that there isn't much in it." Self-interest was everywhere.

—The "war of religion" is also a war of corruption, as we see at the top of scene 3, when Courage and an Ordnance Officer bargain over bullets. In Brecht's version, her son Swiss Cheese sat apart from this, listening with half an ear "as to something quite usual." His mother did not conceal corruption from him. She merely lectured him about it—later.

—At the peak of the action in scene 3, Yvette brings forth the Old Colonel who will bankroll her purchase of the wagon. In Brecht's words, he was "a purely negative quantity." As the Colonel, Georg-Peter Pilz acted passionately, pressing his walking stick into the ground with unconscious sexual insistence so that it bent and then snapped straight, causing a surprise. The result was properly loathsome phallic comedy, but the gesture demanded "considerable elegance" to remain within the production's taste and tone, that is, within the borders of its decorum.

—Having seen Swiss Cheese arrested, Kattrin greets Courage's return (scene 3) with wild gestures and fiercely urgent sounds. Courage orders her daughter not to "howl like a dog" but to use her hands: "What will the Chaplain think? It gives him the creeps." As Kattrin, Angelika Hurwicz made the character "pull herself together and nod. She understands this argument, it is a strong one." Yes, it is a very strong argument to a young woman with a big problem who still considers herself active in the marriage market.

—At the end of scene 5, which takes place in the war zone, Brecht described a point with double focus: "Kattrin lifted the baby into the air, while Courage rolled up the fur coat and threw it into the wagon: both women had their share of the spoils." The juxtaposition was strengthened by bringing both women to the front of the wagon, into focus.

—In scene 6, a Young Soldier at the canteen sings a song to Kattrin, who smiles back at him. "For the last time before she is disfigured [i.e., at the end of this scene], the spectator is reminded that she is capable of love." Directors, actors, or audiences might make an obvious, sentimental mistake here, so Brecht was quite emphatic. Although she is dumb, Kattrin is not stupid, ugly, asexual, or unloving.

—In scene 8, Yvette returns after years as the Old Colonel's wife. Her accent and her philosophy have both changed, and so has her body, in Brecht's treatment. "She is so fat one has the impression that eating has become her only passion." About the second Berlin Yvette (Regina Lutz), Brecht wrote: "She waddles and carries her belly before her, . . . grasps for air like a codfish on dry land." Once graceful, she is now "grotesquely deformed." Brecht's point here was the spiritual price she had paid for physical comfort. Food and morals are constantly related in this play, and not simply.

—In the famous drum scene, Hurwicz showed "increasing exhaustion while drumming." Not even the dramatic theatre can alter physical limitations.

—In the play's last moments, Courage stands over the body of her dead daughter and receives the condolences of three peasants; however, their gestures were hostile rather than kind. "She has caused them great difficulties and they will have her on their hands if she cannot catch up with the departing army. . . . Besides, she is an unsedentary element." The condolences were at best "customary."

"The principle of epic theatre," Brecht wrote in the *Couragemodell,* was "*one thing after another,*" and that was how he directed, taking up one detail after another after another. Of 103 specific notes in the modelbook of *Mother Courage,* more than 10 percent are entitled "Detail," and many more might as well be. These details can be small, even minuscule. One note is appropriately headed "A tiny scene." Studying this model, we see Brecht working over his long, sprawling play with calipers and tweezers. According to one coworker, that was the secret of his best directing—accumulation of "a large number of details, some of them very small."[15]

The photographs, which play such an important role in the *Couragemodell,* draw our attention to details. Brecht notably chose to teach his theatre technique by using still photography in a time when film and sound recording were increasingly available. Actually, photographic aesthetics almost perfectly complement Brecht's aesthetics: freezing a motion or condition; stopping the action for a closer, longer look; isolating a detail or moment or element or shading and then expanding it into meaning, into an image (e.g., Eilif's yoke). This is the "alienation effect," is it not? Stop a minute. Look here. What are you seeing? How does this work? What does it mean? Think about "one thing" in this way, and you might think about "another." Atomizing the play into details is fundamental to a theatre that is always committed to making its audiences more conscious. Expression of meaning in detail, not by intention, not vaguely—this is how Brecht was political, sociological, economic. From all accounts, he wrote and rewrote by breaking things down into constituent elements, holding them up for reexamination and checking. He was less interested in actors' methods or temperaments than in their roles, which—like little engines—had parts that needed constant adjusting, cleaning, and repairing.

Directing in detail means insisting that small things are important enough to bear detailed attention and emphasis. Brecht made this clear in scene 1 of the *Couragemodell:*

> On the brightly lighted stage every detail, even the smallest, must of course be acted out to the full. This is especially true of actions which

on our stage are glossed over almost as a matter of principle, such as paying on conclusion of a sale.

So a first principle of such a method is to avoid carelessness with regard to small or minor matters. Brecht repeated this general point at the end of scene 9, in a description of Courage and Kattrin leaving the Cook:

> Scenes of this kind must be fully acted out: Courage and Kattrin harness themselves to the wagon, push it back a few feet so as to be able to circle the presbytery, and then move off to the right. The cook comes out, still chewing on a piece of bread, sees his belongings, picks them up and goes off to the rear with long steps. We see him disappear. Thus the parting of the ways is made visible.

Left alone, actors may hurry over bits of action that must last long enough to mean something. And the more tempestuous the scene's action, the more stubborn must the director's insistence be.

It is an incremental rather than psychological or inspirational method, and the endless particulars of such directing, by necessity, slow the process. "The pace at rehearsals should be slow," recommended Brecht in the *Couragemodell,* "if only to make it possible to work out details; determining the pace of the performance is another matter and comes later." When the young director Carl Weber entered his first Ensemble rehearsal, he assumed everyone was on a break until just before the rehearsing ended. All that had happened was smoking, joking, sandwich-eating, and a great deal of horseplay about a man falling off a table—for *Urfaust,* as he later realized, Brecht spent hours on Galileo's handling of his telescope or an apple, hours on Grusha's picking up the baby, hours on any activity that materialized a character's relation to the world. And these hours were spent not talking but trying: "Brecht would say that he wanted no discussions in rehearsal—it would have to be tried."[16]

The rehearsal periods at the Ensemble were accordingly long, even after the lengthy preparation of texts, models, ideas, and designs. Like the Moscow Art Theatre before it, the Ensemble was notorious for its leisure: months spent only on blocking, and weeks devoted to tempo rehearsals, technical rehearsals, dress rehearsals, and something that Weber described as "marking" or "indicating" rehearsals. ("The actors, not in costumes, but on the set, had to walk quickly through all the actions of the show, quoting the text very rapidly, without any effort at acting, but keeping the rhythm, the pauses, etc., intact.")[17] Then previews, adjustments, more tearing down and reassembly of details, and at last an opening. Refinement of the famous *Caucasian Chalk Circle* continued for eight months. Even after shows opened, Brecht continued to tinker obsessively. Only "in the course of many performances" did he discover how Courage's funeral oration (scene 6) gained tension when suspiciously observed by the Clerk. "After some forty performances" he put jewelry on Courage in the same scene to signal her new prosperity. But a few shows later, he changed his mind and had her wear jewelry in scene 7, where she speaks up for the war, now appearing bought and bribed. As Weigel once said, "A Brecht play is not finished even when it is on the stage."[18] Something could always mean more or mean more specifically.

When Brecht approached character, he worked by analyzing detail. I explain this more fully when I discuss Weigel's Courage later in this chapter; for the moment let us consider the director attacking a much smaller part. The *Couragemodell*'s longest note relates how Brecht taught a young actress to play the Peasant Woman—a whining, praying, self-protective older woman—in the drum scene. Brecht here described a familiar theatre problem: how a younger actress playing an older woman ordinarily tries to generalize about the character's age, using stiff and unrealistic alterations of pitch and posture. Brecht and his actress used a different method.

Specifically, they made the peasant not "old" but forty and prematurely aged. The basic age was created with painstaking slowness, working out "from the text, one sound after the next and one gesture after the next" (that is, one detail after another) until "the image of a forty-year-old" eventually emerged "by virtue of this inductive method." They then attempted to approximate premature aging by actively imagining her background: childhood abuse, hard labor, rapes, disfigurations, having to lick boots of many colors. With the character thus far along, they attacked behavioral specifics—problems and movements in need of clarification. When the woman had to "kneel and whine," she did not kneel-and-whine simultaneously, but knelt and then whined. Parsing the actions so carefully showed that they were part of "a deliberate production put on regularly," a well-rehearsed sequence in which it would make little sense for a woman to chafe her knees. Leading Kattrin in prayer, she had to illustrate the gestural form of teaching, had to demonstrate the "act of leading in prayer." She also had to find the proper voice for prayer, "the usual vapid bleating: the soothing sound of one's own voice, the cadence learned from the clergymen." By the end of the prayer, "she almost prayed 'genuinely': praying, so to speak, made her more pious." From beginning to end, the issues were framed as specifically as possible.

Analysis of specific details was vital to Brecht's blocking as well. For some directors, grouping and moving characters on a stage is no more exciting than directing traffic or solving jigsaw puzzles, but for Brecht, working with the Ensemble, blocking was the heart of the enterprise; blocking was the action onstage. "The grouping and movement of the characters has to narrate the story, which is a chain of incidents" *(Antigonemodell)*.[19] So he put photographs in his modelbooks to illustrate explicitly the logic of his blocking as his conception of the action. "If a scene didn't seem to work in dress rehearsal," Weber has said, "the first thing reworked would be the blocking." According to Weber, Brecht believed that "ideally . . . the blocking should be able to tell the main story of the play—and its contradictions—by itself, so that a person watching through a glass wall, unable to hear what was being said, would be able to understand the main elements and conflicts of the story."[20] A visual objective correlative, we might call it.

In the *Couragemodell,* Brecht's first substantial notes to scene 1 concern blocking, specifically the scene between the Recruiting Officer and the Sergeant. A director, Brecht wrote, should not allow these two to wander around during their conversation. Instead, the director should stand them side by side and keep them there, for the usual idle strolling would impair "both the image and the argument." He then gave a stern warning in his best pedagogical manner:

> Positions should be retained as long as there is no compelling reason for changing them; and a desire for variety is not a compelling reason. If one gives in to a desire for variety, the consequence is a devaluation of all movement on the stage; the spectator ceases to look for a specific meaning behind each movement, he stops taking movement seriously. But especially at the crucial points in the action, the full impact of a change of position must not be weakened. . . . If changes of position are needed to make certain developments clear to the audience, the movement must be utilized to express something significant for the action and for this particular moment; if nothing of the sort can be found, it is advisable to review the whole arrangement up to this

point, it will probably be seen to be at fault, because the sole purpose of an arrangement is to express the action, and the action (it is to be hoped) involves a logical development of incidents, which the arrangement need only present.

Look elsewhere for the rococo or for excessive exuberance in movement. Brecht wanted weighted ingredients, buttress for his dramatic structure, thematic or psychological relevance, and logic. Even when describing a confused scene, the surprise attack in scene 3, he told in detail how to create "clearly laid-out confusion."

If Stanislavsky's rehearsal cliché was "I don't believe it," Brecht's was "What's the position?" and it was just as revealing of his nature. He might ask "What's the position?" about subjects as diverse as emotion and class relations, but his question always required a physical response. How could actors make a particular point physically, so that it became apparent or visible on the stage? A similar consciousness informed his ideas about "gestic acting," which was meant to convey information about social relation in the form of physical relation. The term *gest* may require a multiple definition (Brecht called it "overall attitude" and "moral tableau," whereas John Willet has glossed it as "gist and gesture"), but Brecht's basic intention becomes clear through studying specific examples.[21] One character's attitude toward another, especially the socially significant attitude, is displayed through the creation of an onstage picture, through making visible the characters' physical relation. Such gests "are usually highly complicated and contradictory"; they are not an attitude describable in a single word but a "complex" of imagery.[22] Courage described her three children (scene 1) from across the stage "as though better able to take them in from a distance"; Kattrin ran into the burning building (scene 5) as soldiers threatened the wagon, so Courage had to show the physical form of being "tugged both ways" along the fault line of her contradictory (mother-merchant) character. In such images, plastic and thematic are one. And they are so *particular*.

Without details there are no "concepts" in Brecht's theatre, no themes, no broad intellectual perspectives or messages. Brecht underlined this attitude in a memo to the Ensemble describing Stanislavsky's achievements: "*Importance of the broad conception and of details.* In the Moscow Art Theatre every play acquired a carefully thought-out shape and a wealth of subtly elaborated detail. The one is useless without the other."[23] Brecht was, after all, a dialectical materialist who believed that truth was not ineffable but visible, not transcendental but concrete. In his writing and in his directing, he managed thematic issues by finding thematic emphasis in the details of blatantly quotidian activity. The *Couragemodell* is loaded with descriptions of details showing that virtue is dangerous in wartime and that the small business person fails in wartime. After Roland Barthes had examined a series of photographs of the Ensemble *Courage* (second Paris tour, 1957), he summarized this issue neatly: "The details are . . . the meaning, and it is because Brecht's theatre is a theatre of meaning that its detail is so important."[24]

Two objections might be raised here. First, that this is all simplistic and truistic. Of course, general idea and specific moment reinforce each other, "as any good director knows." But in reality not even every decent director realizes that meaning ("bright idea") remains general and, for most audiences, imperceptible until it is specified. Stated another way, no quantity of explicit details will necessarily salvage a poorly thought-out production, but a production that is fundamentally sound will find its rightness endlessly extendible into details.

Second, an interlocutor might reverse the point, charging that all these details with their microscopic meanings are most likely only obscurities. Brecht addressed this very objection while describing some blocking in *The Tutor,* noting that the blocking at the end of a scene echoed an arrangement in its opening. "You may ask if such subtleties are noticed by the audience," he remarked in passing, "but it is an unworthy question."[25]

Meaning conveyed through specific detail was fundamental to Brecht's theatrical art, and he insisted on it from his earliest days as a director. "Stop That Romantic Gaping," said the signs to the audience in *Drums in the Night.* "We've got to get away from the prevailing muzziness," said Brecht to his co-workers in the 1920s, "even from *monumental* muzziness."[26] At the moment of discovering "alienation," Brecht stopped a rehearsal of *Edward II* (1924) and asked: "Well, what is it? What's the truth about these soldiers?" A friend, Karl Valentin, volunteered, "They're pale, they're scared, that's what!" —which Brecht objectified with whiteface, making the meaning visible.[27] In the same rehearsals, the actor playing Baldock informed on Edward by crossing the stage and handing him a cloth in a wooden way. Brecht screamed, "Not so! Baldock is an informer. . . . You must show the behavior of an informer. Baldock goes to the man he will betray with friendly, outstretched arms." When his Gaveston performed the will-and-testament scene with generalized emotions, Brecht launched a disquisition on "finding the particulars" of man and scene: Gaveston was a butcher's son, the place was particular, and the war was civil. Realism and objectivity, scrutiny of the meaning of physical actions and historical conditions, "finding the particulars"—these early instincts were identical with his later preoccupation with "details."[28]

If we compare Brecht's ideas early in his career with his later ideas, we see that the greatest change came not in this preoccupation but in what he conceived to be its purpose, in his conception of theatre's final cause or goal. Early in his career, he believed that theatre should be committed to pedagogy and social change, but by the time he was directing *Mother Courage,* Brecht had turned to emphasizing pleasure and entertainment.

Such objectives will not shock readers familiar with Brecht's later career, though they did shock his young, doctrinaire co-workers in the Ensemble, for here was the master of Marxist theatre talking so often about beauty, charm, the virtuoso, the naive, the pleasurable, the "aesthetic." Even in 1934, when Brecht was most earnestly political, he had a recurrent dream or vision, which he described to Walter Benjamin. A tribunal interrogated him: "Now tell us, Mr. Brecht, are you really in earnest?" No, not completely, Brecht admitted, for "I think too much about artistic problems, you know, about what is good for the theatre, to be completely in earnest." But then he made a "more important" claim, "namely, that my attitude is permissible."[29] Brecht's showmanship was visible from an early age. Wolfgang Roth describes Brecht in the 1920s as "total theatre for me: poet, playwright, creative, intuitive—a practical man who shrewdly knew everything there was to know about 'show business' and I mean just that."[30]

Throughout his career, Brecht based his theatrical critique on this choice: "Theatre for Pleasure or Theatre for Instruction" (the title of an essay from the mid-1930s). The younger Brecht emphasized pedagogy, and this is the man most students still encounter first—the bespectacled German-Marxist theorist, the writer of *Lehrstücke* and author of alienation essays and master of "don'ts" —don't like Courage or Galileo, beware the dread empathy. But by the end of the 1930s, he had moved toward balancing both sides of the dialectic opposition. For example, in his famous essay "The Street Scene" (1938), he said: "It has got to be entertaining, it has got to be instructive." And in a 1939 lecture "On Experimental Theatre," he asked: "How can the theatre be both instructive and entertaining? How can it be divorced from spiritual dope traffic and turned from a home of illusions to a home of experiences?"[31] In this same period, Brecht was telling Benjamin about his "discovery of moderation" in many areas of life, and *The Messingkauf Dialogues* show a weakening hostility toward theatrical emotion.[32] Both audiences and actors should take part emotionally in theatre, Brecht wrote. Empathy he now described as "only one out of many possible sources of emotion," one that he hoped would be "left unused" or "at least treated as a subsidiary source."[33] All this was said, remarkably enough, during the writing of his greatest plays.

Brecht's summary of his later doctrine was *A Short Organum for the Theatre,* written in 1948 (in Zurich) just before he embarked on producing *Mother Courage* in East Berlin. In its opening he stated a new position on the issue of entertainment versus instruction: "'Theatre' consists in this: in making live representations of reported or invented happenings between human beings and doing so with a view to entertainment." Theatre's "noblest function," Brecht announced, is "to give pleasure." Dogmatists beware: "It needs no other passport than fun, but this it has got to have." Moral lessons are always welcome, but they must be made "enjoyable, and enjoyable to the senses at that." "The theatre must in fact remain something entirely superfluous, though this indeed means that it is the superfluous for which we live. Nothing needs less justification than pleasure."[34] Of course, Brecht always stated that his theatre should be instructive and progressive and that thinking could be pleasurable, but this was by way of proviso, a corollary rather than the central position. He had worked a lifetime to discover that the secret to great theatre is fun— enjoyment, pleasure, entertainment.

Particularly in Brecht's last decade, this emphasis appeared repeatedly in his working life as a director. With actors, for instance, he still encouraged "demonstration" and separation from the role, but he now urged them toward virtuosity and a joyful self-indulgence in rehearsal. Combine critical analysis (detail), he advised, with "tasks for the senses," seeking occasions to "divide up [the actor's] part and modulate it, thoroughly savouring it, until it suits him. He must 'arrange' his movements, whatever they are meant to express, in such a way that he gets fun out of their sweep and rhythm."[35] In the *Couragemodell,* Brecht advocated blocking that seems unpremeditated, effortless, and natural, no matter how thoroughly planned in rehearsal or disciplined in execution:

> The actors take their positions and form their groups in very much the same way as the marbles tossed in a wooden bowl in certain roulette-type children's games fall into hollows, with the difference that in the games it is not decided in advance which marbles will fall into which hollows, whereas in theatrical arrangements [blocking] there only seems to be no advance decision.

And precisely this theatrical virtuosity was what made his final productions so famous. John Fuegi describes Brecht's preparation for the Ensemble production of *The Caucasian Chalk Circle* that took the Festival de Paris by storm in 1955: "Polishing and re-editing his text . . . he reduced it to its theatrical essentials. Speeding up his players, he dispensed with the rational pauses his theory had once set such store by." To the critics of that time, "the rather plain caterpillar of the early and theoretical 'Street Scene' had become the lovely butterfly of high dramatic art."[36]

Thus, the director of the *Courage* productions was interested in the charmed and the charming, and most definitely in a play's most serious scenes. Ignore ease and elegance in those scenes, he said, and the product will resemble the heavy, cramped *Kultur*-theatre—serious and sad and "deplorable." Instead, this producer-director looked for entertainment and "production values" just as his counterparts did on boulevard and Broadway. If one studies his work from 1948 to 1956, the same model repeatedly emerges: the absorption and realization of the philosophical-economic-political-social in the joyful-sensuous-emotional. That is why his final work has become so famous. That is why all his details were not dry, trivial, fussy, or obvious to the artistically inclined, but were part of a method of making ideas funny or affecting or vivid.

Space

> For Brecht, for Neher when he worked with Brecht, for Otto
> and von Appen, who worked with Brecht in the fifties, the set
> was primarily a space where actors tell a certain story to the
> audience.   —Carl Weber, "Brecht as Director"

Brecht began his production of *Mother Courage* with a half-curtain concealing the stage. As the house went dark, the four-man orchestra, located in a side box, played the short, brittle overture. Then the audience heard the first verse of the Courage song—its lyrics, music, and delivery all exclamatory—played on a backstage record player. The half-curtain opened. A moment later, the Courage family pulled its wagon across the stage, and Courage sang the second verse of her entry song, which appears in most texts as part of scene 1. This was Brecht's Prologue.

With the opening of the half-curtain, the first image was undefined space—a large, empty stage backed by a pale cyclorama but otherwise quite unmodulated. It was physically and theoretically open to definition, a tabula rasa. "We've got to start all over here, from scratch!" Brecht said when he reentered the German theatre.[37] He hoped that the audiences of *Mother Courage* would realize that the stage had been just this blank when, months before, the actors and production staff had walked in to start the process of production.

On the floor was a large circle. Around the back of the circle ran the cyclorama, and at the front was the arc of the footlights. The sets were placed on this circle, scenes were acted on it, and the traveling—a central production image—took place around its great circumference. This circle was the world of Mother Courage.

And the circle turned. (Reality is change.) As the half-curtain opened to reveal the empty stage, the turntable was already moving. Into view, from up left and moving counterclockwise against the turning floor, came the Courage wagon. As the sons pulled it, Kattrin played her harmonica and Courage sang her signature song. This song would be repeated at the end of act 1 (scene 7), the wagon pulled then by the bandaged Kattrin and the downcast Chaplain, while Courage walked beside it, singing buoyantly. At the end of act 2, the wagon moved through the same empty area, but this time it was led by a solitary figure and accompanied by singing offstage. These repetitions demonstrate one link between imagery and argument in *Mother Courage.*

Across the stage, at a height of approximately twelve feet, ran the set of wires carrying the half-curtain, which closed over the wagon at the end of the Prologue. Brecht used the wires' horizontal division of the proscenium to link action with place. From above came a sign— large, crude letters on a frame made of what looked like metallic branches. Below the sign, projected on the half-curtain, was the title information for scene 1. Seen from the audience, the proscenium picture looked like this:

S   W   E   D   E   N
Spring, 1624. General Oxenstjerna recruits troops in Dalarna for the Polish campaign. The canteen woman, Anna Fierling, known as Mother Courage, loses a son.

Below, subsequent titles described years, seasons, military movements, social conditions, and the events of the Courage family. Above, the place names succeeded one another as the site of the action changed from Sweden to Poland to Saxony to Bavaria to Alsace to Fichtelgebirge and back to Saxony. These signs also remained above the action of the individual scenes, as a stimulus to thinking specifically. The world that Courage lives in may be the circle of the turntable, leading her to believe that life simply goes round and round and round without change. But Brecht, who believed that the round and round theory was an exploitive myth, presented his fiction within a frame that was horizontally bisected, as if stage reality were dialectical and capable of objectifying and particularizing human actions.

After the Prologue and the first title, the half-curtain was drawn aside for scene 1, in which the stage was no longer bare of ornament. Behind the two recruiters, who stood downstage complaining about their lot, was a small clump of grass. Other scenic elements would appear on the stage, most of them less skimpy than this one. A few were frankly conventional, such as the imposing musical emblem (trumpet, drum, flag, electric globes) that flew in overhead to detach the songs from their surrounding action. Also conventional were the large screens (made of dark tenting material stretched on rough-hewn poles) Brecht took from Teo Otto's original 1941 designs to serve as masks for the rear of the camp scenes.[38] But no matter how skimpy, that clump of grass was realistic (Ah, they are in the country!), as were the other settings and props brought onto the stage. The settings included actual structures, like the tents of scenes 2 and 4 and the buildings of scenes 5, 9, 10, and 11. True, these structures were rendered in what Brecht calls "artistic abbreviation, only so much being shown as was necessary for the action." But there was no grotesque, no expressionist distortion, and no "unit set" quality. The three buildings of scenes 9 through 11 were all different set pieces, differently arranged. If this was epic theatre, it was more solid and realistic, less conventionalized, than Brecht's earlier version.

In a *Couragemodell* note describing his scenic style here and in the Ensemble period generally, Brecht called his approach a return to Goethe's style, much as that style, in turn, was a return to Shakespeare's. Like the theatres of 1800 and 1600, his was situated at "a happy halfway point on the road to naturalistic illusionism," with "enough elements of illusion to improve the representation of some aspects of reality, but not so much as to make the audience feel that they were no longer in a theatre." In *Mother Courage,* his stage was a bare platform decorated with enough reality to make her story comprehensible, though never with so much as to fool the eye. Brecht's was an art of partial illusion, an aesthetic mixture in which the partiality and the illusionism were equal and contradictory constituents.

Like the world, Brecht's scene changed constantly. At the heart of that changing picture was always the wagon, indexing the fluctuating fortunes of Courage's life and enterprise by its changing covers, signs, and contents. The wagon was never in quite the same position twice. Neither were the buildings or the camps or the settlements that surrounded it.

One constant was the action's downstage focus. The cyclorama had no part in its middle, so there were no upstage exits and few upstage scenic elements (a flagpole in scene 3, a crucifix in scene 9). Scenes were spread downstage across the large arc of footlights. Lighting was also concentrated downstage, except when the wagon rolled over the turntable. Entrances, exits, layouts, and blocking were strongly lateral (right to left to right) on that relatively narrow down-stage strip. Brecht was virtually making tableaux. He was also pushing the picture and point right at the audience, as was his practice.

Looking too long at the modelbook's black-and-white photographs may give the impression that Brecht's show was gray and drab, an impression he warns against in his notes. First, since the photographs frequently do not show the cyclorama, we should note his description of the background as "always bright gray, almost white," certainly more "bright and clear" than the muddy prints allow. Second, recall the testimony of Edward Kook, head of Century Lighting, on his return to New York from a Berlin visit: "You know, this goddamn communist, he never uses colored gelatins but his stage is so goddamn colorful."[39] Brecht's colors depended not on instruments but on the play's life, emanating from performers and their surroundings rather than from mechanical effects, imposed moods, or theatrical pathetic fallacies. Third, Brecht and designer Hermann Gantz used as much light as their equipment permitted—"an even, white light" or "a dull golden light" in the modelbook—because that intensity and coloration best eliminated "any vestige of 'atmosphere' that could easily have given the incidents a romantic tinge." This was certainly not the hot, shadowless white of Peter Brook's stage. Standing in pools and oblongs of light, the actors were modeled, but the shadows here did not obscure. An audience could see everything it needed to see.

The final thing the audience saw, at the end of scene 12, was the Courage wagon being pulled along, again counterclockwise against the turntable's flow. As at the beginning, the scene consisted of only the cyclorama, the floor, the bright lights, and the wagon (see Plate 2). But to Brecht the meaning of this picture had changed. It still gave an "illusion of a flat landscape with the sky over it." But as a result of what Brecht calls a "stirring of poetry" in the spectators, the same empty scene that in the Prologue offered a "wide horizon" and an invitation to an enterprising family had become an image of "boundless devastation." He seemed to be saying, "You are in East Berlin in 1949 (or 1951, or whatever the production date)—look outside." Time and war had changed everything, but at the same time nothing had changed.

But the wagon was visibly changed. Its cover was now darker and tattered, and wares no longer dangled enticingly from its sides. It was pulled not by two healthy boys but by a single stooped figure moving on and on against the flow of the turntable. It was symbolic, the circle that turned against Courage. It was movement, but not Brecht's kind, which would have been change rather than movement, dialectical and progressive rather than circular. That circle was instead the image in Courage's mind, a modern capitalist wheel of fortune from which there was no escape so long as she remained stooped over, her eyes focused on the ground before her, in suicidal pursuit of profit and war. How could anyone in this posture see another destination, another track, another motive?

Ground Arrangements

As I have already remarked, the modelbook's notes on individual scenes are organized into two parts: *Grundarrangements,* or ground arrangements of the action, and details. Note again how Brecht's mind works: first fundamentals, then details; first structure, then finishing; first the analytical and visual division of the action, then its elaboration into sometimes tiny moments of experience.

As in English, *Grund,* or "ground," has meanings both material (soil, earth, terrain, dregs) and analytical (reason, foundation, cause, motive). Brecht imported *arrangements* to convey a double meaning: (1) blocking, and (2) division or parsing of the text. Ground arrangements (Manheim and Willett call them "over-all arrangements") are primary and crucial to the director because they are the basis of all articulation—of rhythm, tempo, character, variety, and poetry.

In the ground arrangements of the *Couragemodell*—as in the published text of the play, as on the stage—the scenes begin with titles. These are not the titles that audiences or readers see but are pithier. The title for scene 1 is: "THE BUSINESS WOMAN ANNA FIERLING, KNOWN AS MOTHER COURAGE, ENCOUNTERS THE SWEDISH ARMY." For the very long scene 3, the title is: "MOTHER COURAGE SWITCHES FROM THE LUTHERAN TO THE CATHOLIC CAMP AND LOSES HER HONEST SON SWISS CHEESE." Some are shorter still: "THE SONG OF THE GREAT CAPITULATION," "MUTE KATTRIN SAVES THE CITY OF HALLE," and "STILL ON THE ROAD." None is detailed or allusive. But they are thematically consistent, describing Mother Courage in relation to three things: family, business, war. In these titles, Brecht reduced a scene's content to the simplest possible statement.

2. The final image of *Mother Courage and Her Children*.

After these titles come italicized sentences that parse a scene into constituent elements. The division of scene 1 follows:

—*Recruiters are going about the country looking for cannon fodder.*

—*Mother Courage introduces her mixed family, acquired in various theaters of war, to a sergeant.*

—*The canteen woman defends her sons against the recruiters with a knife.*

—*She sees that her sons are listening to the recruiters and predicts that the sergeant will meet an early death.*

—*To make her children afraid of the war, she has them too draw black crosses.*

—*Because of a small business deal, she nevertheless loses her brave son.*

—*And the sergeant leaves her with a prophecy: "If you want the war to work for you / You've got to give the war its due."*

These divisions are not what we normally mean by "beats." Nor are they all Brechtian gests. When translated into pieces of script, some contain only a line or two (ends of scenes 1 and 4), and some even include action without words (end of scene 8), whereas others describe six- or seven-minute blocks of dialogue. Some describe blocking and physical activity alone, others describe theme alone. Twice (scenes 7 and 10), Brecht provided only one sentence for a scene, and he never provided many. For long scenes (such as scenes 2, 6, 8, 11), five or six parts are typical. The subjects of Brecht's outline are predictable enough (Courage and family, business, war), but the proportions are not. Scene 5 is cut into five parts that together take less than five minutes to perform; scene 3 has eleven parts lasting forty-five minutes.

At its best, this outlining of the action connects structure with staging, logic with affect. A very obvious case is scene 2, where one dialogue section (Courage and Cook bargaining) is followed by another (Eilif with the general in the tent), and the ensuing double action is described as follows:

—*Mother Courage recognizes her lost son in the young soldier; taking advantage of the meal in Eilif's honor, she gets a steep price for her capon.*

—*Eilif relates his heroic deed and Mother Courage, while plucking her capon in the kitchen adjoining the tent, expresses opinions about rotten generals.*

—*Eilif does a sword dance and his mother answers with a song.*

The entries are double-focused in imitation of both the action and the picture (stage bisected up-down by the right edge of the tent). At the end, when the moment of shared song merges the two worlds and Eilif runs into the kitchen to see Courage, Brecht jarred his audience by alienating the emotional reunion: *"Eilif hugs his mother and gets a slap in the face for putting himself in danger with his heroism."* Even her emotions were twinned: love and anger.

Following the scene titles and the parsing of the scene comes a third section, the "ground arrangements," where Brecht restated the italicized sentences and expanded each with lines of commentary. As with the descriptive parsing, these commentaries provide a variety of insights into the play. But a frequent stress is visual. Brecht described this picture from scene 3: *"First meal in the Catholic camp.* The chaplain, now Mother Courage's bartender, joins the little family around the cooking pot; Swiss Cheese keeps slightly to one side; he wants to get away." He provided this note on the layout of scene 3: "During the whole scene the wagon stands left with its shaft pointed toward the audience, so that those to the left of it are not seen by those on the right." In scene 6, his stage layout was the basis of the drama:

> The right section of the stage is the private part. To the left are the bar and the guest table at which the clerk and the chaplain are sitting. There is by-play between right and left when the drinking soldier sings for Kattrin . . . while Courage . . . comes over to the table to ask the chaplain-bartender how long he thinks the war will go on.

Some of the commentaries simply describe blocking (scene 7, for example), often with the same detail as the typical realistic playwright uses in stage directions within the text. But since Brecht's published plays are stripped of interpretive stage directions, these notes help us to visualize picture and action more clearly.

Elsewhere, Brecht used the commentaries to emphasize theme. In scene 1, his descriptions place an immediate and strong stress on the connections between business and war. (One of the "Detail" notes states this intention: "The fusion of war and business cannot be established too soon.") Consequently, when Courage's family meets the recruiters, Brecht noted their kinship rather than their antagonism: "The professionals of commerce and of war meet, the war can start." He wanted her "Good morning, sergeant" spoken "in the same curt, military monotone" as his "Good morning, friends." The Sergeant's final prophecy stresses in another way how interdependent are the worlds of business and war: "Laughing, he predicts that if she wants to live off the war, she will also have to give the war its due."

In the ground arrangements, Brecht was insistent about indicating the play's "pivotal points," places where a scene's dynamics or structure are redirected by a discovery or motivational change. ("Legitimate variety is obtained by ascertaining the crucial points and planning the arrangements around them.") He found one pivotal point early in scene 2, between the Cook and Courage:

> In this scene the movement occurs at the pivotal point ("You know what I'm going to do?"). The cook stops peeling his carrots, fishes a piece of rotten meat out of the garbage barrel and takes it over to the butcher's block. Courage's attempt at blackmail has failed.

Pivotal points are often coincidental with a thematic crux. In scene 1, Courage's question, "Wouldn't you need a nice pistol, or a belt buckle?" is answered by the Sergeant's provocation, "I need something else." Here Brecht made the action turn on a central thematic issue, the needs of business versus the needs of war. Later in the scene, other pivotal moments echo this one, until Courage concludes the successful sale of the belt buckle only to discover that Eilif has left and she has been hoodwinked.

The ground arrangements of the action are illustrated in the approximately 100 photographs that begin the photo volume. These are laid out in a scene-by-scene, part-by-part format and include photos of titles projected on the half-curtain, blank pages for blackouts, and caption lines under the pictures with italicized sentences repeated from the notes. The pedagogical, illustrative nature of this section could not be more obvious.

In addition to the photographs keyed to the modelbook's text, there are extra photographs for eight of the twelve scenes, and they are just as informative. Some include elements omitted from the ground arrangements, such as the "Song of the Hours" (scene 3), the beating of the Young Peasant (scene 11), and the covering of Kattrin's body at the end. Others illustrate sequences of intense physical activity, like the surprise attack (scene 3), the wagon's departure (scene 8), and Kattrin's climb to the roof (scene 11). The most noticeable discrepancy between the number of illustrations and the number of parts occurs in the final two scenes. The modelbook provides only six photographs for the five parts of scene 11 (the drum scene), which is filled with tumultuous action. But scene 12—relatively short, involving very little action, and parsed by Brecht into four parts—has thirteen photos. These latter illustrations increase our understanding of how Kattrin's body was handled and how Courage harnessed herself to the wagon and moved off. Similar amplification is provided by the photographs for scene 3 (bargaining and denial) and scene 9 (Courage feeding Kattrin and then starting off). In all these cases, the stressed images are predominantly emotional and maternal.

In general, the principle of the photographs' arrangement is the same as the principle of the written commentary: one thing after another, the linear development of the play. That was Brecht's fundamental approach to action and idea. As I explain in the next section, linear development was also his basic method for creating character.

The Businesswoman Anna Fierling, Known as Mother Courage

> The merchant-mother became a great living contradiction.
> —Brecht, "Two Ways of Playing Mother
> Courage" (1951), in *Collected Plays*, vol. 5

In the modelbook, the photographs illustrating the ground arrangements of the action are followed by ten photographs of Helene Weigel in the title part. Brecht's label for these photos, "The contradictory nature of the figure," epitomizes what the scores of other photographs reveal about Weigel's Courage. Her moods were very distinct but very changeable. She was cocky, contemplative, lusty, skeptical, amused, bemused, ostentatious, self-consciously shy, and desolate. Lovers of tragedy should note that she smiled more often than she frowned. Her activities also changed rapidly, and the objects with which she interacted changed accordingly. Her facial expressions were exceptionally varied; she appears to have been a great mugger. I have received such contradictory impressions from my repeated viewings of these photographs that I sometimes doubt that any actress could blend all of these varied expressions into a single characterization. But then I recall how unBrechtian are the words "blend" and "single." Courage's dialectical existence depends upon the extremity of change in her nature.

Aside from her face, her body was difficult to see. A head scarf covered her hair in all but one scene (scene 8, when she was awakened by the bells of peace), and in that scene her hair was tied up on her head—she did not let her hair down even in sleep. Her body below the neck was draped with baggy, lumpy clothes, leaving only her hands and shoetops visible. Her body betrayed the years of hard labor that had bent her into a graceless clench. She showed little of what is commonly defined as sexual attractiveness. Yet in her rare moments of intimacy and relaxation with the Cook or the Chaplain, Weigel hinted at another time when her body was more attractive, more liberated, and more expressive.

The woman in the photographs—Weigel's figure as much as Brecht's character—shows striking vitality. In the "contradictory nature of the figure" pages, Weigel's Courage appears to have had a basically dynamic cast: she cocked a thumb to accent a question, smartly thrust out a leg during a moment of musical exuberance, struck a match against the wagon while she sat on its steps, let her mouth utter a hearty laugh that her hand tried to smother. She seems to have been always in motion, though she was not always crossing the stage. The changing props (belts, boots, bowls, harness, coins, socks) contribute to the impression that this person was always performing a task, solving a problem, avoiding a danger, and handling the affairs of business and family. But this vitality, in Brecht's view, was itself a contradictory phenomenon. As he wrote about the characters in *The Tutor,* one should never doubt the bottomless vitality of the bourgeois: "Europe has had two hundred years in which to learn how horribly vital their class is."[40]

Weigel's Courage was famously vital but also famously immobile, a symbol of postwar exhaustion and shock. The powerful moments of her desolation were all the more powerful because they were such a stunning change, so apparently "out of character." Naturally, these moments occurred during incidents of grief and failure, when Weigel could show Courage in pain, pessimistic, self-critical, and once or twice in a stupor so deep as to be truly terrifying. Students of Brecht's theory may be full of arguments proving that Courage is not a typical

Western tragic heroine. But she certainly looks like one in these photographs. She looks like a woman in extremities.

Contradiction and change were indeed at the heart of Weigel's characterization. I no sooner call up one of her sharply focused expressions than it produces the memory of its opposite. I no sooner assert one element of her nature than I want to add "But then" or "And yet." She was a woman experiencing extreme despair and desolation, but then she always bounced back to energetic activity and a brighter countenance. And yet, as my understanding of her character grows, I realize that this resiliency was less an indication of vitality than of a failure to learn or to understand. So the viewer's reactions are turned and twisted against each other.

The photographs help us to understand Courage as a physical creature, but we need the descriptions in the modelbook's notes to penetrate her moral character. In truth this imposing character imposes less physically than morally, gains size with her words, questions, ideas, and actions. Courage is preoccupied with people and problems outside herself, with a world to which she stands in relation. She is rarely self-absorbed because in a world such as hers it pays (in several senses) to be outer-directed. And because she is intelligent, she has ideas about that world; she even likes to argue in support of them, when it is safe to do so. As with all public debaters of large questions, Courage puts herself forward as a subject for argument, which is the Brechtian ideal in character: someone about whom we need to think. And since her ideas are largely concerned with personal action, to debate her ideas is necessarily to debate her actions. Thus the play's obvious subject is her philosophic character in action.

(Is such a statement of the play's subject merely a truism, a description of the subject in all good plays? Not to the same extent as in Brecht's mature works. Perhaps the "philosophic character in action" is the subject of all of Brecht's plays? No, for we cannot judge Baal, Garga, or Galy Gay as objectively as Shen Te, Grusha, or Galileo. The early characters' makeup offers no basis for such a judgment.)

The argument over Courage's character always reduces to this vigorously roasted chestnut of moral philosophy: Is she right or wrong? The debaters' voices are varied and inconsistent, for the question has intrigued actors, producers, directors, professors, students, critics, and Brecht himself. The debate is further fueled by serious questions about Brecht's dramaturgy. Did he successfully frame the question in the drama of *Mother Courage?* Did he frame an answer? Is there a single answer? When does the audience hear or see or understand it? In what context is the assessment of her rightness or wrongness made? How are we to judge?

Brecht's dramaturgical method of judging Courage was inductive. He placed one thing after another until a final conclusion was obvious. In the opposite (and more usual) method of characterization, authors immediately reveal the general nature of their characters. In the typical melodrama of any century, characters—dirty villains, virtuous maidens, clever sidekicks, and spotless heroes—are fixed elements in a schematized moral universe and are valued precisely for their one-dimensional sturdiness of type—their consistency of personality. In most modern playscripts, the characters' general natures are described in headnotes, either at the play's beginning or on their first entrances. For example: "Lady Britomart is a woman of fifty or thereabouts, well dressed and yet careless of her dress, well bred and quite reckless of her breeding," and so on for another 125 words.[41] "Mrs. Boyle . . . her face has now assumed that look which ultimately settles down on the faces of the women of the working-class," and so on.[42] "Cabot . . . his face is as hard as if it were hewn out of a boulder, yet there is a weakness in it, a petty pride in its own narrow strength."[43] Of course such explanatory notes are useful, but the authorial habit of generalizing at the beginning can condition the expectations and generalize the reactions of readers, directors, and actors who should be asking questions of the characters. Perhaps that is why Brecht never used headnotes in his plays, preferring instead to present experience, especially a character's behavior, in a moment-by-moment or linear mode, so that conclusions could be reached rather than received.

This is how he approached the character of Courage in his *Couragemodell* notes and in his directing of Helene Weigel. Avoiding headnotes or initial summaries, he began by dramatizing her experiences, her changes, and her contradictions. Only at the end of his twelve scenes did he offer a general judgment: that she was wrong for having failed to learn from her experiences.

At the beginning, in his Prologue, he offered the audience little but Courage's intention: to head someplace (the war zone, as the song makes clear) and to "shake a leg" so that she can sell to the troops. Weigel showed a great zest for business and an eagerness for experience, but this introduction was imagistic and impressionistic rather than evaluative and expository.

In scene 1, Brecht saw Courage as combining this same zestfulness with a graver tone, since she was now in contact with the war. Meeting the recruiters, she combined her lighthearted "Courage act" with another act performed for her children—a fortune-telling routine that included dire prophecies about the horrors of war. She overtly managed the early part of the scene but lost control of events when she tried to sell the Sergeant a belt buckle while trying to watch her children. By the scene's end, she had lost Eilif to the war. Weigel did not play Courage as stupid or unmindful of the threat posed by the recruiters. Her Courage wanted to keep her son, but she also needed to make her sales pitch, for that son might starve if she failed. So Weigel and Brecht made it immediately clear that her story was about the conflicting claims of business and motherhood, that her character was poised between contradictory demands ("merchant-mother," or "businesswoman–Mother Courage"), and that the inevitable consequence of certain actions in her contradictory situation would be loss.

At the conclusion of scene 1, Weigel's Courage was dismayed. At the beginning of scene 2, however, she bargained with the Cook in an artful and flirtatious manner. This change in her character carried an important lesson for the spectator: never again could one assume that her personality would be continuous between scenes. Nor could onstage characters trust her to be consistent from moment to moment. At the end of scene 2 she hugged Eilif, then immediately slapped him.

At the beginning of scene 3, the audience saw Courage from a new angle. In the model, Brecht stressed how hard she worked, her "energy and competence" and her "unflagging readiness" for work. "She is hardly ever seen not working." Even in the surprise attack, moving quickly from task to task amid confusion, she consciously attempted to save money and lives. This combination of business and family obligations absorbed her energies throughout the three extended sections of scene 3. When the captured Swiss Cheese returned and the Sergeant interrogated Courage, Weigel sat rummaging in her basket pretending to be what she usually was, "a busy businesswoman with no time for formalities." But at the end of the questioning, she lost control and ran after her son and his captors, almost revealing her motherhood. At the scene's climax, Courage's ability to manage business and family simultaneously was put to the sternest tests when she bargained for Swiss Cheese's life and again when she had to deny his corpse. Brecht brought the dramatic tension and suspense to a peak in order to provide another schematic illustration of her conflicting necessities (the wagon or the boy) and her contradictory motives (stay in business or protect the family).

A spectator might wonder what Courage will do after enduring such extraordinary suffering. Weigel changed. Brecht recommended that scene 4 ("The Song of the Great Capitulation") be played bitterly, stressing depravity rather than dejection or righteous anger. Weigel surprised the audience by changing, during the scene, from a distressed mother with a grievance to a cynical spokeswoman for capitulation to the powerful. She changed again in scene 5. Brecht wrote: "*A new Courage.* A change has taken place in Courage. She has sacrificed her son to the wagon and now she defends the wagon like a tigress. She has been hardened by the hard bargains she drives." To emphasize the cost of her change, Weigel downed several glasses of schnapps at the scene's beginning. For scene 6, which shows the Courage camp at rest during Tilly's funeral, Brecht noted: "Again Courage has changed. Increasing prosperity has made her softer and more human." The transformation is so attractive to the Chaplain (though Brecht was amusingly skeptical of his real motives) that he eventually proposes to his boss. Weigel accentuated the contrast of Courage's physical relaxation and ironic gaiety with her previous moods. When the bleeding Kattrin ran in, however, Weigel's Courage showed her distress and instantly reversed her position on the war. She had just decided to invest in its future, but now she cursed it with all the vehemence of an offended mother.

Courage again reverses her position on war in scene 7, the short scene that is mainly another rendition of the Courage song. Now she will not listen to anyone "running down the war," because the war provides. Brecht prefaced this scene with a projected title that told the audience she was at "the height of her business career," and he made her success visible by draping her in jewelry. Thus her endorsement of war was undercut by her "bribed" appearance and by the endorsement's juxtaposition with the ending to scene 6. Nevertheless, Weigel, marching at the side of the wagon, showed the prosperous Courage to be "cheerful" and in "full possession of her vitality." She showed how thoroughly agreeable riches could be to Mother Courage.

In Brecht's production of this play, scene 7 was the end of act 1, and its startling contrast with the end of scene 6 epitomized the contradictory and rapid changes that Brecht and Weigel had shown in Courage during the first act. Change, after all, is primary in Brechtian drama. Characters can change, the wagon can change, circumstances can change, the world can change. And these changes take place in his work so that the audience will see a changing world as a model for their own world, in which change is always needed and possible. Writers who dramatize unchanging characters in an unchanging world are often guilty of an unconscious pessimism. "Things long unchanged appear unchangeable," said Brecht.[44]

The second act of *Mother Courage* (scenes 8–12) is only half as long as the first, but in it Brecht continued the dramaturgic pattern of scene-by-scene contrasts and strengthened the pattern within Courage's character of contradiction leading to loss. He filled scene 8 with images of change: Courage changes men for the first time in years; the Chaplain changes clothes and vocations; and war changes to peace, which changes to war again. In major sections of scene 8 Brecht analyzed characters from earlier scenes (the Cook, Yvette, and Eilif) and how they had changed, usually for the worse, under the impress of time and war. Brecht directed the degenerative cases strongly. He made Yvette—now "The Countess Starhemburg, my good people"—snooty, vulgar, and grotesque and portrayed Eilif as apparently prosperous but coarse, surly, and degraded by violence. Prospering in this war, the episodes argued, imperils the soul.

As she crossed the terrain of act 2, Helene Weigel showed the steadily downward curve in Courage's material conditions and humanity. She began with a lighthearted treatment of scene 8, specifically, Courage's decision to invest once more in the war's continuation. She showed Courage suffering from cold and hunger in scene 9 and behaving like a draft horse under the desperate conditions of scene 10. In the final scene, she sank further into a blank, animalistic condition. Through these scenes Weigel and Brecht simplified the character's line until little remained but the problem of whether to stay with the war and the assessment of the damages. When she discovered that the war had started again at the end of scene 8, Weigel was "overjoyed" and "in high spirits." She packed up her wagon and her company with the certainty that both business and family matters would now improve, because "Now there's a war again, everything will work out all right" (her line was cut from the play's final edition). But the optimistic mood of this moment was crosscut by dramatic irony (the audience and the other characters knew of Eilif's execution) and by juxtaposition with her about-face in scene 9 when she was once more caught in the snares of the merchant-mother contradiction. When she understood that Kattrin could not accompany her to the Cook's inn at Utrecht, "Weigel showed plainly that Courage thought the proposition over—she thinks every proposition over," but no matter how long she calculated, she could not avoid recognizing the necessity of loss. In scene 12, Weigel created two unforgettable images of Courage—an image of grief when singing the lullaby over the dead Kattrin and an image of eternal enterprise when she marched off into the endless war zone represented by the turntable, pulling her empty wagon. She was the merchant-mother at the nadir of her life.

In the modelbook, Brecht developed each of these twelve scenes, each of Courage's many moods, and a host of details about her character and behavior. On his penultimate page, he gave a general note on the leading character of his production. Entitled "*Mother Courage learns nothing,*" it begins, "In the last scene Weigel's Courage seemed to be eighty years old. And she understands nothing." In the scene with the peasants at the end, Weigel reacted "only to remarks connected with the war" and missed their barbed accusation about Kattrin's death. After all this loss and suffering and punishment, after all these opportunities to change her basic situation, she was no smarter than she had been at the beginning. If she had more children to lose to the war, she no doubt would. This graphic and compelling conclusion came from a playwright who had originally written his play (in the fall of 1939) as a warning against failing to learn from a war that was just beginning. In 1949–1951, with the war behind him, Brecht the director could add the pedagogical imperative: if Courage failed to learn, if it was too late for her, then an audience could (must) learn by studying her failure. And such study was easiest, this note made clear, in a theatre of alienation where the leading actress attacked the part of Courage with "a way of playing it which does not lead to audience identification with the principal character (heroine)."

With these words of judgment at the model's end, the argument over Courage's moral character can begin. (Courage could have stayed home or otherwise avoided the war, goes a familiar argument. Brecht believed that the historical character could have done so, though her modern counterpart in the age of global warfare could not.) But before the argument becomes too involved, we should note the obvious: the argument begins at the end of the model, as we leave the metaphorical theatre after having observed her changes, decisions, necessities, and failures. If we finally reject her, we must not reject her at first (in the Prologue or in scene 1), for at that point she has not yet failed to learn from the war; she has only failed to know about it, which is different. If we judge Courage too quickly, we may fail to learn, for moral condemnation frequently leads audiences to cease evaluating characters and analyzing their actions. First study, then moralize, Brecht might have said.

Is such a treatment of his leading character surprising in a writer so often termed "didactic"? He should instead have been called "dialectic," particularly because that is what he called himself in the years 1948–1956, and that is how he thought. In Brecht's mature theatre, his dialectic held contraries in suspension—anger and hope, condemnation and sympathy, the analytical and the sensual. Such opposites were related actively, held in a state of tension where contraries neither dilute nor resolve one another but become energized by contact with each other. His goal was to make theatre experience lively and enjoyable. Eric Bentley put this typically well when he called Shaw and Brecht "the only good 'Marxist playwrights'—partly, no doubt, because they regarded the dialectic as dramatic and not just as valid."[45] Here in particular, the method strikes me as Shakespearean, building character of great scope and size, yet also modernist, achieving such magnitude through complexity and contradiction rather than through high social status or sheer sublimity of language.

"The contradictions that pervade the play were not taken over ready-made, but worked out," Brecht wrote about the "epic element" at the end of the *Couragemodell*. He directed his own play by working out the collisions and frictions between its short beats and scenes. The model contains a host of specific notes showing dialectical collision in very ordinary moments of Courage's life. Some brief examples of Weigel's portraiture can be cited.

In scene 1, when the recruiters first eyed her sons with interest, Weigel instinctively displayed "maternal pride," but then a leading question from the Sergeant made her remember that the boys were in danger from such compliments.

Defending her sons from the recruiters, Weigel pulled a knife, but she did so without "savagery," since this was in fact a comparatively normal situation for the Courage family, a situation she could handle in a routine, if forceful, manner.

Later in scene 1, Weigel turned meaningfully toward Eilif before the Sergeant drew to determine his fate. Thus she made the audience and the son understand why she was playing this game.

At the end of the first scene, after losing Eilif, Weigel showed "dismay rather than horror," for horror would have been excessive considering that her son was still alive. But she let her belt buckles trail along the ground and then slammed them angrily into the wagon before moving off, showing that she knew why she had lost him.

Weigel's Courage showed a rich mixture of responses to Eilif's military triumph in scene 2—first pride, then opportunism, and finally anger that he had put himself in danger by acting heroically.

When Kattrin attempts to run away in scene 9, Courage must forcibly drag her back. "While saying the words 'Don't go thinking I've given him the gate on your account,' Courage puts a spoonful of soup into Kattrin's mouth." Weigel's words protested, but her actions gave away her maternity.

Two slightly longer episodes also show how dialectical directing can produce rich and complex results. The first is Courage selling the belt buckle to the Sergeant in scene 1. On the one hand, Weigel projected the positive energy and forcefulness of a self-assured saleswoman, but on the other she constantly checked her flanks and rear. As she climbed down to begin the sale, she looked around "anxiously" for the other recruiter. After making her pitch behind the wagon, she left to get schnapps, but she took the buckle with her—it had not yet been paid for. Taking the Sergeant's coin, she bit into it. Brecht's general point was: "If the distrust at the beginning were omitted, we should have a stupid, utterly uninteresting woman, or a person with a passion for business but no experience." He wanted instead a clever, fascinating woman who is very proficient at conducting business, but a clever, fascinating woman who loses. "The distrust must not be absent, it must merely be too weak to do any good."

The second is the reunion of Courage and the Cook (scene 8)—an informative and intriguing episode after Brecht had applied a few touches. Weigel laid the groundwork in scene 6 by telling the Chaplain how "nice" the Cook was, saying it with just a bit more emphasis than was necessary to put off the Chaplain with a "good-natured rebuff." Since the audience was already aware of Courage's special weakness for the Cook, Weigel could treat him ironically in scene 8, using "a dry, matter-of-fact tone." They sat on a short bench down right, to the side of the wagon, and talked in a relaxed fashion about all they had lost. Courage's hand slipped under the Cook's arm and grasped his hand. "Knowing what it knew, the audience could be touched as well as amused that the subject of their love dialogue should be the fact that they were both ruined."

If we widen the context a bit, those lovers' hands may tell us more. Is the conjunction of love and ruin inevitable in war? Will love develop only in conditions of ruin? Or, more darkly, does love cause ruin? Brecht hinted at the latter in his modelbook summary of three major themes in *Mother Courage*. One of these themes is "war, which is a continuation of business by other means, makes the human virtues fatal even to their possessors." Of all people, Anna Fierling might deserve some love in her life, but that love will do no one any good in this topsy-turvy moral universe.

"Look, it's Mother Courage!" said the German housewives as they held their children up to see Helene Weigel marching with Brecht in a May Day parade. It was 1950, a year and a half after the production had been first mounted in Berlin. Her Courage was already Brecht's showpiece; it would become her greatest role and make *Mother Courage* the star production in the Ensemble's repertory. Today, the face of Courage graces the covers of anthologies and books of criticism. Theatre historians who describe the nineteenth century by reference to the Macready Virginius, the Booth Hamlet, or the Bernhardt Phèdre will no doubt refer to Weigel's Courage, along with Olivier's Richard III and Brando's Kowalski, as icons of the mid-twentieth century.

Kenneth Tynan memorialized Weigel's 400th appearance in the part (1961) with these words:

> When I say that this piece of acting is earthy, you may imagine something plodding and laborious; but Frau Weigel's earthiness is light and springlike, even skipping and so utterly devoid of personal assertiveness that the life of the character appears to derive from the wares she handles and the trade she plies.
>
> Her performance, in short and as ever, is devotedly Brechtian; it is not as an individual, separable from history and social circumstance, that we recognize Mother Courage, but as the owner of a broken-down canteen wagon at a particular time in a particular place. She works,

therefore she is. Her function determines her loyalties, her friendships, her loathings and her blind, unwitting drive toward calamity; it
is her love of bargaining, not any lack of maternal affection, that
causes the death of her elder son, who is executed while she haggles
over the amount of money necessary to save him. What Brecht pre-
scribed, his widow, Frau Weigel, embodies: the maxim that there is no
such thing as a character ungoverned by a social context.[46]

Brechtian? we might ask. Well of course Weigel was, living and working with him nearly all his adult life. But she was also more Brechtian
than Brecht; she was a stronger political presence and had a keener
economic sense, according to many accounts.

Weigel's economic sense was evident during the rehearsals of the
Prologue's Courage song. Brecht and Eric Engel wanted "a dramatic
entrance, lusty and cocky," because they wanted to observe the an-
cient show business maxim—open vigorously—and because they
could contrast this vital first image with the show's finale, when the
wagon, the woman, and the song conjoined again with sharply different meaning. But according to Brecht, Weigel saw through the Ethel
Merman–like obviousness of their lusty-cocky woman. She thought
the Prologue song should be "a realistic business song and suggested
that it be used to picture the long journey to the war." So Weigel's
Courage entered relaxing confidently on her wagon box, arms
akimbo and ready to deal, and then looked back after her entrance in
the direction from which the wagon had come. We have been traveling like this for days or weeks, the look said. We are ready to go on as
long as necessary to reach the war zone, the song said. The reality of
the image lay in her self-definition as a businesswoman in war.

One of the great challenges in staging *Mother Courage,* as Brecht
and Weigel both knew, is to force an audience to analyze and criticize
the world of business. In either a capitalist or a Marxist culture, "business" can be viewed as "business as usual," a set of ideas and relations that we accept as normal, natural, and unchanging (unchangeable). Brecht's model notes summarize what happens in the mind of
the audience:

> A deeply engrained habit leads the theater-goer to pick out the more
> emotional utterances of the characters and overlook everything else.
> Like descriptions of landscapes in novels, references to business are
> received with boredom. The "business atmosphere" is simply the air
> one breathes and as such requires no special mention.

By extension, audiences can conclude that war—which Brecht called "a continuation of business by other means" —is likewise an inevitable part of the human experience, a "timeless abstraction." That such thinking went unexamined was the target of his theatre. And yet even *Mother Courage,* as Brecht knew from reviews and from interviews with members of the audience, induced this strange uncritical acceptance of business. So he tinkered with the text in order to strengthen the connections between business and war, giving Courage a new penultimate line in the Munich production: "I've got to get back in business." As a director, he fought to eliminate the uncritical spirit by introducing various devices and juxtapositions that alienated the world of business.

Weigel set to work on the same problem by inventing a small detail, the kind of odd gesture or habit that often centers a character: she quite audibly snapped her purse when concluding a financial transaction. Snapping the purse was a crisp action that closed a sale and signaled her degree of satisfaction. It would be characteristic of Courage to snap her purse—and to carry it always, in all weathers and all situations, on her right thigh. Weigel's Courage had only one other prop with as much value, the large metal spoon that she usually wore attached to her top garment just to the side of her left breast, displayed like a flag. The sound of the purse constantly reminded the audience that work was central to her life; the spoon was a reminder why.

Weigel thus used reminders of economic necessity to augment audience awareness of the existence and importance of business. She also demonstrated in Courage's behavior a constant awareness of value—she seemed never to look at or touch an object without automatically computing its worth. But, most importantly, Weigel forced the audience to see the economic implications of the most dramatic scenes. For instance in scene 3, where Courage bargains for Swiss Cheese's life, the actress did not let the thrilling, suspenseful situation overwhelm the implacable situational realities. Giving up the wagon too easily would be foolish (as Brecht said, "she has fought too hard for it"), and Courage is never conventionally foolish, no matter how right or wrong she is. But when the bribe was reduced to 200 guilders, Weigel clearly made a decision: "Now she is willing to pay." Each of these momentary reflections acted as a check on the audience's inclination to blame Courage for bargaining over a human life. Brecht framed Weigel's bargaining with contradictory attitudes, for Yvette demonstrated "anger at Courage's betrayal of her son," but

Kattrin did not. "The portrayal of mute Kattrin," says the note, "is not realistic if her goodness is stressed to the point of making her oppose her mother's attempt to get the amount of the bribe reduced." Yvette portrayed the audience's first, emotional reaction, but Kattrin pointed to the recognition of necessity.

Weigel's most brilliant example of connecting business to the travails of war came at the end of scene 6, when Courage curses the war. Wounded by the soldiers, Kattrin returns to the camp. Courage tries to pick up her daughter's spirits with light words and even the offer of the red boots. But Kattrin is more than inconsolable—she is angry, and refusing the boots, to Brecht, is a "protest." "She blames her mother for what has happened to her." Courage is angry too. The last child remaining at home has lost her chance at happiness—her chance for marriage, children, peace, and a normal life. Courage is now saddled with a handicapped spinster. But she is also scared and hurt, like any parent who sees her child bleeding. "That's war for you!" she says, expressing bitter anger. "A fine way to make a living!" A soldier "stuffed something in [Kattrin's] mouth when she was little," causing her dumbness. Now this. Swiss Cheese is dead, Eilif is somewhere else—and why? "God damn the war."

Could "God damn the war" be a signal that Courage is learning about war? In his writing and directing, Brecht made sure to deny any such suspicion, for after one of the performance's shortest intervals, she returned in scene 7 to say, "Stop running down the war. I won't have it." In her acting, Weigel was able to alienate the curse of war even as she uttered it. Kattrin had entered the camp scattering the supplies she carried from town among the other goods awaiting inventory. After watching Kattrin retreat into the wagon, Weigel returned to these goods and gathered them up, then knelt among them. "Courage has cursed the war while gathering up the supplies in defence of which her daughter has been disfigured," Brecht wrote. "Resuming the inventory begun at the start of the scene, she now counts the new articles." Manfred Wekwerth describes Weigel at this moment as letting "flour run through her fingers to test its commercial grade—the flour which her daughter was procuring when she was attacked."[47] Weigel thus dislodged the curse of war by cursing while subconsciously calculating. The contradiction and the contradictory principle were in plain view.

Will Courage never understand the second of Brecht's themes, the economic one, that "in wartime the big profits are not made by little

people"? The moral perversity of war makes virtue fatal to its posses-
sor. The economy of war makes enterprise futile for all but the powerful and the well connected.

Reason and emotion, those seventeenth-century dramatic antino-
mies, are balanced contraries in Brecht's later theory, as I have already observed. In Weigel's acting the same was true. The model
Brechtian actor, Weigel combined an actively critical scrutiny of the
character she portrayed with a sympathetic presentation of this
charming woman.

Consider another example of the quick play of Weigel's intelligence, this one from scene 4, "The Song of the Great Capitulation."
At the end of the previous scene, when Swiss Cheese was shot, Courage suffered devastating grief. After a blackout, she must immediately change focus and attempt to teach a chance acquaintance an
unpleasant home truth. "Sitting, aren't you?" she observes of the
Young Soldier beside her. "Oh, they know us like a book, they know
how to handle us. Sit down! And down we sit. You can't start a riot
sitting down." Making such a switch from scene to scene and from
grief to cynicism—in particular, making it so quickly and without
emotional transition—is usually difficult for an actor unfamiliar with
Brecht's theatre or overtrained in Stanislavsky's. But Weigel
whipped the audience around. Brecht's note reads: "In no other
scene is Courage so depraved as in this one, where she instructs the
young man in capitulation to the higher-ups and then puts her own
teaching into effect." But this antipathetic behavior had its dangers,
and Brecht warned against them. If capitulation is seen as the inevitable answer to outrage (scene 3), or if "by hypnotic action the actress
playing Mother Courage invites the audience to identify with her,"
the results will be both wrong and "socially disastrous." So Weigel
showed "a glimmer of wisdom and even of nobility, and that is good.
Because the depravity is not so much that of her person as that of her
class, and because she herself at least rises above it somewhat by
showing that she understands this weakness and that it even makes her
angry." In her acting, Weigel never projected charm without including something repugnant; she never exhibited repellant or incorrect
behavior without adding a touch of the wise and humorous. Brecht
called this evidence of her "masterful sense of proportion."

But, as Weigel moved the audience away from Courage to a critical distance, she simultaneously aroused sympathy. Almost everyone

who saw the Ensemble production testified to this point: in the end it was impossible to avoid "feeling for" Courage. I mean that spectators could feel concerned about her, feel sorry for her, and even share a fellow-feeling with her, that feeling we normally term "empathy". To Brecht and Weigel, such reactions were not lapses or failures in their work but the proper and predictable results of their intentions.

The greatest instance of audience sympathy for Courage came during her emotional crisis at the end of scene 3. Bargaining for Swiss Cheese's life, Courage eventually loses control of the situation and is unable to resolve her financial-family dilemma. Off goes Yvette with a last desperate offer. Courage waits in a state of dreadful anticipation, and then hears the shots that kill her boy. Yvette returns with the news that the soldiers will arrive momentarily. Finally Courage denies knowledge of her son before his killers. It is little more than one page of text and contains no memorable statements beyond Courage's line, "Maybe I bargained too long," but it was and is a heartrending sequence on the stage—the first of *Mother Courage*'s two great dramatic crises. Earlier, when she lost Eilif to the recruiters, Courage was merely dismayed and angry because of her loss. Now she is devastated and heartstruck. The moment challenged Weigel's genius, her conscious artistry, and her virtuoso ability.

After Yvette's departure on her final bargaining mission, Weigel sat at a round table (down left) and scoured knives while the Chaplain, to her immediate right, dried glasses. A long silence ensued. When the shots rang out offstage, Weigel's face was seized by what Brecht called "a look of extreme suffering," an "unscreaming open mouth and backward-bent head." The famous modelbook photographs show this moment clearly. Weigel's hands, still in her lap, did not betray any special tension, but her body was bent by some mysterious force thrusting up against her lower back. That force pushed her chest out, her shoulders up, and her head back. Her eyes were closed and unreadable. The audience's focus was on her silent mouth, frozen open in an agonized expression. The Chaplain, who suddenly discovered himself inappropriately in the middle of this scene, was barely noticeable as he moved discreetly toward the wagon. Weigel was still stationary, her body still stricken, her mouth still open.

We have come to call this "the silent scream." Weigel's agonized face (an expression apparently inspired by a newspaper photograph of a suffering Asian woman) is remembered as one of the most powerful and disturbing images of Europe after the war. As an emblem, the face tells of suffering in war, whether among soldiers on the battlefield, prisoners in a concentration camp, or innocent civilians behind the lines. More particularly, it tells of passive suffering, the suffering of survivors left to mourn. It is, as traditionally, a feminine version of that condition. And its highest metaphorical value is that the scream is not heard. Most revealing of Brechtian method is the fact that Weigel needed much experience in the part before she could discover this image of shock and grief.

Weigel then collapsed. Her face was drawn down into a tight frown, and her eyes were again hooded and unreadable. Her body seemed to frown too, for her shoulders were drawn forward. She had been sitting thus a long time when Yvette walked in slowly and announced the execution and the approach of the soldiers. Kattrin crossed to stand at her mother's left, but each avoided the other's eyes. Weigel even grasped Kattrin's right hand in her own left, but her eyes remained down, and her expression remained "obstinate," to use Brecht's word. As during the scream, audience attention was concentrated on her face, specifically on her mouth, for her lower lip was thrust forward. It remained so as she walked over to deny knowledge of the body, then returned to her seat. As the soldiers crossed to the left behind her, she leaned her head against her daughter's arm, releasing her hold on herself for the first time since the shots—and then only a little. End of scene.

Brecht said that "Weigel's recklessness in throwing away her character reaches its highest point" in this denial scene. I take this to mean that she rejected the conventional opportunity to overplay a dramatic scene and in doing so realized both character and drama to an extent seldom rivaled in the history of the art. What is strange is not that Weigel acted with such emotional power but that Brecht's followers should have been surprised that such acting took place in his theatre. In his last conversation with Eric Bentley, Brecht reproached Ernst Busch for having missed "the whole tragic side" of the marvelous Azdak in *The Caucasian Chalk Circle*.[48] Bentley flinched on hearing Brecht speak in support of tragedy, pity, and sympathy. Then he realized that the new dimension of Brecht's final work was its incorporation of conventional dramatic techniques (emotion, identification, suspense) with the techniques of epic theatre (criticism, detachment, alienation).

Characters, Brecht believed, should both attract and repel because they should be as contradictory as people are. He said that Lauffer in *The Tutor* (1950) "claims our sympathy for being so utterly crushed, together with our contempt for letting this happen." About Coriolanus he said (a few years later): "Not too likable, and likable enough."[49] In the *Couragemodell* he repeatedly displayed his appreciation for such character interpretations by his actors, particularly Erwin Geschonneck (the Chaplain), Regina Lutz (Yvette), and Angelika Hurwicz (Kattrin). The original (1949) Chaplain, Werner Hinz, showed that "the character of the chaplain is based on a contradiction. . . . part scoundrel, part superior intelligence." Hinz's portrayal coupled "a wooden, awkward, comical quality, which he retained in his role of good Samaritan [in scene 5]," with a human vulnerability: "When he helps the injured it becomes clear that he too is to be pitied."

In Brechtian theatre, contradictory characters are understood by a duality of perception that Darko Suvin, in an influential article on Brecht's late aesthetics, calls a "tension between a future which the author's awareness inhabits, and a present which his figures inhabit; this tension is at the root of the most significant values of Brecht's work."[50] Whether we consider the duality to be between the future and the present or between reason and the emotions is not so important. If we judge Courage from both perspectives, we can find her wanting at the same time that we sympathize with her suffering and ignorance. This is perhaps the most effective way to achieve a true understanding of the central contradiction (merchant-mother) of her character.

Weigel used the finale, scene 12, to summarize Mother Courage's character and to create a final symbol. She began kneeling down center and sang the lullaby to her daughter's corpse, which lay face up, right to left across the stage, her head in Weigel's lap. The farm set from scene 11 had been pulled off during the title break, so the floor was bare of everything except people (three peasants stood a few feet away) and the wagon, which was right facing down left.

Singing a lullaby over a dead daughter, like singing "Howl, howl, howl," has a certain built-in pathos, but Weigel alienated it. She sang the lullaby "without any sentimentality or desire to provoke sentimentality." There was even something hideous about the song—she stressed the words in such a way that Courage would be interpreted as selfish: "The neighbor brats whimper / Mine are happy and gay. / They go in tatters / and you in silk down / Cut from an angel's / Best party gown." That was appalling at this point in the proceedings.

So was the "almost bestial stupor" with which Weigel acted the whole scene. Her head constantly down until the end, Courage had not only not learned anything, she appeared to have lost the capacity to learn, the ability to think. She was blankly absorbed in Kattrin, and the peasants roused her only with news of interest about the war's progress. Even in her stupor, Weigel was the mother, then the merchant, constantly in alternation.

The mother had not quite lost all capacity to feel. In the middle of the scene, now on her feet and dealing with reality, Weigel crossed down right near the footlights and walked around to the back of the wagon, then returned with a canvas to cover Kattrin. The bare stage floor (or the barren earth it symbolized) was a poor resting place for that beloved body.

But then she had to confront the matter of paying for Kattrin's burial. (Courage cannot stay for the burial itself, of course, because the war—that is, business—is moving on.) This sequence showed Weigel at her most thoughtful, for she took an apparently trivial moment, extracted its meanings—notably its economic meanings—and translated them into actions. She reached into her purse for what little money she had left. The peasants gathered around, watching her purse and her hands. She surveyed her money, kept one coin back, and gave them the rest. This was a reminder that Courage always saved, always calculated against the future, even though her subconscious mind sometimes had to attend to the arrangements. However, it should also be noted that Courage's funds were nonetheless reduced to one coin. The peasants picked up Kattrin's body and started out, but Weigel remained standing, her head bowed, looking at the coin in her hand. As the body disappeared, she popped the coin back into her purse and snapped the purse shut. With this sound, all the previous purse snappings returned to memory with cumulative force. The moral is that conducting business during a war leads to destitution.

Brecht was extravagant in praising this image, which was altogether Weigel's invention. It "did not in the least detract from the overpowering effect of desolation," and more generally, it had realistic truthfulness:

This little gesture has the power and suddenness of a discovery—a discovery concerning human nature, which is molded by conditions. To dig out the truth from the rubble of the self-evident, to link the particular strikingly with the universal, to capture the particular that characterizes a general process, that is the art of the realist.

The peasant woman now shook Courage's hand and started off to the left. But she paused part way out, turned to Courage and said, "Hurry up!" in a not very pleasant tone. (If closer, she would not have risked saying it like that.) Weigel had been standing down center with her head bowed since the handshake, but now she bowed down low from the waist, very low, her head nearly touching her knees. Brecht called it a "beautiful" bow.

Alone, she slowly and carefully got into harness, saying, "I hope I can pull the wagon alone. I'll manage, there isn't much in it. I've got to get back in business." As the final music started up, she started off. "Hey, take me with you!" she called to the soldiers. Tugging the wagon left across the turntable, she bent her body against the weight. Would she always be bent over? Or would she continue to change? The stage was empty except for the woman and the wagon, traveling counterclockwise. Because the overhead "SAXONY" sign had been removed at the scene break, the stage became everywhere and anywhere. The play was moving into the mythic mode.

The music played and the wagon rolled. There was no illusion here of an offstage army marching into an offstage distance. The words of the Courage song came directly and vigorously from offstage:

> With all the killing and recruiting
> The war will worry on a while.
> In ninety years they'll still be shooting
> It's hardest on the rank-and-file.

The audience learned how hard when the music modulated and the army chorus continued:

> Our food is swill, our pants all patches
> The higher-ups steal half our pay
> And still we dream of God-sent riches.
> Tomorrow is another day!

"Tomorrow is another day"? It is all too reminiscent of "Hey, take me with you!" In Brecht's opinion, the final song gave "powerful expression to [Courage's] still unshattered hope of getting her cut from the war." Do these people never learn? Or is a different "tomorrow" implied? Does the chorus mean what it first meant? Although the tempo slowed, the rhythm still insisted:

> The spring is come! Christian, revive!
> The snowdrifts melt, the dead lie dead!
> And if by chance you're still alive
> It's time to rise and shake a leg.

(The *abab* pattern of Manheim's translation is true to the original, but the "dead-leg" rhyme, weak in both vowel and resonance, is not. Bentley's version of the chorus is more appropriate to the mood, music, and play: "Christians, awake! The winter's gone! / The snow departs. Dead men sleep on: / Let all of you who still survive / Get out of bed and look alive!"[51])

As Weigel continued to pull the wagon around the rumbling turntable, the audience had time to survey its varied reactions to the whole of Mother Courage's story (pity and terror at her losses, anger at her stupidity), as well as to consider how she might have acted otherwise. But Weigel kept pulling that wagon around and around. Brecht's note on this final image reads:

> Of course the audience would understand if [the wagon] were simply pulled away. When it goes on rolling there is a moment of irritation ('this has been going on long enough'). But when it goes on still longer, a deeper understanding sets in.

Directors frequently use such insistent repetition, to and past the point of irritation, to turn an activity into an image. In this case, the desire to stop the wagon brought the audience to Brecht's third theme, one unstated on stage but deeply imbedded in the story and production: "No sacrifice is too great for the struggle against war."

The Brecht-Weigel productions of *Mother Courage and Her Children*, one of the few great antiwar plays, enunciated humanity's evolutionary imperative and the theme of postwar Europe: *Never again*.

"Giehse's Courage"

There are eight notes in the *Couragemodell* with the title "Giehse's Courage." Along with twenty photographs and several more remarks scattered among the notes, they are what Brecht preserved from his 1950 reinterpretation of *Mother Courage* at the Munich Kammerspiele. Watching Thérèse Giehse test, refine, and develop Weigel's version of Courage was Brecht's first experiment with this model as a model. As he said about the lights in his theatre and the curtain rods in his apartment. "One must be able to see how things work."

The historical irony here is that this second Courage was actually the original. Giehse had taken the title part in the 1941 Zurich *Mother Courage,* which Brecht never saw but which he disparaged on the strength of reviews comparing Courage to Niobe, a sure sign to him of excessive empathy. In the *Couragemodell,* the only substantive reference to the Zurich production concerns the end of scene 4. In 1941, Giehse had feigned militaristic obedience when saying "No complaint." In 1950, she followed Weigel's example in lowering her head and walking off past the officer, showing a woman demoralized but convinced. Particularly in view of the times, the first choice was certainly as meaningful as the second. This is only one indication that the 1941 *Courage* may in fact have been quite good. Thornton Wilder among others thought so. Giehse was an enormously talented actress. She and some of her colleagues in the refugee ensemble had already worked with Brecht, and she was one of his first recruits to the Ensemble. She was still powerful in her penultimate film, *Lacombe Lucien* (1974).

Giehse's 1950 Courage had as characteristic a look as Weigel's. The latter's facial expression was changeable, but it was also hard and calculated. Weigel's faces often looked planned—surely part of the alienation effect—whereas Giehse's Courage showed a face patently more innocent. Giehse was chubbier and seemed younger, at least in spirit. Her Courage appeared more often with her head uncovered (as in scenes 3 and 5), and more of her arms was visible in certain costumes. A wonderfully expressive photograph shows her greeting the Cook in scene 8, her body—arms, neck, back, legs, elbows—bent into angles, simultaneously curtseying and shaking hands, while her right foot sticks up at yet another angle from the floor, a final silly mark. It is a pose in which I cannot imagine Weigel.

Brecht was delighted by Giehse's individual style and its effect on his play. Feeding Kattrin in front of the presbytery (scene 9), Giehse shook the last drop of soup into the spoon and spoke the word "wagon" with a particularly Bavarian intonation, suddenly expressing "the unconscious politeness of many little people who attribute

to their sacrifices personal motives in order to spare others the humil-
iation of accepting charity." Having used Eilif's triumph to raise the
price of the capon (scene 2), Giehse's Courage held the guilder up
and executed a small, appropriately "triumphal" march. When Swiss
Cheese was led off to be executed (scene 3), Giehse was screened
from the soldiers by the wagon, doing a "dance of despair, stamping
wildly on the ground" at the same time that she yelled, "And don't
twist his shoulder off." Giehse put the canvas over Kattrin's dead
body (scene 12) as Weigel did, but when she drew the sheet up to
cover Kattrin's head, she angled it so that it covered her bowed head
as well. The final farewell was masked from all invading eyes.

In scene 7 Weigel was cheerful and decorated with jewelry,
whereas Giehse was "stumbling drunk," swinging her bottle boldly
and singing as the wagon passed behind her. The latter interpretation,
said Brecht, would "avoid any misunderstanding."

In the final moment of the play, when Courage hitches herself to
the wagon and prepares to go off, Weigel seemed to be a brute quantity. Giehse, however, "looked into the distance, to figure out where
to go," a realistic impulse. And in the second before she pulled the
wagon off to begin her endless journey, Giehse "blew her nose with
her index finger"—another "beautiful variant" and a rehumanizing
and demystifying of the character.

In scene 9 Courage must choose between going to Utrecht and
continuing on the road. While the Cook sings about men undone by
dangerous virtues, she decides not to leave her daughter. After she
informs the Cook of her decision, they see the light in the house and
start inside for some soup. Halfway up the steps, Giehse bowed
deeply in the direction of the opened door. It was difficult to bow so
deeply and difficult to raise herself up. "That difficult ascent showed
the age of the woman who here was refusing a place of refuge. The
bowing of the beggar shows the life she can expect on the street."
She made the same bow again, when placing her plate on the steps.
Weigel later executed these bows in Berlin. They were among the
clearest social gests in Brecht's production.

Giehse's interpretation of Courage's reaction to Swiss Cheese's
death (end of scene 3) was a virtual copy of Weigel's version up to the
point where the corpse is brought in. She sat far down left on the
stool by the table. Kattrin stood beside her, although reluctantly, and
Courage leaned up against her "in a moment of weakness" and held

her hand. But with the entrance of the soldiers, Giehse's Courage became animated. She sat on her stool looking across at the military men with her body cocked, elbow pointed, chin out. Her manner of walking across to inspect the body was "swaying and bold." Standing beside the stretcher, her posture was erect, revealing a "challenging, even vain, attitude, as if she were simply responding to an offensive accusation." She returned to the stool in the same energetic way and sat looking across at the incredulous officer with her hands on her knees, her back straight, and her head tilted. Slowly the men took the body off behind her, and Giehse continued to hold her pose on that stool. Suddenly, after they left the stage, without any warning or transition or noise, she fell frontward off the stool and landed in a heap on the floor.

These "beautiful additions" that Giehse "consistently invented" proved to Brecht the great value of models. Of course, models were rationalized and ideologically coherent. But the most interesting thing about them was the way in which they created their own improvements, allowing even a "great actor" to use their arrangements and ideas to bring to life "an individual and unmistakable figure"—something all his or her own. Models not only preserved but generated art. They were not only mass production machines but poetic instruments.

Short Subjects

Titles. The titles projected onto the half-curtain during scene changes were the same titles found in the play's authoritative text, with a few minor variations (for example, Tilly's victory in scene 5 was originally at Leipzig, not Magdeburg) and one addition (scene 12 has no title in the text, but Brecht projected a quatrain from the final song). Brecht did not use the projector, as he and Erwin Piscator had in earlier German productions, to provide background pictures or general information about war and its effects.

Dialect. Brecht's most interesting note on dialect concerns Weigel's first appearance as Courage, in the Prologue. In the first production she did not sing the opening Courage song with dialectal inflection, though she used dialect elsewhere in the play and with success. Later this first song also "came to life" when she changed into dialect. "It should never be forgotten that our stage-German is artificial," Brecht said in the modelbook. All but the most bookish texts can be improved if actors rehearse or perform them in everyday folk language.

Properties. Brecht repeated his usual line about onstage objects, especially instruments for work and eating: they "must have been most lovingly made" and must be realistically usable, whether or not they are historically accurate. For scenery, Brecht often advocated a "beautiful approximation" only. But with props he demanded more, for they were intimately connected with behavior. Thus, "the imagination of the audience can add nothing."

Costumes. The same rule applies to costumes as to props: aim for realism without historicity. Brecht wanted the costumes of *Courage* to reveal character, class, and experience of the war. He expressly forbade the "folklore festival" approach or excessive concern with period detail. "Learn from History," he told Wolfgang Roth during the 1940s, "but at the right moment throw it away. Don't be hindered by historical accuracy."[52]

Size. Although he worked in a very large stage, Brecht displayed no impulse to expand the scale of his operation. As dramatist, he kept the population of *Mother Courage* to a functional minimum, quite avoiding the crowds that were available to the dramatic situation. This strengthened the audience's impression that Courage's camp stands off to the side of the action. As director, Brecht added no extras or tableaux or interpolations to change that impression. This was typical. In a note to *The Caucasian Chalk Circle,* he remarked of the palace revolution scene: "What we have to do is replace our extras with good actors. One good actor is worth a whole battalion of extras. I.e., he is more."[53]

Songs. The modelbook's note on music begins, "Paul Dessau's music for *Mother Courage* is not meant to be particularly easy." It is neither easy nor so good that its difficulty is happily overcome. But, as Brecht said, "Art is not a land of Cockaigne."

The frequently sung Courage song came from a French melody that Brecht had already used for one of the songs appended to the *Manual of Piety.* When he played it for Dessau, the composer was "quite taken aback by the banality of this melody, and by Brecht's suggestion, which he made quite politely, that he would like to use it as the model for the opening song of Mother Courage." The composer told Brecht, "It would require a great deal to enable such a theme to carry an important song," and Brecht agreed—that was his point.[54] The melody is no more pretty or accessible than its singer, but its thumping, aggressive line is quite memorable after one has heard it repeatedly.

Beyond the general assertion, familiar from his early epic theatre writings, that songs should be "musical insertions" that break the play's action and mood, Brecht's notes explain that the musical alienation effect depends on the divergence between the character's singing and the song's lyrical or melodic content. Courage's bitter lullaby in scene 12 is one example of such ironic treatment. So is Brecht's preference for an arrogant, unfeeling, self-satisfied voice in the offstage shelter song of scene 10; he realized that this tone made the song surprisingly "provocative." A more complex example is the Chaplain's song about Christ's crucifixion (scene 3). Brecht recorded his admiration for the way in which Erwin Geschonneck, the Chaplain in the 1951 production, revealed with his rendition of the song both his younger, more idealistic self—"the young minister of the university-city of Upsala" who had joined the war—and the older, more battered Chaplain he had become. Geschonneck thus demonstrated that people change in war and that the war itself had changed ("it began not without ideals"). A second example is the duet between the Cook and Courage that is commonly called the "Solomon Song" (scene 9). Weigel sang as she considered the Cook's offer; Ernst Busch (1951) sang the Cook's part "short of breath and with a strained voice," implicitly justifying the hard terms of his offer "by attacking the times." Brecht always urged actors to multiply and intensify the meanings of each musical moment.

Pace. Pacing the performance is a subject that receives little mention in the modelbook. Brecht dropped occasional hints about a scene's tempo and mood. At the end of scene 6, where Courage curses the war, he suggested extended pauses for increased dramatic effect. He provided fairly detailed markings to indicate pauses and music cues in scenes 5 and 11. A note on the Prologue includes the useful advice that pacing should not be, as it so often is in the theatre, simple hurrying. While rehearsing, he decided to condense the Prologue by cutting out the song's second verse. But he found that the scene seemed longer in this version and that only by restoring the second verse and lengthening the pause between the verses could he quicken the tempo of his material. The moral of that story is found in the title to his note: "Too Short can be Too Long." In the model-book's final note, Brecht urged a "carefree lightness" in the theatri-calizing of this play, adding, "Even in their instructive aspects, the arts belong to the realm of entertainment." But in general, no clear idea of overall or localized pace emerges from his notes.

The timings for his production (not mentioned in *Couragemodell 1949* but published in *Theaterarbeit* and distributed with the Ensem-ble's model) indicate that Brecht was extremely deliberate in present-ing his material.[55] Act 1 (scenes 1–7) lasted a few seconds less than two hours—virtually unimaginable in contemporary American the-atre—and Act 2 (scenes 8–12) lasted an hour. Even more revealing is the length of the intervals between scenes, during which settings were changed and title information was projected on the half-curtain. These intervals averaged seventy-four seconds; only one was less than fifty seconds long. The audience had to wait fifty seconds be-tween Courage's curse of war in scene 6 and her endorsement of war in scene 7—considerably longer than any self-respecting stage crew would need to strike the camp set and turn the wagon around. Gener-ally, scene followed scene so slowly that the tempi, rhythms, and emotions were no more continuous than the narrative. This rigorous separation of story elements reflected Brecht's basic intention: to re-inforce the spectators' awareness that they were in a theatre watching a story, a history, or an objective fiction artificially inserted into the reality of their present.

The Drum Scene

Scene 11 of *Mother Courage*, the drum scene, is the most famous piece of drama in any of Brecht's plays. In the following para-graphs, I describe a composite version of this scene as presented in the 1949 and 1951 productions.

The audience had been in the theatre for nearly three hours and, for ninety seconds following scene 10, had seen and heard scenery pieces being moved in and out behind the half-curtain. On that cur-tain appeared this title:

> January 1636. The imperial troops threaten the Protestant city of Halle. The stone speaks. Mother Courage loses her daughter and goes on alone. The end of the war is not in sight.

Now that the spectators knew what would happen, they could watch how it happened ("eyes on the course").[56]

The house of three peasants, standing right, was represented by a fragmentary building front with a sloping thatched roof supported by two posts. Downstage of its door, a chopping block stood on the floor. At left was an even more skeletal building front that represented the peasants' barn. Upstage of the barn was the partially obscured Courage wagon. Except for a few lighting accents, most noticeably on the house roof, the lights were grouped in the farmyard implied down center between the buildings. The cyclorama was still quite visible, and the stage was not nearly as dark as it could have been in a more realistic depiction of this nocturnal visitation.

Four soldiers came onstage. "I don't want any noise," said their leader, the Lieutenant. They spoke a few short lines, then knocked at the door; the Peasant Woman emerged and was muzzled. Perhaps the audience noticed that the Lieutenant was the Young Soldier to whom Courage had taught capitulation in scene 4. Now he was "a void, cold, and brutal officer." This irony would sharpen as the scene progressed.

The soldiers rounded up everyone—the woman's husband and son, and Kattrin from the wagon. The Lieutenant threatened to brutally repress their agitation: "keep quiet, one squawk and you'll get a pike over the head." One soldier forced the Young Peasant to agree to lead the surprise attack on Halle by holding a pike at his throat while the Lieutenant and another soldier threatened to destroy the farm animals. To this the peasants (down left) responded by whining, "Captain, spare our animals or we'll starve." After the Young Peasant consented, the Peasant Woman said, "And thank you kindly for your forbearance, Captain, for ever and ever, amen." Like some forelock-tugging Irishman's address to his landlord, this was feigned obsequiousness. Brecht's note describes it as follows:

> The lamentations of the peasant woman . . . must have a certain routine quality about it [sic]; it must suggest a "set behavior pattern." The war has been going on too long. Begging, lamenting, and informing have frozen into fixed forms: those are the things you do when the soldiery arrive.

(Here we note again the gest as socialized behavior, "the things you do when" the soldiers arrive.)

Against the already accelerating momentum of the scene, the gestic acting worked as a drag. Brecht explained the alienation effect:

It is worth forgoing the "immediate impression" of a particular, seemingly unique episode of horror so as to penetrate a deeper stratum of horror and to show how repeated, constantly recurring misfortune has driven people to ritualize their gestures of self-defense — though of course these ritual gestures can never free them from the reality of fear, which on the stage must permeate the ritual.

Brecht wanted the audience to admit the melodramatic horror of people carted off in the German night but also to find a deeper, more relevant point—postwar Germans suffering under a plethora of masters and ritualizing their behavior accordingly—so that the horror, "the reality of fear," can be given the immediacy of personal experience. That is a strategy of meaning in the moment.

After the Young Peasant led the soldiers off toward Halle, the two older peasants and Kattrin were stranded in the yard wondering what would happen. In an attempt to find out what was happening in the countryside, the Old Peasant put his ladder up against the barn and reported seeing "more than a regiment." After discussing the threat to the city and their own cowardice, the Peasant Woman urged Kattrin to "Pray, poor thing, pray!" The woman's long prayer revealed that the city was full of children, including some of her own young relatives, so Kattrin rose and slipped away toward the house. She grabbed a drum off the wagon and hitched her skirts up around her waist so that she could more easily climb the ladder to the roof. A spectator might remember here that the drum had been part of the merchandise she carried when she returned bleeding and crying in scene 6.

Because the prayer sequence I have just described comes between more superficially exciting activities, it is the type of scene that directors frequently gloss over, leave for last or otherwise ignore. In his rehearsals, Brecht took special care to work out its details and values. He used his most famous rehearsal technique ("said the man," "said the woman") to make the actors stress the peasants' failings, "how they fortify each other in the belief that there is nothing they can do." He emphasized specific movements, as when the Peasant Woman, having decided that there is nothing to do but pray, "shuffled up to" the motionless Kattrin, "looking reproachfully at her: 'Pray, poor thing, pray!' —as if she accused the stranger of an unforgivable omission." Brecht took similar care with preparations for the prayer and with the vocal qualities and points of the prayer itself. In the modelbook he strongly recommends similar procedures to other directors. This is the art that became the Ensemble's trademark: a complete thinking through wedded to a complete working out, or realization, in the acting.

Kattrin's drumming brought the stage alive, yet she almost immediately stopped. The Old Peasant started across the stage toward the house waving his arms, while his wife waved hers awkwardly and hurriedly pulled herself up from prayer. But Kattrin hauled the ladder across the roof, leaving them to flap about on the ground. She stared off toward the city (left) and continued to drum furiously as the peasants shouted first at her, then at each other. The Lieutenant and his men ran in, and his cry, "I'll cut you to pieces!" stopped the drumming. But four speeches later—when he said, "Throw down that drum. It's an order!"—she brazenly started drumming again.

Because this was the most exciting scene Brecht had ever written, he took great pains in his directing to provide it with a solid foundation in character. Throughout rehearsal, he determinedly humanized Kattrin, building a complex of traits and motivations for her: love of children, fearlessness under certain conditions, and a mature intellect. "It is necessary to show an intelligent Kattrin from the start," he urged. "The whole point is missed if her love of children is depreciated as mindless animal instinct" (note from scene 5). He took similar care to clarify her immediate motive in scene 11: she groaned and stood up "horrified" as the woman prayed for the innocent children. It is critical to appreciate that Kattrin's "saving of the city of Halle is an intelligent act." It is just as critical to realize "that here the most helpless creature of all is ready to help." But her bravery, however truly impressive, should never be merely "conventional heroism." As an intelligent human, Kattrin must combine "her fear for the city of Halle" with "her fear for herself."

Kattrin sat on the roof with her drum beside her, waving the two mallets high over her head, while confusion reigned on the ground below. Brecht's answer to the staging of such a "tempestuous scene" was to demand clarity and precision. He highlighted certain points by giving instructions for Kattrin to stop drumming. He inserted specific moments for the military men, as when the Lieutenant, growing desperate as a result of Kattrin's continued drumming, "stops yelling at his men, and begs them for advice instead." His men showed their amusement when his back was turned but responded with "complete apathy" otherwise. When a soldier ran off to get the musket, Brecht had him trot out "with the well-known kind of tardiness that cannot be proven." Brecht encouraged directors to have "a certain amount of stubbornness to make miming of this sort [the chopping block episode] last long enough." Otherwise, "general hubbub" would result, and "everything worth noticing" would be lost. Noticing "everything worth noticing" is, of course, the point of Brechtian theatre.

Put another way, a director needs the strongest alienation in the drum scene because it arouses the greatest amount of empathy. Watching Kattrin on the roof, an audience must want her to raise the town, must cheer for her to win, must make an emotional investment in her struggle to protect the pitiful children of Halle. At the same time, the audience must watch the bulk of the scene in fear of her death. Pity and fear—the tragic emotions—are also what Kattrin feels in her effort to save the innocents from slaughter as she stands in the jaws of death.

In the modelbook, Brecht acknowledged the force of this scene and put it in perspective:

> Audiences were especially stirred by the drum scene. Some explained this by saying that it is the most dramatic scene in the play and that the public likes its theater dramatic rather than epic. In reality the epic theater, while capable of portraying other things than stirring incidents, clashes, conspiracies, psychological torments and so on, is also capable of portraying these. Spectators may identify themselves with Kattrin in this scene; empathy may give them the happy feeling that they too possess such strength. *But they are not likely to have experienced such empathy throughout the play—in the first scenes, for example* [my emphasis].

Nor would an audience experience empathy after this scene. In fact, the empathy for Kattrin in scene 11 makes harsher the audience's judgment of Courage when it sees her again in scene 12. Because it has cared so much for her daughter, it blames Courage, and such blame diminishes the understandable tendency to empathize with Courage in her final desolation.

The climax of the drum scene was noisy and frantic. The Old Peasant chopped wood, the Young Peasant beat listlessly on the wagon with a plank, the Lieutenant shouted and bustled about, though he was beginning to tire. So was Kattrin, and her drumming revealed that fatigue. Suddenly the Young Peasant turned and threw away his plank, shouting up at Kattrin, "Keep on drumming! Or they'll all be killed! Keep on drumming, keep on drumming." Hundreds of silent voices in the auditorium joined him. One of the soldiers threw the Young Peasant down and hit him with a pike. As he raised the pike again, the mother ran upstage toward them, her arms raised in defense and supplication, crying, "Don't hit him in the back! My God, you're killing him." Kattrin's crying was now audible, but she kept on drumming. The musket was brought in and set up (down left) as the Lieutenant yelled one last warning to the girl on the roof (right). She was crying and drumming at full pitch, her arms and mallets curving high above her head. The Lieutenant yelled, "Fire!" No matter that the soldier holding the musket was the same saucy soldier who had loafed when he ran to fetch it before. "Nevertheless, he fires," says Brecht. (Did a spectator have a chance to catch that? *Nevertheless,* he fires.) The musket boomed and Kattrin was hit. She brought one mallet down on the drum for a full beat. Her other "drooping" hand came down for a last "feeble" beat and she fell forward onto her drum, silent at last. The Lieutenant, momentarily triumphant, said, "Now we'll have some quiet," but before the drum's rhythm could fade, it was picked up by the cannon of Halle. The Lieutenant, Brecht noted, "sits down and beats the ground with his fists like a child." Over the roar of the cannon came the last words of the scene, spoken by one of the soldiers: "She's done it." The audience's empathic fears and hopes had all been realized.

For the next seventy-eight seconds, four lines were projected on the half-curtain. Bentley's translation is as follows:

> Dangers, surprises, devastations—
> The war takes hold and will not quit.
> But though it last three generations
> We shall get nothing out of it.[57]

These were the first four lines of the Courage song's last verse, which the audience would hear in just a few minutes.

"Art ought to be a means of education, but its purpose is to give pleasure," Brecht wrote in his journal at the end of 1952.[58] His exciting and suspenseful drum scene, like so much else in his directing of *Mother Courage and Her Children,* illustrates how he could acknowledge the conflict of intentions and emphasize the primacy of pleasure. As he said in *A Short Organum for the Theatre,*

> Even when people speak of higher and lower degrees of pleasure, art stares impassively back at them; for it wishes to fly high and low and to be left in peace, so long as it can give pleasure to people.[59]

3

Elia Kazan and
*A Streetcar
Named Desire:*
A Director at Work

The Primary Colors (Kazan, Stanley, Brando)

Streetcar had no problem, all you had to do was cast it right, and anybody could have directed it.

> —Kazan (1970s),
> in Michel Ciment, *Kazan on Kazan*

THIS QUOTATION is a useful beginning because it is typical of Elia Kazan, who talks about art in plain, rather than highfalutin, terms, and because it is reminiscent of the theatre's conventional wisdom ("75 percent of directing is casting"). More seriously considered, this quotation shows that Kazan treats stage direction as a primarily human activity, in which the most important element is the actor who becomes the character. In his directing, he certainly had other strong suits, including an ear for theme and a talent for devising physical climaxes, both of which could get the better of him. But his greatest fame came in being what we call an "actor's director." Julie Harris remembers rehearsing with Kazan as being "like working in the middle of a whirlwind," and Kim Hunter (Stella) adds, "I was blinded by his halo."[1] Deborah Kerr recalls that in rehearsing *Tea and Sympathy*'s sexual initiation scene, she learned things about herself that "I didn't even know" until Kazan "told me so."[2] He pushed Mildred Dunnock through Linda Loman's "Attention must be paid" sequence in *Death of a Salesman*, yelling "Attack, attack!" and waving a fencing foil at her: "I want more, more!"[3] As a director, Kazan was both a scourge and an inspiration, and he was famous for his brilliance at working the seam between player and part. Eliciting the character from the actor and drawing the actor into the character, he made plays meaningful in the area in which all Stanislavskians think plays should be most meaningful—revelation of character, the mystery of drama's human nature.

Kazan's flair for casting "on instinct" and against type is part of his legend. Peggy Meredith was too young to play the mother in *All My Sons*. Gusti Huber was too unknown for the lead in *Flight Into Egypt*. Kerr was too English for *Tea and Sympathy*, Barbara Bel Geddes was too refined to be a *Cat on a Hot Tin Roof*, and Carroll Baker—cast without so much as a screen test—was preposterously inexperienced for the title role in *Baby Doll*. Casting to type, of course, is casting to a physical mold, to a restrictively external image of a person. One of its advantages is the time it saves. In Kazan's theatre the standard rehearsal period was less than four weeks, and much of the final week was devoted to technical matters. A difficult assignment like MacLeish's *J. B.* he accomplished in nineteen days. Human transformations on a step-by-step basis might seem ruled out in such a system. But Kazan's way was to cast to the actor's inner possibilities, to the protean human spirit as he understood it. So he took actors to dinner instead of to auditions, on walks instead of into rehearsal halls. He tried to spend time with them outside the theatre in order to observe them being themselves. Justifying his involvement in the personal lives of his Actors Studio students, he said, "The material of my profession is the lives the actors have led up till now."[4]

Kazan has also said, "I never cast by looks because looks are false. And I don't believe in heroes anyway, so good looks don't mean anything to me."[5] Marlon Brando was lucky that this was the case, for in 1947 he was extraordinarily good-looking. He was blond and pouty, and his nose was not yet broken—that would happen when he sparred with some technicians offstage during a performance of *Streetcar* (after which he came onstage and bled all over Jessica Tandy). At twenty-three, Brando had an innocent, even pretty look that contrasted markedly with the greasy, simian strength of Stanley Kowalski. In the mid-1940s the actor was still a *jeune premier,* a Marchbanks to Katharine Cornell's *Candida.* And yet Brando not only succeeded with Kowalski but used the part to begin transforming the American myth of heroism. The director who helped him the most to effect that transformation was Elia Kazan.

Kazan has said that directing is "half conceptual, the core of it—you get into what the events mean, what you're trying to express," and half executive, "just work. But if you are careless with the first stage, you make something which is flaccid at its center."[6] We may study both stages of his work on *Streetcar* in some detail. Kazan's conceptual planning has been preserved in a famous set of notes, which I shall call his "notebook." First published in 1953, selections from these notes have been widely republished since, most notably in the revised edition of the seminal text and anthology, *Directors on Directing.* To find evidence of Kazan's second phase, the "work" that turned his idea into theatrical reality, the interested student can turn to *A Streetcar Named Desire: Acting Edition,* the playbook for performers published by Dramatists Play Service and the guidebook for most later productions. This acting edition is a reprint of the 1947 production's final, official promptbook, complete with textual changes and detailed accounts of movement and inflection. (The standard literary text, the 1947 New Directions hybrid script, is of value to my discussion because it retains many of Williams's prerehearsal lines, but throughout this chapter I have usually referred to and quoted from the dialogue and stage directions of the acting edition.) The 1951 film serves as a useful supplement because its cast includes almost all the actors who had appeared on Broadway and because Kazan made it with the clear intention of "filming the play" as straightforwardly as possible.[7]

Kazan organized his notebook not by action segments nor by ideas but by descriptions of the four major characters, beginning with a statement of the "spine" of each part. He used this familiar theatrical term because his mentors in the Group Theatre had learned it from their mentor in the late 1920s, Richard Boleslavsky of the American Laboratory Theatre, who had learned it from his teacher, Stanislavsky, back at the home office. All these people used "spine" as a handy metaphor to describe two things: the play's main action and a character's main action. Though Kazan too employed both uses, his *Streetcar* notes refer only to the character's spine, which means the character's "through line"—the dominant action of a character's soul that unifies his disparate activities, thereby lending structure and coherence to the actor's work on and in the part. In orthodox Stanislavskian practice, the key to defining a character's spine is to use an infinitive verb or phrase, usually with an object on the end ("to get to Moscow," "to avenge my father's death," "to wait for Godot" are familiar examples). The importance of such definitions, to quote Francis Fergusson, a distinguished literary alumnus of the Boleslavsky-Ouspenskaya school, is that the verb phrase pictures a spine as "the *movement* of the psyche, not a passive state, like a mood."[8] In a dramatic role, the best kind of spine is a line that turns into an arrow, a vector. It is a desire. Directors in rehearsal frequently call to the confused actor, "But what do you *want?*"

Kazan has said: "I put terrific stress on what the person wants and why he wants it. What makes it meaningful for him. I don't start on *how* he goes about getting it until I get him wanting it."[9] Think of this as step one in a three-stage process in the rehearsal of actors. Consider that it accounts for Kazan's famously energetic productions. ("All my actors come on strong, they're all alive, they're all dynamic—no matter how quiet."[10]) The method's dangers, such as oversimplification and monotony, result mainly from failure to progress beyond this stage of psychologizing. Step two in the process introduces the actor to "the circumstances under which he behaves; what happens before, and so on"—what Stanislavsky called the "given circumstances."[11] That phrase, which Harold Clurman and Stella Adler had brought back from a visit to Stanislavsky in 1934, had caused a controversy in the Group, for Lee Strasberg had held out for the primacy of inner identification and emotional memory. But the new word from the master, clearly influential in Kazan's career, was that the opposition of given circumstances to a character's desires was the source of dramatic conflict and the stimulus of a character's actions. "I will say nothing to an actor that cannot be translated directly into action," Kazan said in 1944.[12] Twenty years later, he was still expressing the same thought: "The life of a play is in behavior."[13] So the third step in the rehearsal process sets the actor loose to try to accomplish his desire: "I try to find the physical behavior without preconception on my part if possible, but from what the actor does to achieve his objective under the circumstances."[14]

Kazan began the *Streetcar* notebook with this statement of his first principle: "*A thought*—directing finally consists of turning Psychology into Behavior." Then he defined the characters' spines. Blanche wants to "find protection." Stanley wants to "keep things his way." Stella wants to "hold onto Stanley." Mitch wants to "get away from his mother." Compounded, these desires account for much of the conflict. Stella must try to hold onto Stanley while first accommodating, then competing with, her sister. Stanley fights for continuation of the status quo in spite of Blanche's invasion. Mitch uses Blanche as the lever in his fight for freedom from Mother. Looking for protection, Blanche appeals to each character, and each finally rejects her— their needs do not match hers—so she goes mad. These characters are each other's given circumstances.

Before proceeding to an extended analysis of Stanley and Brando, I shall briefly illustrate the director's method as applied to Mitch. In the notebook, Kazan observed that the play relates "the crucial struggle of Mitch's life." That struggle is certainly unconscious (Mitch seeks in Blanche a mother substitute to oppose a mother who keeps him eternally adolescent), but the struggle is visible and real on stage. Mitch's friends gibe at him constantly for his attitude toward Mother, and "in his guts he knows they're right. Mitch, in his guts, hates his Mother." Kazan admitted that the reverse is true, that Mitch loves her—out of habit, because of some lingering early affection, and because of his admiration (however grudging) of her clever manipulations. But at bottom, "he *hates her*. It is a tragedy for him when he returns to her absolute sovereignty at the end." Kazan thus explained the character in the psychologizing of the notebook.

When he went to work on the actor, Karl Malden, Kazan did not lecture about these thoughts but waited until a specific problem created the need for a solution that had a potential for generalization. Late in scene 6, when Blanche learns that Mitch has discussed her with his mother, she is touched. "You love her very much, don't you?" she says, and Mitch replies, "Yes." (By opening night, this monosyllable had been replaced by Mitch's miserable nod.) Malden describes his struggle with this emotional admission:

> Now, the first week of rehearsal I couldn't do anything with that, it was a nothing line. And one day I'm going through it again when I look up and see Gadg pull the most terrible teeth-gnashing face. I said, "What's the matter?" And he said, "Did you watch me? That's how

you should feel when you say that line. Because you hate your bloody mother. Sure, you have to say you love her—you even have to think you do. But deep inside you know she's got a double nelson on all your emotions and she's the reason why you can't develop and mature."

As soon as I understood that, I'd licked not only the line, but the whole character. He didn't bawl me out like a great big director because my approach was wrong. He just pulled a funny face like a buddy with a sense of humor giving me a tip.[15]

With this few seconds' silliness over the reading of a single word, Kazan revealed the basic character motivation. The actor found the spine, and hence the unity running through disparate moments, lines, and scenes. That is Kazan's "Method" when it works.

If *Streetcar* is, conventionally speaking, "Blanche's play," its first act belongs to Stanley Kowalski. He is its first event—laughing, joking, throwing meat to his wife. Blanche and Stella provocatively discuss him in their first substantial dialogue. He enters casually but dramatically. And he produces a very dramatic finish to scene 1: when he asks Blanche about her marriage he uncovers her fragility, and Williams marks that moment with his first expressionistic effect, the "Varsouviana". Stanley completely dominates both halves of scene 2, which centers on the wardrobe trunk. Scene 3, his greatest scene, is the poker night; his violent moods orchestrate the poker game and interrupt the rhythms of Blanche, Stella, and Mitch in the bedroom. As cause and principal of the brawl, Stanley holds the focus until the end of scene 3, when he stands at the bottom of the stairs bellowing "STELL-LAHHHHH!" with "heaven-splitting violence" (Williams's description). This may be the actor's most demanding moment, but it is certainly the character's greatest contribution to the play's thematic drift, for the poker night must make the audience feel what Blanche feels—how strong desire can be. In scene 4, when Blanche pleads with Stella on behalf of civilization, decency, and tenderness, Stanley sneaks in to overhear her bold conclusion, *"Don't—don't hang back with the brutes!"* At the curtain he decisively wins the opening round against Blanche as Stella flies past her into his arms.

Those first four scenes, the spring sequence, are played as *Streetcar*'s first act, and they constitute nearly half of the play, both in the book and on the stage. Describing this first act, Rosamund Gilder wrote that "gigantic, tragic forces are implied, not stated: the furies hover in the wings and have not yet gained admittance. The audience is caught up into the dark, menacing mood with its flashes of raucous humor and exuberant high spirits without knowing or caring about the conduct of a plot."[16] The menace, the humor, and the high spirits all come from Stanley Kowalski. Early in the play, Blanche is seen in relation to Stanley—in his house, with his wife, handling his objects, reacting to his views. He brings out the best in her, as in the trunk scene or scene 4, where she appeals to Stella to go beyond his admittedly wonderful "animal force." That animal force is the most likely topic of conversation at the first intermission of any good production of *Streetcar*.

In his notebook Kazan described Stanley as Blanche's antagonist and as Stella's lover. In relation to Blanche, he is a cultural symbol, standing for "the crude forces of violence, insensibility and vulgarity which exist in our South." In production, these qualities became associated with the North, for Brando's accent was distinctly Northern, and Williams changed a line accordingly. (In the acting edition, Stanley changes his T-shirt in scene 1 saying, "Be comfortable. That's my motto up where I come from.") But regional associations aside, his harshness and bluntness, his modern, urban, antimagical, antiromantic brutalities continually undermine Blanche. The same character is elsewhere the romantic lodestar of a good woman's life. In his notes on Stella, Kazan hardly talked about anything other than her fascination with Stanley. For example: "She is waiting for night. She's waiting for the dark where Stanley makes her feel *only him* and she has no reminder of the price she is paying. She wants no intrusion from the other world. . . . She hopes for no other meaning from life. Her pregnancy just makes it more so. Stanley is in her day and night." Thus Stella's crisis of belief in Stanley is terrible for her. But he proves too strong: "In the end she returns to Stanley."

Discussing Kowalski individually, Kazan found him deeply conservative. "He's got things the way he wants them around there and he does *not* want them upset by a phony, corrupt, sick, destructive woman." Kazan agreed with Stanley (how could he not?) that Blanche is dangerous, that she will wreck his life and home. Blanche may think Stanley is her "executioner," but she is the invader, she has brought herself within range of the blade. *"This makes Stanley right!"* Kazan noted, finding it easy to appreciate the problem she presents to a character who wants to "keep things his way." But then Kazan chafed at his own insight: "Are we going into the era of Stanley? He may be practical and right . . . but what the hell does it leave us?" For the director, as for later audiences, contradictory sympathies were the order of the day.

Kazan saw contradiction in the character as the source of personal and interpersonal conflict. For instance, Stanley can be hard, but he can also be soft. At times he is implacable, positively case-hardened, bitterly envious of anyone higher in station or enjoying greater fortune. That is Stanley losing at poker, Stanley giving orders to the bowlers, Stanley pulling Stella down from the columns, the "hoodlum aristocrat" Stanley who finally rapes Blanche because she has pretensions. But he also displays "sudden pathetic little-tough-boy tenderness toward Stella" and "cries like a baby" in scene 3. Kazan found more "soft" moments: "Somewhere in Scene 8 he almost makes it up with Blanche. In Scene 10 he *does* try to make it up with her." Another note describes a naive Stanley who means no harm to anyone until threatened. Such perceptions on the director's part, along with an appreciation of the irrepressible humor written into the character, helped Kazan arrive at a deeper or more rounded understanding of Kowalski. Stanley may be a Lawrentian "gaudy seedbearer" (Williams's epithet) or a Male Chauvinist Pig, but he is both more savage and more boyish than he seems on first acquaintance.

Complex conceptions led Kazan to complex details in performance. In scene 2, while Blanche is still flirting with Stanley and before he cuts off her "re-bop," she airily asks him for a cigarette. In the Broadway production, Brando reached for a cigarette that he had earlier slid behind his ear and offered it to her. Any person as finicky as Blanche could find such an unhygenic offer shocking, repulsive, and offensive. But in Brando's version, Stanley had no intention to offend. He offered the cigarette straightforwardly, unself-consciously, just as he would to his buddies at work. As in his use of the phrase "shack up" near the end of scene 1, Stanley shocked Blanche and his audiences with behavior that, to him, was natural.

Kazan worked to fill his production with interesting social behavior. (Later in this chapter I discuss one of Kazan's hypotheses about Blanche: "All her behavior patterns are those of the dying civilization she represents.") Stanley's social behavior "is the basic animal cynicism of today. 'Get what's coming to you! Don't waste a day! Eat, drink, get yours!'" Kazan noted that "God and nature gave [Stanley] a fine sensory apparatus . . . he enjoys!" Brando sucked on cigarettes, cigars, and bottles with hedonistic and provocative gusto. In the early rehearsals of scene 1, Kazan had him chomp on a carrot while introducing himself to Blanche. In the final version of scene 2, when Stella explains why Blanche is upset by the loss of Belle Reve, Brando chewed away at his cold dinner in an abstract fashion, demonstrating, as Kazan noted in the planning stages, "a most annoying way of being preoccupied—or of busying himself with something else while people are talking with him, at him it becomes." Such a Stanley is a monster of selfishness, an orally fixated infant-God.

Kowalski is commonly called "a slob" (as Brando was when young), so I wish to point out his unslobbish behavior in Kazan's version. However vigorous and lower class the style of Brando's movements, he was neither careless nor messy. This Stanley kept his house in order. Returning from work, he always put his lunch box in the same place, on top of the icebox. He changed clothes frequently and put away his laundry. When he licked his greasy fingers, Brando licked them methodically. He was particular about how he enjoyed life, whether he was spraying beer all over the room or nursing it carefully in his idiosyncratic way. Kazan wanted Brando to imitate Stanley by bringing into rehearsal "the things he loves and prizes: all sensuous and sensual."

But this is hedonism rather than epicureanism, a stilling rather than an awakening of the soul—a losing of consciousness. The aim of Stanley's self-absorption in pleasure is to lose the self in pleasure. And it leads ineluctably to cynicism, the vice Kazan perceived behind Stanley's rape of Blanche. Kowalski's self-esteem comes not from being above others, but from keeping others below him, and we should see a sexual implication in that attitude. Stanley is certainly a familiar species of sexual marksman; he is weak and insecure, with a "silenced, frustrated part" that "breaks loose in unexpected and unpredictable ways and we suddenly see, as in a burst of lightning, his real frustrated self." Kazan also saw the social ramifications of the hedonistic tendency, for such a person "simply stores up violence and stores up violence, until every *bar in the nation is full of Stanleys ready to explode.*" Stanley's lapses are especially in evidence when he is losing, at cards or in arguments. And "a loser" he finally is, for he loses those sympathies which he claims in act 1 as the audience's interest and imagination become fixed on Blanche during acts 2 and 3. In the end he wins a battle by raping and expelling Blanche only to lose his friends' respect and, to a large extent, Stella's affection and loyalty. She stays, of course, but as Kazan thought, "At the end of the play, her life is entirely different. It will never be the same with Stanley again." Standing with her in his arms, murmuring in her ear, the Stanley the audience sees at the final curtain is just another loser.

But at least Stanley is a fighter. Modern drama, like modern literature, is not so full of fighters that any of them should be undervalued. Stanley Kowalski will make a contest of anything—poker games, bowling matches, legal arguments, or who will have a better meal. Thus he does not so much "hate Blanche instinctively" as he accepts her challenge. In Kazan's mind, Stanley is initially indifferent to his sister-in-law's arrival. But then his pleasures are disturbed (the cold dinner, the screen around the bed) and his interests are threatened (the loss of Belle Reve), so he bridles and fights to dominate this perplexing woman. Her "brutes" speech to Stella assures him that his sister-in-law really does hate him. So he naturally tries to uncover Blanche's past, then uses it to destroy her relationships with Stella and Mitch.

But as late as the rape scene, he is still ready to make up with Blanche, to turn his foaming beer bottle into a loving cup. And Kazan thought Stanley might have made up, if only she had not done "the one thing that most arouses him, both in anger and sex." That "one thing" was her display of fine sentiments, her queenly lies. Munching on pretzel sticks in scene 10, Brando listened to her repudiation of transitory physical beauty in favor of "richness of the spirit." "How strange that I should be called a destitute woman! When I have all of these treasures locked in my heart. I think of myself as a very, very rich woman! But I have been foolish—casting my pearls before—" In cutting off the last word of Williams's script so that Brando could guess it himself ("Swine, huh?"), Kazan accentuated a recurrent pattern of behavior in the play: Stanley hears himself called a "brute" or an "ape," and he retaliates. (Soon after Blanche's arrival she calls him "a bit on the primitive side," so he shouts at her to cut the re-bop. When he throws the radio out the window during scene 3, Stella calls him a "*Drunk —drunk —animal thing,*" so he hits out at the pregnant woman with his fists. When Blanche jokes about Stanley's being a Capricorn—"the Goat!"—he responds with a contemptuous laugh over her being a Virgo and adds a hint of menace by mentioning Shaw and the Hotel Flamingo. When Stella calls him a "pig" at the dinner table, he smashes dishes.) In the rape scene, Blanche continues, "Yes, swine! Swine! And I'm thinking not only of you, but of your friend, Mr. Mitchell," and regally dismisses Mitch. It is more than Stanley can take, this pretension to social superiority, and in a woman, too. In Kazan's conception, Stanley's arousal is sexual as well as personal. So, in his last mindless attempt to pull Blanche down to his level, down from the columns, he reenacts his conquest of Stella, which presumably was the greatest conquest of his tawdry life.

Kazan understood Stanley so well because he could identify easily with characters, was able to project himself into all sorts of people. In the notebook, he reminded himself: "The only way to understand any character is through yourself. Everyone is much more alike than they willingly admit." Since Kazan understood Kowalski's force and contradiction so well, how fortunate that he found a young actor whose instinctive genius enabled him to capture those same qualities: Marlon Brando, whom Kazan called "as close to a genius as I've ever met among actors."[17]

Kazan's estimation of Brando as an actor is that he "has everything"—a unique combination of often contradictory traits and talents. For instance, Kazan said that Brando, in his work life as an actor, combined an enormous emotional intuition with "a brain . . . a very good analytical understanding of a dramatic problem."[18] In terms of sexuality, Kazan described him as "bisexual in the way an artist should be: he sees things both as a man and as a woman." Brando's contradictory nature was also evident in his working methods, for Kazan called him "a very honest man, in that he speaks plainly to you" and "a very devious man, in that he conceals his processes and reactions; they're none of your business."[19] Describing Brando's personal qualities, the director called him "one of the gentlest people I've ever known" but also used him as the foremost example (along with Bogart, Gable, and Cagney) of a man who projects the danger necessary for male stardom:

> With men it's essential to have something unpredictable and dangerous. If they're too tamed, too responsible, too civilized, they're bores. Women should never know if they're going to fight them or love them. The best male actors . . . have a quality of mystery and strength, the strength to implement the mystery.[20]

Stella Adler said that "Marlon never really had to learn to act."[21] Certainly he has always known more than most directors about the parts he has played. Kazan describes the process of working with Brando as follows:

He was on a level apart. There was something miraculous about him, in that I would explain to him what I had in mind, and he would listen, but his listening was so total that it was an amazing experience to talk to him; he would not answer right away, but go away and then do something that often surprised me. You had a feeling of "God, that's better than what I told him!" You had a feeling "Oh, I'm so grateful to him for doing that!" He was, like, giving you a gift. It was essentially what you'd asked him, but in feeling so *true,* so re-experienced through his own artistic mechanism. It's almost like directing a genius animal. . . . He even surprises the other actors. Sometimes you don't even know that he's acting: he does something and you say: "Oh yes, he is! He is doing it!" He's very, very underground—you don't know *how* he gets to what he gets. Part of it is intuition, part of it is real intelligence, part of it is ability to be empathic—that he connects with the people.[22]

And so, to his partisans and fans, Brando's genius lies in his capability to astonish. It was as visible in *Streetcar* as it was later in *The Godfather* and *Last Tango in Paris.*

And yet, before rehearsals began, Brando tried to telephone Kazan so that he could back out of his contract. He was afraid that the part "was a size too large for me."[23] Saved from resignation by a busy signal, Brando went to rehearsal and spent days muttering to himself, shuffling props around, napping in the theatre. He told Kim Hunter that he was wrong for the part and that the producers should have stayed with an earlier choice. Only gradually, and only through the very technical means of voice placement and diction, did Brando find his way into the part. "I'm an ear man," he has explained, and once he had located Kowalski's particular coarseness of speech, the character came into focus around that hard, flat, unSouthern voice, a voice big enough to have grandeur in screaming "STELL-LAHHHHH!" and nasal enough to bite when Stanley confronts Blanche with "So what?" or *"Ha-ha-ha!"*[24] Brando also understood Stanley's curious attitude toward speech. "Stanley didn't give a damn how he said a thing. His purpose was to convey his idea. He had no awareness of himself at all."[25] So Brando was able to demonstrate how peculiar Stanley sounds when he handles a body of information (as in the trunk scene and in his revelations about Blanche), and how he loses control of language ("especially when you've been exercising hard like bowling is," and "they requested her to turn in her room-key—for *permanently!*").

If Stanley is only dimly aware of his own language and thought, he is almost completely oblivious to other people's. This was the biggest of Brando's problems. As a man, Brando has always been noted for sensitivity, with regard to both his own emotions and those of others. As an actor, he found Stanley "everything I'm against—totally insensitive, crude, cruel," untouched by people's pain and unmoved by their need.[26] Worse, Brando thought, was the character's violence: "Kowalski was always right, and never afraid. He never wondered, he never doubted himself. His ego was very secure. And he had the kind of brutal aggressiveness I hate. I'm afraid of it. I detest the character."[27] Such antagonism between actor and part, particularly when complemented by deep similarities, can produce exciting results. Brando responded as Kazan wanted him to, by emphasizing the sensual and the physical: "The only way I could zero in was to say, 'This guy is a big, lusty, eating animal with no sensitivity.'" Brando said this lustiness left him too little room to develop the character's good humor: "I always wanted to come out laughing, but I was always too frozen."[28] But he overstated his failure, for whatever else they thought of him, few reviewers in 1947 missed the character's lighter side. His first entrance, his triumphant grin at the end of scene 4, and his rejoicing with the foaming beer bottle showed that Brando's Stanley could be positively sunny and buoyant.

As a result of the play's long run on Broadway and its famous re-creation on film, Brando's Kowalski became one of the century's most famous and controversial pieces of acting. At first, however, Jessica Tandy naturally commanded primary attention as Blanche, and many journalists—such as Brooks Atkinson in two *New York Times* reviews—treated Brando, Hunter, and Malden as the supporting players and described their work with a single adjective. Since Brando's career on Broadway had been distinctly erratic, some critics wrote longer and more admiring notices of Malden, who had compiled a string of solid successes. Among Brando's few forceful detractors was Eric Bentley, who belittled his acting ("an Odets character: Stanley Kowalski of Brooklyn whose tough talk is but the mask of a suffering sensitive soul") and his masculinity ("Brando has muscular arms, but his eyes give them the lie . . . a rather feminine actor overinterpreting a masculine role").[29] Fortunately, Brando was not so discouraged that he seriously considered Elsa Maxwell's suggestion after she saw *Streetcar*—to change that "terrible name" to either Marlow Brandon or Brand Lowmar.[30]

Brando received rave notices, to be sure. Robert Garland called him "our theatre's most memorable young actor at his most memorable."[31] Wolcott Gibbs called him "brutally effective," "almost pure ape."[32] John Chapman said he was "magnificent as the forthright husband, in his simple rages, his simple affections and his blunt humor."[33] A typical review was that of William Beyer: "Brando, who has never impressed us before, is excellent as the virile Kowalski, creating a clearly defined and consistently projected character, sparing nothing in making the man a figure of contempt."[34] John Mason Brown thought Brando's Kowalski was much better than his "weak and plainly inadequate" Marchbanks: "he is now all force and fire; a Rodin model; a young Louis Wolheim [the original *Hairy Ape,* 1922] with Luther Adler's explosiveness."[35] In what was probably the most favorable notice, Irwin Shaw described how Kazan and Brando manipulated the audience's sympathies throughout the play:

> Marlon Brando arrives as the best young actor on the American stage. Most young men in our theater seem hardly violent enough to complain to a waiter who has brought them cream instead of lemon. Brando seems always on the verge of tearing down the proscenium with his bare hands.
>
> Representing the healthy, driving forces of the flesh, Brando plays a useful trick on us. He is so amusing in a direct, almost childlike way in the beginning, and we have been so conditioned by the modern doctrine that what is natural is good, that we admire him and sympathize with him. Then, bit by bit, with a full account of what his good points really are, we come dimly to see that he is one of the villains of the piece, brutish, destructive in his healthy egotism, dangerous, immoral, surviving. By a slouching and apelike posture, by a curious, submerged and almost inarticulate manner of speech, by an explosive quickness of movement, Brando documents completely a terrifying characterization.[36]

The most widely quoted rave for Brando's acting came not from a journalist but from an anonymous director at the New Haven premiere: "It was awful and it was sublime. Only once in a generation do you see such a thing in the theatre."[37]

Brando's portrayal revealed just those contradictions which the part demands: light and dark, grin and glower, a curiously canny intelligence contrasted with stupidity and powerfully sensual physicality. His Stanley was easily perplexed, which made him amusing, even cute, in the early scenes with the women. "I have a lawyer acquaintance will study these out" was memorably silly. So was the conclusion to scene 2, when Brando put away the legal papers and sat "*lumpishly on [the] bed, staring straight ahead.*" Blanche and Stella went off for the night, Pablo and Steve came in with the beer for the poker party (scene 3), and a vendor passed, crying "Red-hot!." Stanley continued to concentrate, staring straight ahead. Brando could be unexpectedly gentle, as when he almost tenderly told Hunter (Stella) about Blanche's last years in Laurel. But he could be terrifying too, as in scene 8, the birthday party. When Hunter ordered him to clear his place at the table, he smashed his hand down on the meat platter, faster than anyone could have expected, his fist pressing the broken plate fragments onto the table. Then, just as suddenly, he swept plate, food, and silverware off the table, upstage past a gasping, shrinking Blanche. We customarily call such violence "volcanic," and for once the metaphor was not a cliché.

Brando's Stanley eminently met another of the script's major requirements—sexiness. Beyond the commercial appeal of a muscular physique and the importance of the physiological in "presence," I mean that the themes and actions of the play demand a sexy Stanley. The audience must see the attraction between Stanley and Stella that foils Blanche's pursuit of protection and reminds her how she fears "brutal desire—just—Desire!" Kazan also demanded physical magnetism in Stanley as a basis for the mutual sexual attraction that brings Blanche so close to her rapist. Sex is a drug in *Streetcar,* as exemplified by the narcotized condition of Hunter's Stella when she was in proximity to Brando. During the rehearsals of scene 1, Williams passed Kazan a note urging him to slow Hunter down, suggesting thereby a drugged languor. In scene 2, when she told Brando her plans for the evening and begged his indulgence for Blanche, Hunter kissed and stroked him so powerfully, so unembarrassedly, that the audience could easily imagine how obsessed these two were with their sex life. Brando confirmed this in scene 8, on the porch: "Stell, it's going to be all right after she goes and after you've had the baby." Hunter testified most persuasively to the force of Stanley's sexuality in scene 4, the aftermath of the poker night brawl. In his notes, Kazan envisioned her as "drugged . . . in a sensual stupor . . . buried alive in her flesh . . . half asleep . . . glazed across her eyes." In performance Hunter stretched her legs and torso under the sheet while sighing, smoking, and eating chocolates, and then gurgled and whinnied as she shuffled around the apartment. No wonder Blanche was upset.

The test of Stanley Kowalski's masculine power and sexuality comes in the last minutes of scene 3, when "The Poker Night" (as the scene is subtitled) erupts into violence and passion. In Kazan's version, the scene began slowly with the card game, gathered tension during the double-focus sequence after the women returned, and reached its climax with Stanley's outburst over the radio. With the radio blaring, Blanche dancing, Stella applauding, and Mitch beginning to cut bearlike capers to the music, Brando lost a hand of poker—he held three aces against a straight. Out of control, he ran into the bedroom, snatched the radio and its cord, and threw the offensive machine out the window. This began a lengthy and carefully choreographed sequence of running, shouting, and tussling. Malden fought with Brando as Hunter pushed the other players away, until Brando broke free and punched Hunter. The frenzy increased as the two women ran noisily up the outside steps to Eunice's. The cardplayers subdued Brando, pushed him onto the couch, and then forced him through the bedroom into the shower, left. From the bathroom came sounds of their struggle—breaking glass, splashing water, curses, and groans. Malden ran out, crossed the stage muttering about poker and women, and left. As Steve followed, he tended a bloody nose. The blues tune that the orchestra began during the peak of the offstage melee was now audible. The lights in both interior areas were beginning to dim.

Brando came out of the bathroom dripping wet. He telephoned upstairs for Stella, then walked sobbing through the shambles of the house to the patio (down right) and cried out for her, sometimes in a choked voice, sometimes in a bellow. From upstairs, Eunice chastised, but the effect was only to increase the volume and intensity of his calls for Stella. The two-minute fade of the interior lights was just concluding, leaving a shaft of light from the bathroom, a faint glow from the Chinese lantern in the bedroom, and some dim light on the patio. The blues continued with a prominent clarinet. Brando stood with his back to the auditorium, a magnificent animal in a wet, torn T-shirt, commanding and imploring in a sound already past the stages of meaning or naming: "STELL-LAHHHHH! STELL—" Hunter came onto the landing, then walked down the steps above him. Rosamund Gilder has described this moment: "She comes slowly down the steps, bathed in an intense white light, her head bent, her nightrobe trailing behind her—drained of will, drawn by a primordial force beyond her understanding into the arms of the man who waits for her at the foot of the stairs."[38] Brando fell to his knees, pressing his face into her belly and crying like a baby as the clarinet moaned and soared. He murmured against her: "Don't ever leave me . . . don't ever leave me . . . sweetheart . . . baby." Displaying some of the modern stage's more triumphant sexuality, Hunter fluttered over Brando's shoulder, putting herself in the perfect position to be picked up and swept away. He carried her, embracing her against him, through the kitchen door and over to the bed. As the music faded, Jessica Tandy descended to peer incredulously into the house. The episode was capped by her quiet, touching exchange with Malden's Mitch. "I need kindness now," she said, anticipating her famous line in the final scene. Street cries came up in the background and were heard throughout the blackout that led into the next scene. The colored lights might not have been visible, but they were turned on.

Making a Hit

In America you're a success or you're a failure. Any halfway ground . . . isn't recognized.
— Kazan (1964), in Richard Schechner and Theodore Hoffman, "'Look, There's an American Theater': An Interview with Elia Kazan"

In 1947, directing *Streetcar* in his thirty-eighth year, Kazan was already a brilliant success. He was becoming what we call "bankable"—one of the directors that producers scramble to bet on. At the time, he was referred to as "the only director regularly employed today by both Hollywood and Broadway."[39] Hits, stars, and awards were familiar parts of his life by 1947, and his income was over $100,000, or so the newspapers reported. He lived in an upper East Side townhouse with his wife, Molly Day Thatcher Kazan, and a brood of children for whom he had just purchased 100 acres in Sandy Hook, Connecticut. He was so successful that he could retain his folksy ways and ethnic bluntness. He wore tennis shoes, and he picked up his Oscar that year in a tweed suit rather than in the standard tuxedo. Everyone called him "Gadge," short for "Gadget." Success was familiar from his early years, though in his youth he had seen the world through the eyes of an immigrant outsider. His parents, members of a persecuted Anatolian Greek minority, were living outside Istanbul when Elia Kazanjoglou was born in 1909. Soon after, they realized their dream of emigrating to the land he would later call *America, America*. From a Greek ghetto in New York City, where they spoke Greek and Turkish at home, the family followed the paths of assimilation and aspiration by enrolling Kazan in a Montessori school at age five and by moving to New Rochelle, New York, where he graduated from high school. He went on to Williams College and the Yale School of Drama. Along this route, he had the experience of struggling. Jobs like waiting tables in a fraternity house caused him to develop a generalized hostility "to privilege, to good looks, to Americans, to Wasps," made manifest by his tough-guy, proletarian exterior.[40] He also developed a deeply critical attitude toward American society (including a distrust of its rewards) that led him into left-wing politics. Ironically, he proceeded to have a career in which he missed few of American society's hurdles and collected many of its rewards.

After leaving Yale for New York and an apprenticeship with the Group Theatre, Kazan continued to struggle and succeed. The Group did not renew his apprenticeship in 1933, on the grounds that his acting talents were too slight to justify hope, and the result was that Kazan became one of the Group's most prominent actors. He loitered around offices and typed scripts in order to cultivate friendships with Clifford Odets and Harold Clurman. Soon he was rousing the crowd as the taxi driver in *Waiting for Lefty*, playing Kewpie in *Paradise Lost*, and portraying the hero in yet another Odets play, *Night Music*. As Eddie Fuseli in *Golden Boy* he seemed, to Brooks Atkinson of the *New York Times*, "one of the most exciting actors in America."[41] The terms Kazan uses to describe his acting are characteristically deflationary ("narrow," "good" but not "great"), although he says wryly, "I was fiery all right."[42] Another man in Kazan's position might have taken acting as his career when the Group disbanded in 1941.

Instead, Kazan chose directing, a field in which he quickly worked his way to the top. While with the Group he had directed plays by Robert Ardrey and Irwin Shaw, but those credentials were not particularly impressive on Broadway. Nor was the Group, with its reputations for Communism and overwrought acting, an auspicious place for a hit-maker to emerge from. When his first post-Group assignment, *Cafe Crown* (1942), attracted Thornton Wilder's attention, Kazan suddenly found himself in big league commercial theatre, directing Frederic March, Florence Eldridge, Florence Reid, and the dragon lady of the period, Tallulah Bankhead, in *The Skin of Our Teeth*. In the midst of titantic backstage feuds and screams for his dismissal, Kazan waged the "one fight that makes or breaks" every fighter. He said, "That was my fight. After that I knew I could handle anyone" —even Helen Hayes, the following year in *Harriet*.[43] Soon he was demanding casting rights and, as the years passed, he gained more artistic control and achieved more success. For Arthur Miller's *All My Sons*, which opened early in 1947, Kazan received his first producer-director credit and won the first Tony Award given by the American Theatre Wing to a director.

When Tennessee Williams saw *All My Sons* in the spring of 1947, he was more than a disinterested customer. He needed a director for a new play that had begun, late in 1944 during the Chicago rehearsals of *The Glass Menagerie*, as a scene entitled *Blanche's Chair in the Moon*. By March 1945, when *Menagerie* was playing in New York, the new play had already been given two more titles (*The Moth* and *The Primary Colors*) and three possible endings: Blanche departs, Blanche goes insane, Blanche throws herself under a train. The thematic importance of the Mitch-Blanche plot waxed and waned while Williams changed the locale (Chicago to Atlanta to New Orleans) and the ethnicity (Italian to Irish to Polish). But throughout he was basically telling a story about a lonely Southern schoolteacher who comes to the big city to visit her sister and brother-in-law on *Electric Avenue*, as another early title had it. Between 1945 and 1946 Williams moved around the United States with lovers and relations, writing both *Summer and Smoke* and this play, now called *The Poker Night*. Late in 1946, when he read the new work to his friends Margo Jones and Joanna Albus, they "were shocked by it. And so was I. Blanche seemed too far out."[44] After making another revision in Key West, Williams sent *A Streetcar Named Desire* to his agent, Audrey Wood, who liked it enough to proceed immediately to production.

Wood quickly found a producer in Irene Mayer Selznick, Louis B. Mayer's daughter, David O. Selznick's ex-wife, and an independent woman "supposed to have 16 million dollars *and* good taste," Williams wrote to a friend.[45] Selznick's taste had not helped Arthur Laurents's *Heartsong*, which failed to reach New York, but she liked *Streetcar* right away and contributed a quarter of the required $100,000, getting the rest from Cary Grant, Mrs. John Hay Whitney, Audrey Wood, Clinton E. Wilder, Jr., and some anonymous Broadway investors. Selznick signed Williams at a meeting in South Carolina that the author found dramatically clandestine, especially at the end when Selznick sent off coded telegrams about the agreement to her New York office. During this meeting, Williams agreed to drop his idea of Tallulah Bankhead in the leading role. Their next move was to find a director.

Selznick first sent the script to Joshua Logan, whose Southern upbringing and history of mental instability might have made him sympathetic to the material. Logan wired back that he was interested in the play, which he later called "the best play I had read in years; maybe the best play I had ever read."[46] But after seeing *All My Sons,* Williams had other ideas. He had been "so impressed by [Kazan's] staging of that message drama, by the vitality which he managed to put into it," that he urged Wood and Selznick to "do everything possible" to get Kazan.[47] However, Kazan turned *Streetcar* down because he said it lacked interest. Then Molly Kazan twisted her husband's arm, and he agreed to direct it. Later, he would call the play "a masterpiece," "distinguished and beautiful," and "the best play I've ever done."[48]

The production's all-star quality was enhanced by the designers who were hired. In charge of both setting and lighting was Jo Mielziner, whose career had already spanned a quarter-century and 150 shows. (So prolific was Mielziner that at one point in the 1955/56 season he could claim design credits in one-seventh of the current Broadway productions.) Best known in literary and theatrical history for his poetic renditions of great American plays like *Strange Interlude, The Glass Menagerie, Streetcar,* and *Death of a Salesman,* Mielziner was also famous as a topflight designer of musical comedy, a consultant to theatre architects, and the most accomplished second-generation legatee of Gordon Craig. Lucinda Ballard, a costumer trained by Norman Bel Geddes and associated then with Rodgers and Hammerstein, was reputed to be a "genius" designer and a formidable woman with the power to tame both directors and actresses, Ethel Merman included. The shows for which she was known immediately prior to *Streetcar* included *Annie Get Your Gun, Allegro, Show Boat, Another Part of the*

Forest, Street Scene, and the 1944 production of *I Remember Mama,* in which Brando played Nels. She had recently collaborated with Mielziner (twice) and also with Kazan, who had taught her "how to work with actors, and how to think in terms of what the characters are like."[49] Music coordinator Lehman Engel was one of the period's best musical directors and theatrical conductors, having been associated with productions of Shakespeare and Shaw and with such prestigious projects as *Murder in the Cathedral, The Time of Your Life,* and *The Beggar's Opera* (which he staged and conducted in 1941).

By the summer of 1947, the production was coming into focus around two well-known Hollywood actors in the leading roles: Margaret Sullavan as Blanche and John Garfield as Stanley. But Williams raised serious objections on seeing Sullavan audition, so the production team turned to Jessica Tandy with some alacrity. Hume Cronyn, her husband and an enthusiastic producer of Williams's one-act plays, picked up a copy of *Streetcar* in Wood's office and spotted a part that was appropriate for Tandy. Since she had just finished portraying Miss Lucretia Collins in *Portrait of a Madonna* in Los Angeles—and since Collins was Southern, mad, oversexed, aging, and otherwise a study for Blanche—Tandy and Cronyn talked the East Coast parties into coming west to see a June revival of *Madonna.* The choice of Tandy was neither undisputed nor immediately obvious. Experienced she certainly was. Since her London debut at the age of twenty in 1929, she had appeared in classics and contemporaries at London's Old Vic and in the West End. After a New York debut in 1930, Tandy had appeared on Broadway a dozen times in the next dozen years. But she had never had a huge success in either movies or theatre and had not performed in New York in five years, so a producer concerned with the box office might have resisted her, as Selznick did. Kazan did not, however, particularly after he saw Tandy in *Madonna.* She left the theatre that evening thinking she had lost the part of Blanche because of her "absolutely disastrous" performance.[50] Kazan went to bed knowing she was right for it. She signed in July 1947, and Williams wrote a friend from Selznick's beach house in Malibu that they were now set with Garfield and Tandy for a winter opening at the Ethel Barrymore Theatre in New York. New Haven, Boston, and Philadelphia were booked, and press releases were sent out in flurries.

Then John Garfield made trouble on two counts: he wanted Stanley's part expanded to equal Blanche's, and he wanted a short-term contract. Since Selznick anticipated the success that was to come, she could not agree to a contract of only a few weeks; consequently she released him. Surely this was a serious setback. Kazan and Garfield had worked together in the Group Theatre and in Hollywood, most recently on *Gentleman's Agreement*, which was an Oscar winner for Kazan. Although Garfield had not appeared in New York since 1940, when he had been the rising star within the Group, his Hollywood career was cresting during 1946 and 1947 with *The Postman Always Rings Twice, Body and Soul,* and *Gentleman's Agreement*. Not only did he have box office appeal, but Garfield was a perfect Stanley—dark, masculine, proletarian, ethnic, and, in some of his best screen acting, a frighteningly implacable force.

In replacing Garfield, Kazan proved again that he was a gambler by choosing a sensitive blond beatnik who had already offended such pillars as Bankhead, Noël Coward, and Alfred Lunt and Lynn Fontanne. Kazan (who probably would not have attached much importance to their opinions anyway) had worked with Brando in 1946 when he produced *Truckline Cafe* and remembered "a wonderful scene," only five minutes long but full of terrifying realism, in which Brando's character had suffered a seizure.[51] Convinced that Brando was right for the part, Kazan sent him off to Provincetown, Massachusetts, where Williams was staying at the beach. An anecdote well known among Brando fans is that the actor pocketed his bus fare, hitchhiked to the Cape, fixed both plumbing and electricity at the beach house, and then sat down in a corner and read the part of Stanley Kowalski so well that Margo Jones let out a brave Texas whoop. Aside from thinking that this actor was "about the best-looking young man I've ever seen," Williams knew immediately that Kazan was right: Brando could act Stanley, and in a way no one might have predicted.[52]

Kazan had worked closely with Selznick and Williams on casting the two leads. Left to his own devices with regard to Stella and Mitch, he picked Kim Hunter (née Janet Cole), a young actress with a modest film career and no Broadway experience, and Karl Malden (né Mladen Sekulovich), a rising stage actor from Chicago's Goodman Theatre with thirteen New York plays to his credit between *Golden Boy* (1937) and *All My Sons*. Malden had also worked with Brando in *Truckline Cafe*.

Kazan took these actors into rehearsal on October 6 at the top of the New Amsterdam Theatre. He spent the entire first week reading and talking—more time than most Broadway directors devoted to that task. During the second week, he unhurriedly began group work, and focused on emotional expression and gestural elaboration. As the acting developed, Kazan's location in the theatre gradually changed: first he was onstage with the actors, then he moved into the first orchestra rows, and finally, by the end of this second week, he sat in the back of the house. Williams sat beside him passing notes, answering questions, demonstrating such movements as the flower seller's entrance, and filching dialogue from an earlier one-act play to supply some incidental dialogue between Steve and Eunice. Kazan grew to appreciate Williams's help, even at blocking rehearsals, and his habit of staying away from the actors. Williams came to think that Kazan "understood me quite amazingly for a man whose nature was so opposite to mine." Kazan not only understood Williams's desperate sensitivity, but knew how to give drama "vitality" (that was why they hired him) and made his rehearsals "fun."[53] "It's unbelievable," Williams told a friend during these weeks. "This man hasn't made one single mistake in judgment since these rehearsals started."[54] These opinions did not prevent the depressive author from thinking *Streetcar* "a certain failure," but his gloom went generally unshared.[55] For example, Tandy has remarked: "It was marvelous to be working on a play of such quality. . . . The quality of that play was so absolutely remarkable that it never bothered us whether it was going to be a hit or a failure because it was so fascinating to work on. And Kazan is a remarkable director with a great sensitivity to everyone's needs."[56]

Sensitivity to various needs proved valuable when differences arose between Brando and Tandy. Her acting method was to discover what worked and then set it, whereas he preferred to experiment, which meant both exploration and horseplay. In temperament they were also dissimilar. In 1950 Brando said: "We don't see eye to eye. She gives her name for advertising. She thinks you should shave before a day in the country. She doesn't like peanut butter."[57] Once the run had begun and Kazan had left the production, these differences became disruptive, for Brando insisted on experimenting during performances, bringing his moods and problems onto the set with Stanley. Tandy needed more precision, and twice in the show's first month she demanded disciplinary rehearsals with Brando and Kazan. (Brando was late both times, so both sessions were canceled.) On the other hand, Brando's unpredictability during the eighteen-month run was a joy for Kim Hunter, who found him playing the trunk scene differently every night, always devising some new way of handling the clothes and jewelry. No matter the innovation, she said, "he'd always yank me into his sense of reality."[58] Their three and a half weeks of rehearsal passed happily enough, however, and they soon found themselves in New Haven performing on Mielziner's set, a wide, shallow affair of the interior-exterior variety that he did so much to popularize. The interior of the Kowalski apartment was bisected up-down by a curtain between the bedroom (left) and the kitchen-cum-living-room (right). Interior walls and furniture were covered with unmatched floral prints. The patio (far right) began outside the kitchen and included the circular staircase up to Eunice's and an outlet down right. This same outside area was connected to a narrow upstage alley that ran behind the apartment's back wall and was visible—along with a pattern of French Quarter ironwork—when the apartment walls were lighted for transparency. The whole was high and vast, gloomy and gray-greenish, with a characteristic Mielziner effect—decreasing realism as the eye traveled up and out from the realistic props and furniture down front. A "brooding atmosphere . . . like an impressionistic X-ray," the designer later wrote.[59]

Technical rehearsals began October 28 for the four-show run (October 30–November 1) at New Haven's Shubert Theatre. Kazan, Engel, Williams, and Selznick had sorted through scores of jazz tunes before picking their opener, "Claremont Blues," written by their pianist John Mehegan. They brought in the Novachord, a primitive synthesizer that they used for the haunting "Varsouviana," the "Good Night Ladies" cue in scene 10, and the chimes at the end. Mielziner spent hours banging away at the Kowalskis' kitchen door so that it would have just the right "kicked-at" verisimilitude. The Kowalskis' bathroom also required attention, for Kazan had decided that steam should come from behind the bathroom door (twice) and that the toilet's flushing should be audible. The crew rigged a telephone so that it would click realistically when left off the hook. By this time, Kazan had finished editing Williams's script into pictures and movements. He had composed first drafts of street scenes, poker games, love scenes, and fist fights. He had eliminated some passing trains and repositioned some yowling cats. A Streetcar Named Desire was now a cast and a crew in search of an audience.

At the premiere, the play received a typically uncertain hearing. Both locals and New Yorkers agreed that *Streetcar* was a bit too long and a bit too slow, particularly in its first scenes. The *Variety* critic called it "spotty as a checkerboard" and recommended serious consultations on pacing.[60] But both the *Variety* and the *Billboard* reviewers sent another message back from New Haven—that this play was going to be a hit. Thornton Wilder disagreed, telling the company at his house after the show that the play was "based upon a fatally mistaken premise. No female who had ever been a lady [Stella] could possibly marry a vulgarian such as Stanley."[61]

In Boston *Streetcar* ran for a fortnight (November 3–15) at the Wilbur Theatre but encountered censorship, and Kazan muted the end of the rape scene after stemming an effort to eliminate it altogether. Meanwhile, the reviews improved. Elinor Hughes described a "pitiful" and "nakedly honest story" with a wonderful performance by Tandy and "evocative and brilliant" directing.[62] Elliot Norton criticized the play for lacking pity and compassion and noted the show's occasionally "jerky pace," but admitted that the production was basically strong and confident.[63] The run at Philadelphia's Walnut Theatre (November 17–29) was also successful. A headline in the *Philadelphia Inquirer* called it "strong dramatic meat."[64] "Elia Kazan has done his most inspired work," said the *Evening Bulletin.*[65]

The production had only two problems, which were related: length and pace. The play was finishing just under the stagehands' deadline for overtime. Along the tryout road Kazan had made a few small cuts in the final scene, but these had not changed the impression regarding the play's duration. When Hume Cronyn argued that the show might profit from being twelve to fifteen minutes shorter, Williams agreed to consider any additional cuts. So Cronyn sharpened his editorial pencil and retired to a Philadelphia hotel room to do some doctoring, only to emerge later, convinced that nothing could be taken out of the play. Reviewers had complained from the beginning about occasional sluggishness. One reason the show seemed to drag was that *Streetcar* is composed of eleven discrete scenes, and between them Kazan had been using a blackout without curtain. This practice was an innovation, and no one took to it—neither the *Variety* reviewer (who called it "anything but satisfactory") nor the Philadelphia journalists, who complained about seeing the running crew dashing around in the dark.

So in New York Kazan made two changes intended to revise the subjective perception of theatrical time. First, he closed the curtain during scene breaks, creating an impression of smoother, hence shorter, transitions. Second and more important, he decided to redivide the play into three acts. In New Haven, Boston, and Philadelphia, *Streetcar* had been presented in two acts (scenes 1–6 and 7–11). The first act had lasted ninety minutes, which even then exceeded the attention span of most American audiences. On Broadway, with an additional act break between scenes 4 and 5, the play ran in segments of 62, 29, and 48 minutes that followed the plot's seasonal divisions (spring, summer, autumn). Staged in this manner, the piece seemed shorter.[66]

Installation of *Streetcar* at the Ethel Barrymore Theatre was technically complicated. The production had five stage managers, including Robert Downing as production stage manager; Joanna Albus and Clinton Wilder were among Downing's assistants. Mielziner's light plot was not particularly complicated by the standards of the 1980s— it consisted of realistic changes and a few long fades—but it required five backstage electricians working five switchboards, six or seven auxiliary boards, and a jungle of cable. A follow-spot operator stationed out front provided what Mielziner recalled as "a subtle heightening of the faces of those who dominated the scene," though the surviving cue sheets give the impression that the light shone exclusively on Blanche.[67] The Novachord was installed on the backstage floor, but the jazz ensemble (clarinet, trumpet, piano, and drums) was located in a soundproof room three flights above. These musicians responded to buzzer and light cues from an assistant stage manager who controlled volume as their music was piped down to the stage.

Business was booming when the production came in from Philadelphia to play one dress rehearsal with audience (December 1) and one paid preview (December 2). Parties were booking fast. Investors were coming around, since *Streetcar* had taken in nearly $100,000 on the road, ringing up record grosses from SRO houses in both Boston and Philadelphia. Kazan was already an investor, with what one trade report termed "a record share" for a director.[68] His optimism was thus both artistic and financial when he said to Williams, while they watched the audience assemble one night in Philadelphia, "This smells like a hit."[69] New York was full of competition during the week of their opening. There were popular hits (*Oklahoma, Annie Get Your Gun, Allegro, Brigadoon, Born Yesterday,* and *Finian's Rain-*

bow), classics (Godfrey Tearle and Katharine Cornell in *Antony and Cleopatra,* Maurice Evans in *Man and Superman,* John Gielgud directing Judith Anderson in *Medea*), and sturdy commercial vehicles starring Thomas Mitchell, Helen Hayes, Basil Rathbone, and Wendy Hiller. Nevertheless, the word on the street about *Streetcar* was that it promised to be a hit.

Williams called the opening on December 3, 1947, a "smash."[70] Kurt Weill, Cheryl Crawford, Joshua Logan, Dorothy Parker, Lillian Hellman, and Stella Adler were all there, along with Gypsy Rose Lee, Jock Whitney, Lawrence Langner, Alan Lerner, Ruth Gordon, Garson Kanin, Cole Porter, and a Hollywood contingent composed of Samuel Goldwyn, David O. Selznick, George Cukor, Olivia de Havilland, Gene Tierney, and John Garfield. The Kazans sat across the aisle from Margo Jones and the nervous author who drank double scotches during intermissions to soothe his tension headache. The final curtain came down to a loud ovation. Tennessee was called to the stage and took such a charmingly bewildered bow that everyone remembered it. Kazan slipped out to an adjacent alley to listen to the conversations of his departing audience and found to his satisfaction that some individuals were audibly upset.

At Cukor's 21 Club party, the principals toasted each other and waited for reviews. Atkinson called *Streetcar* "a superb drama" by a "genuinely poetic playwright" featuring an "almost incredible" Tandy.[71] John Chapman's review in the *News* was headlined "Season's High in Acting, Writing," and his prose was studded with phrases like "tragic overtones of grand opera," "a New Orleans Camille," and "an answer to a playgoer's prayer."[72] Richard Watts, Jr. *(Post)* described the play as a "feverish, squalid, tumultuous, painful, steadily arresting and oddly touching study of feminine decay," staged "brilliantly" by Kazan and written with a "lyric originality in his [Williams's] pessimism that gives it an inescapable vitality."[73] Among the dailies the final score was six wild raves and three mild criticisms, but Charles MacArthur's pronouncement that "those aren't raves, those are Valentines" erased any doubt that this was a hit show.[74] Williams reluctantly admitted to Audrey Wood that he now felt himself to be "a completely fulfilled young man."[75] By the end of December, he was fleeing to Europe, largely because of the publicity crush surrounding *Streetcar.*

After this successful opening, *Streetcar* ran eight shows a week for eighteen months with the four original principals still in the cast. During the first year, the box office took in gross receipts of $1,438,271 and sold standing-room tickets at every performance, even during the blizzard of December 26, 1947. On June 1, 1949, Uta Hagen, Ralph Meeker, and Carmelita Pope opened as Blanche, Stanley, and Stella. Anthony Quinn, who had been Stanley to Hagen's Blanche earlier in Chicago, replaced Meeker on August 29. On December 17, 855 performances after the opening and six months over the house record, *Streetcar* closed at the Barrymore. By this time, royalties were coming in from London (Laurence Olivier directing Vivien Leigh as Blanche) and Paris (Cocteau's adaptation, with Arletty as Blanche). Film rights had been purchased for $350,000. In January 1950, a national company started touring with "Elia Kazan's Production of" Williams's play, and by the spring, when this road company returned to play at New York's City Center, the show's gross was estimated at $4.5 million.

Among the trophies given to this production were a Pulitzer Prize for drama and a New York Drama Critics Circle Award for best original American play (Williams's second such award). Kazan and Williams did not win Tony Awards in 1948, at least in part because Kazan and Arthur Miller had won for *All My Sons* in the awards' inaugural year. (Tony Awards for best play, best director, and outstanding actor went to *Mister Roberts,* Joshua Logan, and Henry Fonda—the second famous graduate of Dorothy Brando's Omaha Community Playhouse.) Tandy's Blanche did win a Tony for the 1947/48 season, putting her performance on the same level as Cornell's Cleopatra and Anderson's Medea. The filmed *Streetcar,* released in 1951, won Academy Awards for best actress (Vivien Leigh), best supporting actress (Kim Hunter), and best supporting actor (Karl Malden), and thus became the first film in Hollywood history to win three of the four Oscars for acting.

The film of *Streetcar* deserves a paragraph, for it is a chapter in the story of the play's impact and reputation. Prior to the beginning of production in the summer of 1950, Joseph Breen's Production Code office censored the filmscript, and Williams's dialogue immediately lost its rather mild profanity and its more shocking vulgarisms. The Code censors insisted on the suppression of Allan Gray's homosexuality and thereby made nonsense of the Moon Lake Casino sequence in scene 6. Fighting to save the rape scene from the censors, Kazan and Williams agreed to "punish" Stanley at the end: as Blanche leaves with the doctor, Stella shrinks from Stanley's embrace saying, "Don't you touch me. Don't you ever touch me again," and takes her baby upstairs to Eunice's. Prior to the film's release, Jack Warner cut the final print behind Kazan's back because Warner feared Legion of Decency protests over the poker night finale. But even without the parrot joke, the toilet humor, and Blanche's "*Voulez-vous coucher avec moi ce soir?*" the heat and sordid intensity of *A Streetcar Named Desire* came through in the film version. Kazan and Williams salvaged a quiet victory from the dispute over punishing Stanley at the end. In the final frames, Stanley shouts "Stella!" from below, and his shout, according to the screenplay, is "reminiscent (in the reading) of the cry he gave at the bottom of the steps at the end of the poker night." Hearing that cry, the audience could remember—even if the Breen office forgot—what happened next. However lamentable the deletions and changes forced on Williams's script because of the moral standards of Hollywood in the early 1950s, the film survives as a classic by virtue of cinematic additions and wonderful acting. The film's lighting brought to Blanche's collapse a chiaroscuro quality reminiscent of the psychological extremities of German expressionist film. The film's plot improved the theatrical original by focusing on Blanche in the opening and by compressing the middle of the story. Most important to the film's success were the well-honed performances of Brando, Hunter, and Malden and the stunning intensity of Vivien Leigh as Scarlett-become-Blanche.

Streetcar was thus a hit in all the conventional ways: it won awards, aroused controversy, and held the attention of massive numbers of spectators. It also brought about gradual, though pervasive, changes in American theatre. "The style of *Menagerie* and *Streetcar* stimulated a whole wave of new actors and playwrights," said Anne Jackson. "Tennessee's lyric style was a departure from the naturalistic acting and writing of the Group Theatre."[76] The fact that Edward Albee, Woody Allen, and Neil Simon refer knowingly to *Streetcar* in their works indicates how deeply its imagery, style, and emotions have penetrated the fabric of American dramatic culture. Its influence extended to England as well; in the 1950s a generation of theatre artists was influenced by films by Kazan, William Wyler, Orson Welles, and Billy Wilder, and by the plays of Miller and Williams. Of that decade, Kenneth Tynan said that for "the first time in its history, the English theatre has been swayed and shaped by America."[77] (For evidence, one may compare the plot lines of *Streetcar* and *Look Back in Anger*.)

It is all the more important to note, then, that a few significant voices were raised in opposition to the play. George Jean Nathan led the attack, saying that Williams had fallen into the "shadowy borderline between the unpleasant and the enlightening." Nathan called the play *The Glands Menagerie* and his review included some typical one-liners, such as "There is a considerable difference between Wedekind and Wedekindergarten."[78] Another critic, and a fascinated one (for he saw the production several times) was Eric Bentley, who found it sentimentally flawed and psychologically excessive. But he could not help acknowledging the "liveliness of the dialogue, a liveliness quite different from the machine-made slickness of the play-doctors, a liveliness that the American theater has heard from only two or three native playwrights."[79] A few other critics (Mary McCarthy, for example) attacked the play, its conclusions, or its characters, but—like the majority of those in the audience and in the profession—fell under the trance of *Streetcar*'s dialogue rhythms and sexual intensity. American theatre had not produced a more interesting success since *Mourning Becomes Electra* (1931) and would not produce another until *Who's Afraid of Virginia Woolf?* (1962).

For all concerned, success bred success, and for no one more than Tennessee Williams. He had won the 1945 Critics Circle Award because a living legend, Laurette Taylor, had made a masterpiece of the role of Amanda Wingfield in *The Glass Menagerie*. But reviewers always need to see their enthusiasms confirmed, and *Streetcar* did that. Critics relayed the news that Williams was now the leader of the post-O'Neill generation of serious American playwrights, in a class with Odets and Saroyan. The highbrow endorsements of Joseph Wood Krutch, John Mason Brown, and Irwin Shaw were even seconded by *Time* and *Newsweek* critics. (The latter claimed that though Williams had "lustiness and neurotic tinge," he was "tender" too.[80]) Thus Williams was launched on his "Streetcar Named Success" and he would be, until the mid-1960s, the most eminent and publicized writer in American theatre.

Jessica Tandy, the only *Streetcar* actor not to get a movie contract, was also the one who would in later years be most associated with the theatre and New York. In the 1960s, for example, she appeared there in three Shakespeare plays, two by Chekhov, and one each by Shaw, Congreve, Miller, Dürrenmatt, and Williams. In the 1970s she became prominent in the theatres of both Edward Albee and Samuel Beckett. In 1983/84, she appeared on Broadway in a perhaps inevitable *Glass Menagerie*. Karl Malden reappeared in New York in *Peer Gynt* (1951), *Desire Under the Elms* (1952), *The Desperate Hours* (1955), and Molly Kazan's *The Egghead* (1957). But his great success came in Hollywood, with movies in the 1950s, television series in the 1960s, and television commercials in the 1970s. Kim Hunter returned for various Broadway engagements, but she, too, became notable in Hollywood—as a personality actress (somewhere between Barbara Stanwyck and June Allyson) with personality enough to make engaging the *Planet of the Apes* films in which she was featured.

Brando's later career is well known and has been the subject of much debate. The actor called his professional situation a "mess" in 1957, and both fans and detractors would use even harsher words in later years.[81] As Kazan has said, Brando at his worst represented "an enormous waste of a great talent."[82] At his best, he has seemed to be what Williams once called him: "the greatest living actor . . . greater than Olivier."[83] From the perspective of theatrical history, Brando's career is most notable because he completely abandoned the legitimate stage soon after *Streetcar*. How poignant it is to recall Williams's prophecy in the telegram he sent to Brando on their opening night in 1947: "FROM THE GREASY POLACK YOU WILL SOME DAY ARRIVE AT THE GLOOMY DANE."[84] When Brando rejected Hamlet's black mantle and dramatic verse for the black leather and fierce mumbling of his famous screen parts, he left behind a tradition of almost three centuries, in which a serious candidate for the title of "the greatest living actor" was tested against the greatest roles in the repertory. By electing to work in Hollywood not only for the high salaries (a motive that had drawn actors west for decades) but also for the artistic opportunities and social impact of film, Brando did more than any other contemporary actor to legitimize film acting.

The reviews of Kazan's directing of the stage version of *Streetcar* described it as "superb," "brilliant," "evocative," "sensitive," "magnificently done," "vigorous and engrossing," showing "lots of punch" and "uncanny prescience." Combined with *All My Sons* and *Death of a Salesman* (early 1949), *Streetcar* put Kazan on top of the New York directing world. "After *The Skin of Our Teeth* I was offered a lot of plays," he has said. "And after *A Streetcar Named Desire* I was offered any play."[85] For the most part, he chose to direct new American realistic plays: Robert Anderson's *Tea and Sympathy* (1953), William Inge's *The Dark at the Top of the Stairs* (1957), and most frequently plays by Williams (the unrealistic *Camino Real* in 1953, then *Cat on a Hot Tin Roof* in 1955 and *Sweet Bird of Youth* in 1957). In 1964 he returned to Miller's plays; he chose *After the Fall* to inaugurate the Repertory Theatre of Lincoln Center, of which he was a codirector with Robert Whitehead. Kazan's film career also gained momentum and visibility after his receipt of an Oscar for directing *Gentleman's Agreement* (1947). After the movie of *Streetcar,* he made *Viva Zapata!* (1952), *On the Waterfront* (1954), *East of Eden* (1955), *Baby Doll* (1956), *A Face in the Crowd* (1957), and *Splendor in the Grass* (1961).

For Kazan, commercial success meant gaining power, and power meant exerting creative control. This dynamic is apparent in the progression of his career—from actor to director to producer to film maker to novelist. As his roles changed, so did his attitudes to the art forms he worked in. At the time of *Streetcar,* he said this of the theatre: "If you get a play you believe in and if you get the money for it, why, then you can do it any way you want, and say in it anything you want to say. The theatre is free."[86] Soon after, he was complaining that "our stage today is essentially a playwright's medium," and he decided to concentrate on film, establishing an independent film production unit with money supplied him by Warner Bros. In the heyday of *auteurism* (the mid-1950s), he said he preferred being "a film maker, not merely a director."[87] His decisive break with theatre came in 1964, when the Lincoln Center theatre was struggling through its first year: "it suddenly struck me that if I was ever going to make it as a writer, I'd better get going." So he walked into Whitehead's office and resigned, saying, "I'm never going to do any more plays—I'm through."[88] He also withdrew from the Actors Studio and from substantial involvement in the Hollywood movie industry. *The Arrangement* was a best-selling novel in 1967, and it showed how quickly he could learn the ways of success in another new medium. Since then four more of Kazan's novels have appeared on the popularity lists. During the 1970s, Kazan confessed that he "can't even read plays."[89]

Stage offers have come from time to time (he almost directed Richard Burton in *King Lear* in the late 1970s), and he has admitted to dreaming about theatre work at night. But in the morning, facing reality, Kazan works on novels and films.

The Moths (Williams, Blanche, Tandy)

A plague has stricken the moths, the moths are dying,
their bodies are flakes of bronze on the carpets lying.
Enemies of the delicate everywhere
have breathed a pestilent mist into the air.

—Williams, "Lament for the Moths,"
in *In the Winter of Cities*

Remembered today for being both an actor's director (in the sense of making actors' performances stronger and truer) and a producer's director (in the sense of making producers richer), Kazan was also famous during his stage directing days as a director who was keenly sensitive to a writer's needs. He called himself "a writer's director," and so did many of his writers, and I take the sense of that expression to be that he respected their plays while making them more dramatic and more theatrical.

Tennessee Williams said that Kazan "understood me quite amazingly" and knew "how desperately much [my work] meant to me and accordingly treated it—or should I say its writer—with the necessary sympathy of feeling."[90] Robert Anderson was struck by Kazan's "contagious enthusiasm," by his "simplicity and honesty," and especially by his respect for writers. On the long walks they frequently took during the production of *Tea and Sympathy,* Kazan would tell Anderson, "Be patient. I'm still discovering your play." Or, "You wrote the play. You know better than anyone what you want, and that's what we're going to give you." When Anderson suggested a change that Kazan disliked, Kazan said, "No, this is the way you saw it when you were working quietly and alone. This is the way it will be."[91] This latter statement, of course, translates "I prefer the first version," but it also shows he possessed a talent useful in a director— the ability to protect writers from the momentary panic that can seize them during rehearsals.

Kazan summarized this kind of directing and its psychology when reminiscing during the 1970s:

I tried to put myself in the author's shoes. I used to try to say: "I'm now speaking for this author." Each author is different. I said to myself: "I'm doing *Tea and Sympathy* by Robert Anderson—this should be like a Chopin prelude, light, delicate, without over-stressing" or "I'm doing a play by Tennessee Williams: he's morally ambivalent, he admires the people who destroy him, he doubts himself, he is afraid of certain people and yet he is drawn to them. I must see life like he sees it." When I did a play by Arthur Miller, I said to myself: "This man deals in ethical absolutes (at least he did through the plays I directed), he is absolutely certain where he stands on issues. He is certain maybe because he is afraid of facing ambivalences, but I must not introduce ambivalences. I must keep it clear, forceful. I must save up force for the last part because he makes a final summation statement at the end of every play." And so on, and so on. In other words, I tried to think and feel like the author so that the play would be in the scale and in the mood, in the tempo and feeling of each writer. I tried to *be* the author.[92]

This quotation leads logically to a discussion of: how "being the author" is not "being oneself" and how Kazan viewed Williams and his work.

Being "a writer's director" is inherently alienating for anyone who, like Kazan, possesses an independent creative mind. The preceding retrospective quotation does not end with "I tried to *be* the author," but continues, "I was many men but none of them was myself." Being many men is diverting, instructive, and broadening, but trying to "be" another can ultimately retard personal growth and run contrary to one's ego, taste, belief, or need. Kazan "put the writer on top" in his theatre, and to a lesser extent in his films, because he secretly "envied and admired" writers; he wanted to be one.[93] In the theatre as he knew it between the 1930s and the 1960s, a director could not find avenues for becoming a writer-creator-*auteur* unless he became a playwright. A director could, of course, choose plays selectively or manipulate plays to make them vehicles for self-expression. Kazan was accused of manipulation as early as *Streetcar.* One critic called "Elia Kazan's Production of" above the title "a strange steer, accenting a kind of false virtuosity in what should be the most objective job of all."[94] Another, who was more sympathetic, assessed the manipulation more positively: "the real job of pulling [*Streetcar*] together and transforming it into a play has been done by Elia Kazan rather than by Mr. Williams."[95]

Eight years later, when Kazan convinced Williams to alter the ending of *Cat*, the debate about whether directors should serve the writer or assert their creative independence again flared up around these two.

Kazan said he was "overwhelmed" by Williams's talent and his "positive genius" for emotion, and startled that with his plays there was "always a new brilliant illumination." In particular, Kazan said Williams's plays resembled life, where "you cannot anticipate what will happen next." The characters were "wrong and right, magnificent and foolish, violent and weak," full of "the mystery and confusion that is part of every human soul." Williams did not express his opinion about life; rather he created indecipherable life itself, making "audiences instinctively feel Williams is writing about their real problems."[96]

The same moral ambivalence that Kazan saw in the playwright he saw in *Streetcar*'s leading character, Blanche DuBois, and he knew that in this case similarity came from identity. Blanche and Williams did share opinions (for instance, about deliberate cruelty) and obsessions (with death and desire). In making the comparison, Kazan points out this shared ambivalence:

> Blanche DuBois, the woman, *is* Williams. Blanche DuBois comes into a house where someone is going to murder her. The interesting part of it is that Blanche DuBois-Williams is *attracted* to the person who's going to murder her. That's what makes the play deep. I think one of the best things I did for the play was to cast Brando in it— Brando has the vulgarity, the cruelty, the sadism—and at the same time he has something terribly attractive about him. So you can understand a woman *playing* affectionately with an animal that's going to kill her. So she at once wants him to rape her, and knows he will kill her. She protests how vulgar and corrupted he is, but she also finds that vulgarity and corruption attractive. . . . I saw Blanche as Williams, an ambivalent figure who is attracted to the harshness and vulgarity around him at the same time that he fears it, because it threatens his life.[97]

Thus, in his work on *Streetcar*, Kazan drew on his sympathy with the playwright in attempting to gain a deeper understanding of the play's mysterious central character.

Blanche reveals herself most fully in the play's second act, scenes 5 and 6. In the first rehearsal script, Williams put a note at the head of scene 5 to emphasize its pivotal nature:

Some weeks later. The scene is a point of balance between the play's two sections, Blanche's coming and the events leading up to her violent departure. The important values are the ones that characterize Blanche: its function is to give her dimension as a character and to suggest the intense inner life which makes her a person of greater magnitude than she appears on the surface. [This note reappears in the acting edition.]

Act 2 is indeed a point of balance with regard to plot structure. Stella's growing stomach, Stanley's growing hostility, and the increasing signs of Blanche's presence in the small apartment have created a charged atmosphere. But Stanley's suspicions are as yet unproven, and since he appears less frequently in this act than Mitch, the household is also permeated by an air of cease-fire. During this brief respite, Blanche tries to put down roots and to avoid bad dreams, and the audience has the opportunity to better understand her psychology and the past that has twisted her mind.

With the revelations about Blanche's inner life in scenes 5 and 6, and particularly her disclosure about her early trauma over Allan Gray's life and death, the audience's sympathies are transferred from Stanley to Blanche. What may have begun as distaste for or perplexity at her behavior turns into pity for her lot. Kazan noted this in his planning even before he had a three-act structure in mind:

> The variety essential to the play, and to Blanche's playing and to Jessica Tandy's achieving the role demands that she be a "heavy" at the beginning. For instance: contemplate the inner character contradiction: bossy yet helpless, domineering yet shaky, etc. The audience at the beginning should see her bad effect on Stella, want Stanley to tell her off. He does. He exposes her and then gradually, as they see how genuinely in pain, how actually desperate she is, how warm, tender and loving she can be (the Mitch story), how freighted with need she is—then they begin to go with her.

The second act's words and actions reveal much about "how genuinely in pain, how actually desperate she is." At the beginning of scene 5, when Blanche is in a happy mood, she laughs at herself "for being such a liar." When her brother-in-law, in his question about the Hotel Flamingo, touches the subject of her lies, she panics, and she gives an excessively piercing cry when the Coke foams over. As the scene progresses, Blanche reveals more and more about her desperate need for protection from a brutal world: "I don't know how much longer I can turn the trick," and "They think a girl over thirty ought to—the vulgar expression is—'put out.'" The atmosphere of mental disturbance and suffering intensifies at the end of scene 5, when the Young Collector arouses her sexuality and the weather irritates her nerves.

The smallest details of scene 5 indicate that Blanche is "in pain" and "desperate" about sex. The scene's light beginning is interrupted by an argument over "that blonde" between Steve and Eunice—Wolcott Gibbs of *The New Yorker* called them "perhaps the least inhibited married couple ever offered on the stage."[98] The astrology is openly sexual, and the Coke foaming over is metaphorically so. The authorial tone turns to a wicked deadpan in Blanche's exchange with the paperboy about his drugstore soda:

BLANCHE: Chocolate?
COLLECTOR: No, ma'am. Cherry.
BLANCHE: *(Laughs.)* Cherry!
COLLECTOR: A cherry soda.
BLANCHE: You make my mouth water. *(Touches his cheek lightly, and smiles.)*

In scene 6, the sexual intensity between Mitch and Blanche builds (*"Voulez-vous,"* and so on) and reaches a peak in Blanche's passionate reminiscence-revelation about Allan Gray. In that speech—Albee would call it an "aria," and Williams provided a well-orchestrated polka-locomotive accompaniment—Blanche reveals her deepest secret, about an experience that has caused her the greatest pain. The scene ends with the ominous hint that thwarted sexuality can breed self-destruction.

It may be hard for younger generations to realize how strongly both *Streetcar* and Tennessee Williams were associated with sex and sexuality. Blanche's sexual adventures aroused striking reactions. In *Theatre Arts* magazine, Rosamund Gilder described Blanche's discovery that Allan preferred sex with men as a "shattering experience when her most intimate happiness was destroyed at its source."[99] Less ladylike, Elsa Maxwell called Blanche "oh-so-genteel yet a real slut at heart, with a street-walker's complex."[100] Many reviewers routinely called her a "prostitute" or a "whore." A New Haven reviewer called her a "nymphomaniac," as did a writer in Boston. Once the play reached New York, the term "nymphomania" appeared in reviews in *Newsweek, The Nation, The New Yorker* ("simple nymphomania"), *Commonweal* ("A mess of nymphomania, plus a hundred further psychoses"), and even *School and Society* ("nymphomania which culminates in insanity"). Intellectuals such as Joseph Wood Krutch used the word, and ten years later another intellectual, Robert Brustein, was still using it.[101] Feminists in particular should note that it was fashionable among critics of the time to use "nymphomania" to describe Blanche's psychosexual needs, which were hardly, as in the clinical meaning, female sexual desires of an uncontrollably excessive kind, equivalent to satyriasis in men. But the word had a psychologically fashionable Greekness, and in the 1940s even streetwalkers had "complexes." Little wonder that questions were raised in the British Commons when Olivier produced *Streetcar* with a government subsidy.

Behind the footlights, the author, director, and leading actress were more interested in Blanche's complexities than in her complexes. Williams's descriptions of Blanche stress her variety and range of qualities or aspects, including quick humor, truth to life, cultural symbolism, and demonic grandeur. He wrote her as such a strong example of female sexuality that she appeared to be a nympho, but he called her "*blanche*" (originally, "Bianca")—white, with associations of purity, frigidity, cleanliness, and emptiness. Williams also explained that Blanche is not only a complex character but an argument for the acknowledgment of complexity in our judgment of character. He called her a heroine of "delicate half-approaches to something much finer" and made her argue (in the play) for ambiguity and for broad-mindedness. Tandy too was impressed by the many parts of Blanche's "intricate and complex character," specifically "her background—her pathetic elegance—her indomitable spirit—her innate tenderness and honesty—her untruthfulness or manipulation of the truth—her inevitable tragedy."[102] In his notebook, Kazan analyzed her personal and social "contradictions" and stated his determination to emphasize them in order to achieve the "variety essential to the play."

In all of Kazan's work, his views on women and his pictures of them have never been simple-minded, but he has tended to repeat some specific images: the tigress, the Beatrice or Marguerite figure who leads men on to higher things, and the vamp. By "tigress" I mean a woman in what Kazan calls her "elemental" or "primitive" aspect, when she must kill for a child or dominate a man in order to survive. It may be a Mediterranean trait that Kazan reveals when he idealizes women and describes them as "civilizing, fair, staunch, undefeatable, encouraging."[103] He appreciates the vamp because she attracts men actively and variously. Finally, like so many other men, Kazan responds to a "yearning" in women and wants a woman to "make you feel her fate matters." "Men expect life to be thrilling to women," he says.[104]

Kazan's three female archetypes all reside in Blanche. Stanley calls her a tiger when he wrestles with her at the end of the rape scene. Beatrice or the virgin ideal is the image that Mitch traps her in. And the vamp is what she plays when she is desperate. But Blanche is also more than this generalized female constellation. If we start with the spine of her part, the need for protection, we can analyze how Kazan defined the character's contradictions and then used them as a basis for developing Tandy's particular acting style.

Blanche's need for protection could hardly be more strongly stated in the play. Her actions show us this need from the beginning, where she appeals to Eunice for help in her confusion, until the end, when she exits in a ruined condition on the protective arm of the Doctor, another of the strangers on whose kindness she depends. The need for protection is a theme also reinforced by the play's structure: Act 1 reaches its climax at the end of the poker scene, where Blanche confesses that she needs kindness now; act 2 ends with Mitch holding her in a protective embrace and confessing his own need. The original rehearsal script contained a forthright statement by Blanche that she had been searching for protection from the storm but found only leaky roofs. This speech was eliminated in rehearsal, but it made Kazan certain that Blanche's dominant action was to search for "someone to hold onto, some strength in whose protection she can live."

In many notebook jottings, Kazan pondered the social dimensions of Blanche's character. His central insight about the role was that Blanche's situation did not result from personal weakness or feminine limitation but from social condition. He ascribed her search for protection to "the tradition of woman (or all women)" who can "only live through the strength of someone else." This view of femininity, along with the Southern social history of which it was an integral part, struck Kazan as contradictory: already extinct, "like the dinosaur," and yet still definitive and crucial to Blanche DuBois. "*Her problem has to do with her tradition,*" he emphasized. "Her notion of what a woman should be. She is stuck with this 'ideal.' It is her. It is her ego. Unless she lives by it, she cannot live; in fact her whole life has been for nothing." In the mid-twentieth century, the traditional behavior of the Southern belle "does not work," for it alienates women like Blanche from society and renders them useless. "She doesn't know how to work," Kazan noted. In the nineteenth century, by contrast, this tradition "made a woman feel important, with her own secure positions and functions, her own special worth." So Blanche must inflate the importance of her life, must transform her fight for Belle Reve into "an act of heroism." She must think of herself as "*special* and different, out of the tradition of the romantic ladies of the past: Swinburne, Wm. Morris, Pre-Raphaelites, etc." However, this need for "specialness" leads Blanche to behave grandly, which is the worst possible behavior in a woman wanting protection, especially from Stanley Kowalski. "The airs the 'tradition' demands isolate her further," thought Kazan. And for Blanche isolation is the opposite of protection. It means defeat.

These remarks, which I have condensed from Kazan's notebook, suggest that the Southern social tradition is responsible for Blanche's tragedy. She can only satisfy her Southern woman's need for protection by pursuing a traditional line of behavior that, given changing times and changes in men, is now the behavior most likely to lead to her destruction. Kazan thus saw her as a character with a tragic flaw, who is comparable to Medea: "someone pursued by the Harpies, the Harpies being *her own nature.*" Kazan's view also implies tragic hopelessness, with Southern society in the role of the Greek gods and Southern womankind cast as the helpless Oedipus, damned for no reason other than having been born.

Social conditioning is the cause of Blanche's psychosexual problems. Her conditioning prompted her to destroy her own early happiness at the Moon Lake Casino. She has encountered nothing but unsatisfactory male types—Allan and the young soldiers on the one side, Kiefaber and Stanley and Shaw on the other. Kazan believed that Blanche had never been taught to understand her "physical or sensual side," so she "calls it 'brutal desire' . . . [and] thinks she sins when she gives in to it." Unable to integrate her sexuality, she rejects it. She then "begins to forget" sex and "to live in fantasy," making

Allan's death "a necessary piece of romanticism" appropriate to her own Rossettian glamour. Finally, she denies her sexuality altogether and projects it onto men. At the same time, however, Blanche never loses her "loneliness," her need for "human warmth."

This alienation from sex intensifies the difficulties of her contradictory position: Blanche needs protection, and protection requires sex or its promise, but sex is the department she understands least and fears most. The results are ontologically threatening. In an early version of scene 5, Blanche explained to Stella that men only admit to a woman's sexual existence (Kazan's notebook paraphrase reads, "Men don't see women unless they are in bed with them"), but that a woman needs her existence admitted before someone can protect her. So Blanche falls into a spiral of self-destruction. Kazan's version is as follows: "the 'tradition' . . . creates an apartness so intense, a loneliness so gnawing that only a complete breakdown, a refusal, as it were, to contemplate what she's doing, a binge as it were, a destruction of all her standards, a desperate violent ride on the Streetcar Named Desire can break through the walls of her tradition." Like the Victorian gentleman before her, the Southern belle flirts with dangerous sexual escapades because she is flirting with psychic suicide, with the destruction of the imagery that defines her very self.

From the perception that Blanche had been influenced and thwarted by social traditions Kazan derived his directing style and a method of portraying Blanche's character. The relevant notebook passage begins, "One reason a 'style,' a stylized production is necessary is that a subjective factor—Blanche's memories, inner life, emotions, are a real factor." This sentence might remind us of Strindberg and expressionism, in which stylistic vision imitates a character's mental state. Kazan continued: "We cannot really understand her behavior unless we see the effect of her past on her present behavior." These words seem suggestive of Ibsenite drama, in which we understand characters in the present by accumulating information about their pasts. (*Ghosts* is the classic example of such plays.) But Kazan meant "see the effect" more literally. He wanted Tandy to "act out" Blanche's tradition, to represent it in her behavior, so that the audience would be constantly reminded of the causes of her action and suffering. "All her behavior patterns are *old-fashioned, pure tradition*," Kazan remarked, "all as if jellied." He expressed this point even more plainly near the beginning of the notebook:

Blanche is a social type, an emblem of a dying civilization, making its last curlicued and romantic exit. All her behavior patterns are those of the dying civilization she represents. In other words her behavior is *social*. Therefore find social modes! This is the source of the play's stylization and the production's style and color.

Such an approach to character is strikingly reminiscent of Brecht, and so is Kazan's summary on the question of style: "The style—the real deep style—consists of one thing only: to find behavior that's truly social, significantly typical, at each moment."

Kazan then translated these perceptions about Blanche into a set of images for the actress. In one note he said that Tandy, physically, "must at all times give a single impression: her social mask is: *the High-Bred Genteel Lady in Distress*." In another note, he developed a much more complicated set of acting problems:

Try to find an entirely different character, a self-dramatized and self-romanticized character for Blanche to play in each scene. She is playing 11 different people. This will give it a kind of changeable and shimmering surface it should have. And all these 11 self-dramatized and romantic characters should be out of the romantic tradition of the Pre-Bellum South, etc. Example: Sc. 2 Gay Miss Devil-may-care.

Here we have a concrete example of social tradition and behavior providing the material for theatrical stylization. (While planning the production, Kazan hardly dared call what he was doing "stylization" and reminded himself to "say nothing about it to the producer and actors." Gordon Rogoff took this remark as the confession of a "cunning diplomat," which Kazan may have been.[105] But directors have frequently agreed that "style," "stylized," and "stylization" are volatile words around the theatre—words carrying associations that can be unusually destructive or useless, and not only for actors.)

Like so many tragic characters, Blanche raises the problem of whether a playwright, or for that matter a director, can believe what the character believes (that is, agree with her) even while illuminating her character flaws and the limitations of her beliefs. Kazan knew that though Blanche's *"Don't —don't hang back with the brutes!"* was motivated by "jealousy and personal frustration, still she, alone and abandoned in the crude society of New Orleans back streets, is the *only voice of light*. It is flickering and, in the course of the play, goes out. But it is valuable because it is unique." To Kazan, *Streetcar* ultimately represented "a message from the dark interior," a cry like Blanche's, that "light and culture" were dying in the barbaric modern world. Blanche herself is "twisted, pathetic, confused," and her cry is "snuffed out by the crude forces of violence, insensibility and vulgarity which exist in our South," but hers remains the standard of value. Therefore her destruction, however understandable, is still intolerable and wrong.

Jessica Tandy's importance to Kazan's production came precisely here, in the nobility she brought to the crazed character. Kazan told an interviewer soon after opening that "Blanche, to be believable, has to be played by somebody you respect instinctively, and Miss Tandy is such a person. She is a womanly woman, fragile and with a quality of helplessness, but underlying the feminine pliability, you sense her essential integrity. It is this attribute of hers that makes you feel, when Blanche disintegrates, that here is a person of real stature, a potentially fine young woman, going down."[106] Reviewers consistently confirmed this perception.

Reviewers also caught the complexity that Williams, Kazan, and Tandy had worked so hard to build into the performance. Joseph Wood Krutch described the production as a study in "subtle and delicate" perceptions, showing "nuances even in situations where nuance might seem to be inevitably obliterated by violence"[107] Did Kazan want something more complex than the story of a nymphomaniac? Atkinson called the part "elusive," the play "a quietly woven study of intangibles," and Tandy "almost incredible" in catching "so many shades and impulses that are accurate, revealing and true," including "the terror, the bogus refinement, the intellectual alertness and the madness that can hardly be distinguished from logic and fastidiousness."[108]

In Tandy's interpretation, Blanche was fragile from the beginning, revealing herself to be in the incipient stage of madness when she made her first entrance. Frenetic and chattering, she was clearly distracted when she found Stella embracing this crude, lower-class life. So explicitly did Tandy portray Blanche's condition that when she left the part and Uta Hagen took over, Brooks Atkinson said, "In Miss Tandy's acting Blanche's mental collapse was closer to the surface throughout the play and the agony of the last act was implicit in the preliminary scenes. Blanche had slipped into the limbo of the psychopathic world before the time of the play."[109] Making the same comparison, Eric Bentley found the same basic difference. "More or less mad from the start," Tandy seemed less attractive than Hagen, because she was more pathetically situated.[110]

Tandy's Blanche was not very Southern in her speech. Unlike such compatriots as Margaret Leighton and Vivien Leigh, Tandy found the dialect of the South difficult to master while retaining Broadway volume, speed, and accuracy. She practiced the accent during dress fittings with Lucinda Ballard, a New Orleans native, but on stage used "only . . . touches of it."[111] She seems to have entered, applied those touches of accent in the earliest moments, and then dropped the Southern manner of speaking almost entirely. "A strange, unintelligible young woman from England," Bentley called her.[112] Richard Watts, echoing many others, said: "She doesn't manage to suggest a chattering coquettish girl from the deep South to anyone's satisfaction."[113]

Nor was Tandy especially sexual in her portrayal. Reviewers seemed to dissociate the history of nymphomania attributed to Blanche from the character of the woman whom Tandy incarnated on stage. Ballard's costumes strengthened this impression, for they dampened Blanche's steaminess and made her look less vampish than Williams had first imagined. But most important, Tandy chose not to emphasize the racier, more physically compelling aspects of Blanche. Itemizing Blanche's traits in the list quoted earlier (p. 175), she made no mention of sexuality. During the Broadway run, the show's reputation for being sexually suggestive bothered her, particularly since she stressed the character's nobility so strongly in her interpretation of the part. This description of her acting squares with a general estimation of Tandy's career. Her characters have never been known for their voluptuousness or sexual passion. Her enduring qualities as an actress are strength, liveliness, and intelligence. In her old age she has added steely bitterness to these qualities. But Tandy is and always has been a proper actress, the high-toned Christian woman being her great type. Her characters, even when they are disillusioned or earthy or lower class, never fail to retain some measure of reserve and propriety.

Tandy's success in the part of Blanche was impressive but not staggering. (Remember that Atkinson called her "almost incredible.") Reviewers were fairly liberal with adjectives such as "superb," "limpid," and "searing," and they generally showed a respect for Tandy's endurance in a part that Kazan said was "about as long as Hamlet."[114] But in view of the inflated rhetoric that characterizes daily reviewing, expressions like "memorable," "steadily rising," and "Miss Tandy never fails his script" can hardly be considered fuel for the star-making machinery. Elliot Norton had this estimate of her success: If Tandy "could only add one cubit to her professional stature and become for the moment a new Eleanora Duse, [*Streetcar*] might well be an overwhelming play."[115] I hope that Tandy had a healthy chuckle at the thought of being asked to become a new Duse, but if Norton's line means anything, it means that her Blanche somehow fell short of sublimity. Is it fair to ask for such greatness? Some measure of greatness was certainly called for in this particular production because of the memory of *The Glass Menagerie* and Laurette Taylor. Most reviewers politely shied away from this comparison, but Irwin Shaw openly said that Tandy's achievement "suffers only from the fact that some seasons back we all saw Laurette Taylor in another Williams play. Everything that talent, intelligence, discipline can do, Miss Tandy does." Shaw admitted that this was a "fanatic standard" of judgment, but Tandy's was simply not the "solitary and touching genius" of Taylor.[116] (There is no shame, of course, in being merely a talented mortal.)

Shaping the Play

Thus far I have described Kazan as an actor's director, a writer's director, and even a producer's director. Guiding the actor—"the talent"—is the great challenge of all directors. Handling writers is a more specialized problem, particularly in those theatres where writers have power. Producers are what directors become if they cannot shape the play. All directors must do that, whether they direct marionettes in the classics or Marlon Brando in Tennessee Williams. If they shape very well, they may be among the "directors' directors," as Kazan most definitely was.

By "shaping the play" I mean editing, molding, handling, orchestrating—controlling the material's immediate and consecutive values by adjusting rhythm, emotion, and texture, by changing mood, speed, brightness, and loudness—in an attempt to render the subject truly or well, in order to give the play grace and meaning. Kazan's assertiveness as a stylist was evident early in his career. Rehearsing *One Touch of Venus* in 1943, he paced around the theatre for some minutes, trying to invent an appropriate piece of business. When the authors (S.J.

Perelman and Ogden Nash) pointed out the stage directions already in their script, Kazan answered: "That chicken shit? I never read that. What do you think my business is in being here? I'm the director; I have to think of the business. I never read that kind of thing!"[117]

My subject in this section is how Kazan shaped or theatricalized the script of *Streetcar* he received. In the discussion that follows, I repeatedly give him credit for ideas and changes that may really have originated with Williams, the actors, or other members of the production staff. However this may oversimplify the collaborative nature of theatre work, my decision to say that "Kazan did" something to the script makes for easier reading and reflects the credit that is conventionally given to the director, who is the one person who must finally decide.

In the fundamental sense of revision—changing words—Kazan revised *Streetcar* substantially. He reworded hundreds of speeches, though he often did little more than change "Now let's cut the re-bop!" to "All right! How about cuttin' the re-bop!" A few scenes, especially scenes 5 and 9, he rewrote almost totally between first rehearsal and opening night. When rehearsing some of the incidental action, such as the street scenes, Kazan inserted new dialogue for the minor players as he experimented with new versions. But he did not alter the central events or the number or order of scenes. He changed characters less than he changed their names: Boisseau became Du-Bois, Poncho O'Shaughnessy became Pablo Gonzales, and the Young Collector, originally a premedical student named Lucio Francesco Romano, lost both his name and his vocation before opening night. A director making these changes is like a gardener cleaning the soil: he turns everything over, but aside from removing extraneous objects he changes nothing. He works over the material of the text with the actor as preparation for the performance.

Consider the following changes made by Kazan. Are they improvements over the original script or simply variations that appealed to these artists at that time?

Scene 1. Kazan rescored the noises of the neighborhood cats. In Williams's version, Blanche is alone in the apartment, where she is visibly nervous. She hears a cat screeching and reaches for a whiskey bottle to calm her nerves. In Kazan's version, the cat screeched after Blanche drank the whiskey, giving a different point or meaning to the whiskey and to the next line ("I've got to keep hold of myself!''). Kazan put the second cat's screech not at the very end of the scene, as in Williams's script, but a minute or so earlier, so that it helped build up to Blanche's breakdown rather than capping it.

Scene 2. Kazan had Tandy sing "My Bonnie Lies Over the Ocean" in her bath, not "From the Land of the Sky Blue Water." When Tandy sprayed Brando with the atomizer, Kazan changed the physical action from "He seizes the atomizer and slams it down on the dresser" to "Seizing her R. wrist," which created a moment of glaring tension Kazan repeated and elaborated during the climactic whiskey-bottle fight in scene 10. He cut out the line Blanche speaks on the porch ("How pretty the sky is! I ought to go there on a rocket that never comes down"), though it reappeared years later in the screenplay. He brought Steve and Pablo in at the end of the scene to deliver the beer and literally to set the stage for the poker game to follow (scene 3).

Scene 3. When the sisters enter, Stella calms Blanche by saying, "You look as fresh as a daisy." Blanche's original response, "One that's been picked a few days," was changed to "What nonsense!"

Scene 5. Before kissing the paperboy, Tandy spoke this new line forcefully, like a mother or teacher: "Come here! Come on over here like I told you!"

Scene 6. Williams and Kazan both intended for Mitch to return from his date holding a statuette of Mae West. Surviving photos (perhaps only publicity shots) show Malden bringing in a Raggedy Ann doll—a disappointing replacement.

Scene 8. Early in rehearsals, Kim Hunter showed Stella having labor contractions at intervals throughout the scene. Later Kazan changed his mind and decided to save the advent of labor for a surprise at the scene's end. He also cut out Blanche's speech admitting to age twenty-seven, since it diverted attention from Stanley's determination to deliver the bus ticket.

Scene 9. In the first rehearsal version, Mitch entered in his dirty work clothes, and Blanche described him as looking as rugged as a propaganda poster. Kazan cut out these words, believing that the visual impression was sufficient. Kazan also added lines to Blanche's mad scene here: "I was true as God in my heart to all of you— *always*—always!" and "I lived in a house where dying old women remembered their dead men."

Scene 10. In rehearsal, Kazan eliminated two of Stanley's jibes to Blanche: "Unless you got somebody hid under the bed," and—when he hears she has an invitation—to "A fireman's ball?" Kazan limited the humor he would allow in this gripping scene.

Scene 11. Kazan added Blanche's speech about the sea and her identification of the Doctor with Shep. Here, as elsewhere, Kazan nudged the character a step or two in a certain direction and altered details, but the character's outline was unchanged.

Kazan was often aggressive about trimming or eliminating some of Williams's most direct thematic statements. He cut out much of Blanche's most explicit cry for protection, her claim that a bit of peace is the poor man's paradise, and a dialogue between the sisters that contrasted Blanche's energy with Stella's self-control. Kazan also deleted Blanche's single most penetrating insight into Stanley's behavior: "He hates me. Or why would he insult me? Of course there is such a thing as the hostility of—perhaps in some perverse way he—No! To think of it makes me . . . (*Gesture of revulsion. She finishes her drink. Pause.*)." This realization that Stanley's hostility may be a mask for sexual attraction was restored later in the filmscript. But in the 1947 rehearsals it must have seemed an unearned insight or an obvious piece of authorial psychologizing. Emended, the speech continued after "why would he insult me?" with "The first time I laid eyes on him, I thought to myself, that man is my executioner! That man will destroy me!—unless—" Kazan's critical faculty stood him in good stead here—he could have employed it more in films and fiction—for it enabled him to shape Williams's themes into a happier mixture of the explicit and the mysterious.

A few months after the Broadway opening, Karl Malden described the interaction between playwright and director as in this way:

> They're a wonderful combination. While Williams is off the ground, Kazan, with his tremendous force, is firmly planted on it. He found the realism behind the play's poetry, extracting the meaning from it in theatrical terms and allowing the poetry to take care of itself. It's there, it's written. For the actors, that left no problem of trying to work up contrived emotions. Our only problem was to get the realistic meaning out.[118]

To an important extent, "realistic meaning" meant "physical meaning," and Kazan started working out physical truths by putting props into the actors' hands. The point of a prop might vary from case to case: for example, giving color to a scene, helping actors turn feelings into behavior, and giving value to objects—making them meaningful properties. The production began with prominent props. Peg Hillias and Gee Gee James, as Eunice and the Negro Woman, sat on the porch eating peanuts. A moment later, when she let Tandy into the apartment, Hillias filched, polished, and ate an apple as she shuffled through Stella's mess. Tandy told Hunter, "You're all I've got in the world" while staring into a *"shaking glass."* Tandy looked in detail at Hunter's hands before asking, "Stella, you have a maid, don't you?" The play turned into a necklace of such realistic activities. Malden took Sen-Sen from an envelope and popped it into his mouth before his second conversation with Tandy in scene 3. Cigarette business, poker business, house-cleaning business were all made meaningful.

Generally speaking, Kazan improved the moments of intense activity and feeling, especially the fight scenes. A good example is the painful moment in scene 9 where Mitch exposes Blanche's face to the light. During rehearsals, Kazan never changed the words of this sequence. Nor did he change the scene's functions—to allow them both to release their anger and to push Blanche a full step toward breakdown. But he did change the activity. At first, Malden merely crossed, turned on the light, and stared at her. Tandy cried out at this and covered her exposed face. Then he turned out the light. Kazan, going to work, had Malden snap the light switch on, return to Tandy, and pull her brutally to her feet. Then he shoved her back against the dressing table, wrestling with her right under the light and *"pushing her face into [the] harsh glare of the naked bulb."* He paused on seeing the physical facts and said bitterly, "I don't mind you being older than what I thought. But all the rest of it—" His voice trailed off into a pause, which was followed by a shout, "CHRIST!" He then dropped her arms and stepped back.

Kazan also created physical intensities from inaction. Near the end of scene 1, Brando in his clean T-shirt stood at the curtain between the rooms (center) talking to Tandy, who stood in the middle of the kitchen. He told her that it was possible to catch a cold from sitting around in damp clothes, and neither person moved. They discussed the teaching of English, how long she might stay, and where she would "shack up," but still there was no movement—the only time this had happened thus far in the play. With tension mounting, Tandy said, "Travelling wears me out," and there was a pause. Brando said, "Well, take it easy," his meaning uncertain. Another pause followed. Suddenly a cat screamed, causing Tandy to start, Brando to smile, and both of them to move about and speak more rapidly. Such rhythmic tension hinted at Blanche's destination and at her need for protection.

In shaping the play, Kazan could not help but emphasize the general bipolar tension that exists in *Streetcar* between Stanley and Blanche. The two principal characters are this play's symbols and spirits. They are aware that their tensions symbolize a cultural warfare—Stanley always sees the columns behind Blanche; she thinks Stanley represents the world she can no longer protect herself from. When Williams was writing the early drafts, he gave the play titles that expressed Blanche's personality *(Blanche's Chair in the Moon, The Moth)*, substituted others suggestive of Stanley *(The Primary Colors, The Poker Night)*, and finally settled on a neutral title referring to place. The casting, with its emphasis on choosing Blanche and Stanley, also revealed the bipolar reality, as did the curtain calls at the end of the Broadway show (company bow, Mitch and Stella, Stanley, Blanche). In his notebook Kazan described the play as a triangle, but he put Stella at its apex, a character who acted less independently than as the object of Stanley and Blanche's struggle. Tandy explained the play's dialectical nature to an interviewer: "What's marvelous about the play is that there are so many opposites all going at the same time. It isn't just violent [Stanley], or just lyrical [Blanche]. It's violence and lyricism all at the same time. And they intermingle. And they're absolutely dependent on each other."[119] Reviewers described the production in revealingly bipolar terms: "grim and bitter, yet somehow softened by a sense of impersonal pity" said one; another remarked that "[Kazan] has woven the tenderness and the brutality into a single strand of spontaneous motion."[120] They used similar dualities to characterize Kazan's style, saying that he "succeeds in combining stylization with realism" and achieves a "triumphantly heightened naturalism . . . combined and contrasted with a verselike elegance of phrase."[121]

A 1948 anecdote shows how conscious the *Streetcar* crew was of the bipolarity of Blanche and Stanley. After the play had been running for some months, Thomas Hart Benton painted a vivid oil of the poker night scene—the men displaying their physiques, Blanche at the curtain with her nipples showing clearly through her slip. *Look* magazine proposed to photograph the cast in an identical pose and to run painting and photograph on facing pages. When Tandy found out that the producers had cleared this idea, she addressed an affectionate but clear-headed protest to "Mr. Intermediator" Williams. She did not want the play promoted like Rossellini's *Rome, Open City* (1945), which had been advertised on marquees as the "most fearless sex picture ever made." She was already having enough trouble with snickering audiences conditioned by publicity to expect the salacious. She urged the producers not to tilt the show's imagery toward "the Stanley side of the picture," which Benton had captured so well. An abashed Williams replied:

> I have such a divided nature! Irreconcilably divided. I look at Benton's picture and I see the strong things in it, its immediate appeal to the senses, raw, sensual, dynamic, and I forgot the play was really about those things which are opposed to that, the delicate half-approaches to something much finer. Yes, the painting is only one side of the play, and the Stanley side of it. Perhaps from the painter's point of view that was inevitable. A canvas cannot depict two worlds very easily: or the tragic division of the human spirit: at least not a painter of Benton's realistic type.[122]

If painting, realistic or otherwise, could not capture the tension and "clash of opposites" at *Streetcar*'s center, theatre could, at least in Kazan's view, and quite easily since conflict was so vital to it. Kazan pictured the play as a world divided—light and culture over here, violence-insensitivity-vulgarity over there—and directed by developing audience sympathy for Stanley and then transferring it to Blanche. Particularly in act 3, when Blanche has the audience's sympathy and is the dramaturgical focus, Kazan wanted the members of the audience to "realize that they are sitting in at the death of something extraordinary . . . colorful, varied, passionate, lost, witty, imaginative, of her own integrity . . . and then they feel the tragedy."

Considered as a tragedy, *A Streetcar Named Desire* is notable for satisfying a rule of thumb in modern dramatic criticism: the best tragic climax is a point at which the theme's definitive statement coincides with the plot's definitive crisis. The critical consensus on this matter obviously derives from Aristotle's preference, in *Poetics* 11, for tragic plots in which recognition, the intellectual or psychological crisis, coincides with the sudden reversal of circumstances essential to tragic action. In this sense, *Streetcar* is well crafted, for its climax— scene 10, the rape scene—shows a collision of principles and people, a conflict of world views combined with a meeting of the flesh in battle. This collision is so central to the play's meaning that, when fighting to save the rape scene from the film censor, Williams described the attack itself as "a pivotal integral truth . . . without which the play loses its meaning which is the ravishment of the tender, the sensitive, the delicate, by the savage and brutal forces of modern society."[123] But the rape is also a crime and a horrifying personal invasion and a failure of two individuals and the cultures they represent to achieve understanding.

The rape scene was likewise the climax of the stylistic progression in both the play and its production. In Williams's version of Blanche's psychological storm, the audience hears her flashbacks (polka, gunshot) and sees the phantoms of her terror and despair projected on the apartment walls. Williams described this style in his preface to *Menagerie* as "a new, plastic theatre" to rival the "exhausted theatre of realistic conventions."[124] Eric Bentley, then a confirmed realist and a young Brechtian, dismissed the innovations as "chiaroscuro" and "phantasmagoria."[125] I call it "expressionism" because of its historical connections with the art of making the invisible visible, as Peter Brook would say.

In his script, Williams carefully plotted out the recurrence of his best expressionistic effect, the "Varsouviana"—the haunting polka from the Moon Lake Casino. Observing a time-honored principle, he always saved it for last. He saved it for last within scenes, as at the end of scene 1, where it interrupts the conversation between Stanley and Blanche. He also used it to end an act—the whole of act 2 is without unrealistic interruption until the climactic moments of Blanche's speech about Allan, when the polka becomes prominent. Finally, Williams reserved this music haunting Blanche's mind for the last section of his play's large arc, making act 3 a sweeping crescendo of expressionistic effects, of which the "Varsouviana" is the most liberally used. In scene 8, as Stanley hands Blanche her ticket to Laurel, the polka "*steals in softly and continues playing*" to the end of the action. In scene 9, Williams used the polka three times, indicating the mounting agitation and madness of Blanche. Kazan followed these "Varsouviana" cues through to scene 11, where he increased the polka's effect by deleting it from Blanche's entrance and playing it instead as an accompaniment to her final exit. The device of ending both the paradigmatic first scene and the play itself with the polka is a piece of orthodox theatricality and more, for the polka explains Blanche's tragedy and signals her end. The "Varsouviana" gives shape to the parts and to the whole.

The second kind of theatrical effect (if we categorize by source) is the realistic or environmentally generated. In his script, Williams brought in the neighborhood "blue piano" in each of his eleven scenes. He was assertive in using quarreling neighbors, passersby, and street vendors to populate the French Quarter in which his drama is set. Sometimes, as with the rainstorm of scene 5, the realistic background was brought forward in order to emphasize mood. More often, Williams used environmental effects to punctuate the action. The blue piano punctuates the announcement that Belle Reve is lost in scene 1, the mention of Stella's pregnancy in scene 2, and Stanley's entrance in the rape scene. In three scenes, screeching trains torment Blanche at critical moments. The neighbors laugh to point up the "colored lights" conversation between Stella and Stanley on the porch. Blanche and Stella leave for Galatoire's, and the vendor cries, "Red-hot!" The chimes ring ironically throughout the finale. Williams was neither delicate nor sparing with such embroidery in *Streetcar.* He multiplied Stanislavsky's crickets by the giganticness of the city and the seriousness of the mental disturbance.

Kazan was more aggressive in some places, more conservative in others. For Blanche's first entrance, he contrived a street scene in which she encountered a young sailor who engaged her in a shadowy, provocative conversation. (In the early rehearsals, she bumped into the Mexican Woman selling "Flores.") But after much reworking Kazan cut out another such street scene between the Young Collector and the Negro Woman in scene 5. He also was less interested than Williams in trains; he eliminated the second train from Blanche's "brutes" speech (scene 4) and the trains from scenes 6 (Blanche's Moon Lake Casino speech) and 10 (Blanche's madness). Kazan perceived the jazz that wafts over from the Four Deuces as intrinsic to the play; in his notebook he wrote that the music expresses, first, "the loneliness and rejection, the exclusion and isolation of the Negro and their (opposite) longing for love and connection," and, second, "the soul of Blanche" in her longing for love and connection.

"It emotionally reminds you what all the fireworks are caused by." However, Kazan used the music sparingly in the production. He introduced it mostly to bridge the blackouts and then, as the scene began, he removed it quickly with the curtain (scenes 3–6, 9, 11) or the speaking of an early line (scenes 2 and 10).

In some of the most decisive moments in his script, Williams experimented with a third kind of stylistic effect, in which Blanche's disintegrating mind is shown to distort a realistic stimulus into a more grotesque or expressionistic form. Early examples include the "goat-like" cries of Steve and Eunice in scene 5 and the distant piano's sympathetic "hectic breakdown" as Blanche weakens at the end of scene 7. Both Blanche and the audience might wonder whether the peddler selling "Flores" in scene 9 is real or is some projection of Blanche's sick mind. In the rape scene, Stanley exposes Blanche's "lies and conceits and tricks" and yells, "*Ha-ha-ha!*" As he crosses near Blanche on his way to the bathroom, his threatening presence is reinterpreted by her projection of "*lurid reflections*" and "*shadows . . . of a grotesque and menacing form*" on the walls. The voice of this man she has called an ape becomes a multitude of "*inhuman voices like cries in a jungle,*" and when he returns in his provocative pajamas with an apelike grin on his face, the sound of the blue piano is gradually transformed into the roar of an approaching locomotive. Realism and Blanche's control break down in concert; the theatrical style is imitating the subject-event.

Kazan altered this scene markedly by emphasizing its social implications and by concentrating on the street sequence. He eliminated the reflections and shadows on the wall along with most of the other expressionistic devices and created a scene that the backstage personnel called "the ballet," using minor actors, understudies, and assistant stage managers. After Stanley's exit to change, a passerby (Richard Carlyle, Brando's first understudy) was mugged and robbed by Gee Gee James (the Negro Woman), who had lured him into the street, and Nick Dennis (elsewhere Pablo), who finished the job. The sounds of this fight and more sounds from the cafe where the fight originated mixed with general street sounds, police whistles, and the groans of the victim. It was a true urban babel, and the noise terrified Tandy, who was trying to reach the long-distance operator and Shep. After she hung up the phone, and as the first mugging victim groped his way offstage (down right), a second mugging occurred, this time of Clinton Wilder, who staggered in (up right) saying, "I'm through."

Three assailants—Dennis, Rudy Bond (Steve), and Vito Christi (the young Collector)—knocked Wilder out, took his money, and began to fight over it as a panicky Tandy lurched through the kitchen door and ran into the street, her arms full of jewelry and gowns. Nearly colliding with them, she froze in horror, amid police whistles and cacophony. The Negro Woman streaked through again. Actors and crew offstage made weird noises by moving their fingers around in their mouths. Tandy saw and heard all this and reeled back through the door in shock. The muggers ran offstage (down right). As the siren moaned low, she crossed to the phone, knelt clutching her possessions against herself, and begged the operator to put her through to Western Union.

By the end of this phone call, all noise and activity had ceased. Tandy was telling the imaginary operator that she was "Caught in a trap! Caught in—" when suddenly a sound came from the bathroom and—"Oh!" she gasped—Brando appeared in red silk. Everything was completely quiet except for the phone's clicking. The lights had been taken down; the interior lights were dimmed first on a long, slow count during the earlier dialogue between Blanche and Stanley, and the exterior lights were taken out after the "ballet." Brando crossed from the bathroom to the phone (left to center) and replaced the receiver. Kazan's picture was now still, focused, and dense. "You left the phone off the hook," Brando said, and he crossed slowly in front of her (she was now upstage of the phone in the kitchen) and closed the outside door. In the course of the subsequent five short speeches, Tandy tried to get out that door by going around Brando, who faced her upstage from the door, giving focus. She then ran to the dressing table in the bedroom, which was as far away as she could go. Brando thus had to cover the entire width of the apartment, from the door (right) to the dresser (extreme down left). He moved toward the curtain, telling her she would not be "bad to—interfere with," then padded forward through the bedroom until Tandy smashed a whiskey bottle against the dresser. When she threatened him with the neck of the broken bottle, Brando laughed at the notion of "rough-house" with a woman, then caught her wrist (compare scene 2, the atomizer), and forced her into a hammerlock saying, "Tiger—tiger! Drop the bottle-top! Drop it!" She did, and then he bent her body backward (see Plate 3), picked her up with both arms, and said his last line: "We've had this date with each other from the beginning!" As

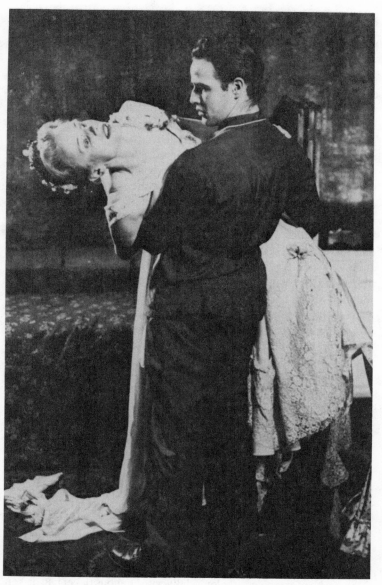

3. The rape scene in *A Streetcar Named Desire.*

he moved toward the bed with her, the "Wang Wang Blues" faded in and the lights faded out. The music continued during the longish blackout before the final scene.

Kazan's rape scene was most remarkable because it was a realistic portrayal of a society gone mad, as I have already said. The single element of the "ballet" that was expressionistic or unreal was the finger-in-the-mouth noise coming from offstage. Otherwise, what the audience saw and heard—and what Tandy saw and heard—had not been exaggerated and was social in origin and point. Tandy neither saw reflections on the walls nor saw through the walls, as in Williams's script. She witnessed real violence outside her door, and though these incidents may only have confused her, they showed the audience social violence that had originated with arguments over sex and money. She heard the sounds of distraught victims of social violence just before she became one. She heard the sirens of the impotent forces of law and order whirring in the distance. And she heard Brando (as Stanley, the symbol of the brutal modern world that was destroying her)—heard the taunt and threat in his voice and the sound of his shoes on the floor as he approached. (Yes, even when in pajamas he wore shoes.) This Blanche was not out of control and projecting evil phantoms; she was out of control and suffering from real, present evil. The threats to her mind and body became more sordid as the scene progressed, but this change accompanied—it did not result from—the change in her psychological condition. The man coming at her was no delusion, no dream, no hallucination. In Kazan's treatment, the horror of the rape scene's final moments was their stark reality.

Instead of fusing Blanche's mad visions and Stanley's all too real aggression, Kazan took care to separate them in directing scene 10. He inserted at the scene's beginning an episode clearly indicating that Blanche had already lost her self-control. In the first rehearsal script, Blanche's obvious collapse had come earlier, at the end of scene 8, when the Kowalskis left for the hospital after the spoiled birthday party. In this version, Blanche peered out of the bathroom, made certain that she was alone, and emerged singing in Spanish a rambling, repetitive song about cornbread. The implication could not have been stronger: Stanley's delivery of her bus ticket had driven her mad. Rehearsing this sequence, Kazan first eliminated the song, then revised the remainder of the beat, and finally excised the whole thing. He added instead the soliloquy scene for Blanche at the beginning of scene 10, with its speech that begins, "How about taking a swim, a moonlight swim at the old rock quarry?"

In this new opening to scene 10, Kazan used the psychological expressionism that Williams had wanted in the rape scene's final minutes. The sound crew executed a segue or cross-fade, taking out the jazz ensemble playing "Morningside Blues" and bringing in the Novachord playing "Good Night Ladies." The Novachord was the instrument associated with Blanche's mind by this point in the production. With its music came phantom sounds of voices and applause, provided by backstage personnel using microphones. These sounds completed the aural flashback to the days of her social success at Belle Reve. Her appearance gave additional emphasis to the flashback to her youth and those earlier historical periods that had, Kazan believed, influenced her development. She stood listening to her mental cacophony in a "*soiled and crumpled white satin evening gown and a pair of scuffed slippers,*" with a rhinestone tiara nestled in her disordered hair. The picture, her speech, and the song all declared that this was Blanche's "Ophelia scene." It was longer in production than in the New Directions text. Brando entered the kitchen and had a moment to observe Tandy as she stood in the bedroom talking to herself: "Oh, my goodness! They're playing 'Good Night Ladies.' May I rest my weary head on your shoulder? It's so comforting." She rested her head instead on her own hand—a meaningful gesture for a woman seeking protection from others—and Brando took note of her condition as the sounds of her mind faded from the theatre. This little vignette told the audience that Stanley completely understood Blanche's madness and raped her anyway. In summary, the opening moments of scene 10, like the entire scene and *Streetcar* itself, showed the progression from psychological disintegration to the social madness that can destroy the already fragile mind (Kazan's larger topic).

A final observation about Kazan's rape scene is that it was so typical of him—it was action packed and rousing. Kazan has described this characteristic in his early film work:

Everybody's problem is his talent, not his faults. My problem is that I can always make things forceful. I used to make every scene GO GO GO! mounting to a climax, and if I had sixty minutes in a picture there were sixty climaxes, *ready?* CLIMAX! *all right, rest a minute*—CLIMAX! That was what I used to do. And it's easy to do, you know, make somebody shout, or grab somebody by the neck or throw somebody out, or slam a door, or open a window, or hit somebody with a hammer, or eat something quick in disgust—it's easy to do. It's bullshit! Bullshit! So you see what I mean, the problem of a man is his virtues, not his faults.[126]

This is the director of primary colors, noted for his power and vitality. Mielziner has said that Kazan is "vigorous . . . never vague or temperamental."[127] Malden admired his "tremendous force."[128] Designer Boris Aronson remarked that "there is nothing precious about him. No half-tones or overtones. He concentrates on structure, plot, character. He strives for power and simplicity."[129] "Kazan's vision of things is very strong and forceful," said Geraldine Page. "He communicates them that way."[130] Eric Bentley, one of his opponents, commented on his speed and its consequences:

Things move fast in a Kazan show. So fast you can't see them. If anything is wrong, you don't notice. If a false note is struck, its sound is at once covered by others. One has no time to think. "Drama isn't time to think" the director seems to be saying, "it's action that sweeps you off your feet."[131]

Reviewers praised Kazan's handling of the action in *Streetcar.* "The Kowalski family and the persistent neighborhood brawls are vigorous and brassy; the sentimental clinches between Kowalski and Stella, muted, lingering, and repeated; and the shrill accent provided by the neighbors, blatantly contrasted and pungent," wrote William Beyer.[132] Irwin Shaw said Kazan "caught the combination of Southern, rambling languor, slashed by moments of blazing violence, that the play calls for."[133] John Mason Brown described the production's strong management: "He knows when to jab a climax home, when to rely on mood, when to focus the attention pitilessly on the principals, or when to establish in Reginald Marsh terms the tenement atmosphere."[134]

Kazan was energetic in places where other directors might let attention slacken. In scene 8, after the exchange about Polacks, Stanley breaks off the argument with Blanche and Stella to answer a telephone call and to give orders about where the bowling team will and will not play. Kazan told Brando that this phone call should not actually interrupt the argument at all. The phone dialogue should "be read with direct dramatic reference to the scene with the women."[135]

Thus while involved in one argument, Brando visibly decided to end another, and then attempted to throw Tandy out as dictatorially as he decided where the bowling team would meet. Facilitating that flow, Kazan trimmed some dialogue from the script between the phone call and the ticket delivery.

Similarly, Kazan energized those scenes where Williams built in dynamic conflict. Consider the famously miserable trio of Blanche, Stanley, and Stella gathered around the birthday table at the beginning of scene 8. Meals shared by antagonists are one of Kazan's specialties, for he enjoys the idea of hostile people being forced by social convention and circumstance to participate in an otherwise intimate and ritualized act ("a perfect example of dialectic in Marxism, where there's an element that holds them together and an element that pulls them apart").[136] The birthday party symbolizes the months of undesired intimacy between Stanley and Blanche. At the table, Brando, sullen at first, became more explosive as Tandy's joke about the parrot dragged on. Hunter's sarcasm prompted him to smash his hand down on the table and to sweep the crockery onto the floor. "Pig— Polack—disgusting—vulgar—greasy!" he mimicked. "What do you think you two are? A pair of queens?" His voice choking over these last vowels, he was now the perfect cock of the walk, masculinity at its most tense and confused and exalted and ridiculous. "Remember what Huey Long said:—'Every Man is a King!' And I am the king around here, so don't you forget it!" Hurling more crockery, he shouted: "My place is cleared!" He leaned across the table toward Hunter and asked, with clumsy irony, "You want me to clear your places?" Soft cries from Hunter sent Brando stalking out onto the porch to light a cigarette. The silence was relieved by music from around the corner; Tandy looked up and said, "What happened while I was bathing?"

Kazan created another memorable set of images in scene 11 by directing this finale with an emphasis on simplicity and emotional truth. Because all tensions had been released during the rape scene, Tandy's departure was anticlimactic and was "reticent" and "muted," as reviewers said. The scene's dominant emotion was pathos. Reviewers called Kazan's version "painful," particularly because of the violence that continued to erupt—among the poker players, between Brando and Malden, between Tandy and the matron restraining her. But when released from restraint by the gentlemanly

Doctor, Tandy smiled coquettishly and radiantly, "*as she would at a new beau,*" and arranged her hood around her face in preparation for the journey. Standing in the bedroom at the arch (center), she smiled as she said to him, "Whoever you are—I have always depended on the kindness of strangers." (Imagine hearing that wonderfully expressive line when it was freshly minted, before her words had been incorporated into the language of the tribe.) Tandy took the Doctor's arm and moved through the kitchen (stage right), crossing behind Brando, who was hanging "loose-lipped and cold-eyed over his poker table, a grunting, laconic, tooth-sucking pig."[137] The kindness of strangers, indeed! Passing Hunter as the heartbroken Stella on the porch, Tandy turned and walked out slowly, from up right to up left, behind the now transparent back wall, through diagonal streams of light, to the accompaniment of the "Varsouviana." Brando moved to the porch steps in response to Stella's crying over her sister's departure, then took Hunter in his arms and "*voluptuously*" murmured a string of phrases: "Now, honey. Now, love. Now, now, love." They were standing in the very spot of his earlier sexual conquest. As Tandy neared the wings and the music began to crescendo, the curtain began to fall. Back at the poker table, Steve started to deal the cards: "All right, boys—this game is seven-card stud." The production's final image showed the DuBois women clinging to their men, their angels of death.

Credit Kazan here and in other work with an instinct for truth that, to a greater extent than his dynamism, distinguished his directing in both theatre and film. This instinct was the basis of his notorious love of "the real thing" on screen and on stage. He liked to shoot films in real places, at a time (the 1940s and 1950s) when location shooting was uncommon. He used nonactors in his lineups, in his crowds, on his docks. He preferred authentic clothing, too, and frequently worked with costumer Anna Hill Johnstone because she knew the secondhand clothing stores so well. In *Streetcar,* the real thing was visible (the kitchen door was kicked and scraped) and audible (the flushing toilet always got a laugh). So real was Kazan's action that Brando and his fellow poker players damaged the offstage "bathroom" with their thrashing about; a few months into the run, the bathroom floor required $400 worth of repairs.

Kazan knew what constituted emotional truth and dedicated his work to finding and revealing it. In 1956 he explained that a play "must have truth. A play has to hit home somewhere, it has to mean something to people. Take *Cat on a Hot Tin Roof.* What was it really about? It was about a woman whose husband wouldn't go to bed with her. That was the story."[138] Discussing *Splendor in the Grass* (1961), he said: "It isn't only that the picture amuses. A little light lights and you're aware of something, you see the truth, and you say to yourself: 'Yes, that's the way things are, somebody said it, they cut through all the mush and said something new.'"[139] In 1956, after he had wrapped up the shooting of *Baby Doll*, Kazan described his directing as an effort to find "a handful of truth . . . that little human thing . . . that little moisture in the girl's eye, the way she lifts her hand, or the funny kind of laugh she's got in her throat." This was "the shine and shiver of life . . . a certain wildness, a genuineness." Reflectively, he continued: "I've always been crazy for life. As a young kid I wanted to live as much of it as possible, and now I want to show it—the smell of it, the sound of it, the leap of it. 'Poetic realism' I call it when I'm in an egghead mood."[140]

In Kazan's novel *The Under-study* (1975), the aging Sidney Castleman notes the importance of expressing fundamental truths.

> It's not cleverness that gets to people, Sonny. The great plays were not great because of cleverness. Today it's all experiments in style. What counts and what endures is meaning, theme. What you have to touch in an audience is their fundamental concerns, what's worrying them now and always will, even if they don't know it, the mind's despair, the heart's hope.[141]

Having called Kazan "an actor's director" and "a writer's director," I should acknowledge finally that he was always his own director, always his own man. In his words, "I work on the premise that the audience will like to see what I like to make."[142] From the mid-1940s until the early 1960s, no American theatre director could point to a more distinguished career as justification for such artistic self-assertion.

4

Peter Brook and Marat/Sade:

Workshop and Production

Process: From Workshop to Production

Phrases came. Visions came. Beautiful pictures. Beautiful
phrases. But what she wished to get hold of was that very jar on
the nerves, the thing itself before it has been made anything.
Get that and start afresh; get that and start afresh.
— Virginia Woolf, *To the Lighthouse*

By 1963 AND 1964, the period that particu-
larly concerns me here, Peter Brook was an internationally acclaimed
director whose star was going nova. After coming down from Oxford
in 1945 at the age of twenty, he rose with dizzying speed from London club theatres to the Birmingham Repertory Theatre to Stratford
in a single year. At age twenty-two, Brook assumed the self-created
position of director of productions at Covent Garden. He succeeded
on Shaftesbury Avenue and Broadway, in film, television, the British
repertory theatres, and the commercial theatre of Paris. He directed
such British stars as Laurence Olivier, John Gielgud, Edith Evans,
Sybil Thorndike, and Flora Robson, and such international talent as
Orson Welles, Pearl Bailey, Raf Vallone, Jeanne Moreau, and Alfred
Lunt and Lynn Fontanne. From the beginning of his career, Brook's

repertory had a high cultural tone, for in the early years he directed works by Shakespeare, Cocteau, Shaw, Ibsen, Dostoyevsky, and Sartre. During the 1950s, Brook added plays by T. S. Eliot, Thomas Otway, Christopher Fry, Jean Anouilh, Tennessee Williams, Arthur Miller, and Graham Greene, as well as six more by Shakespeare. The climax of his first twenty years as a director was the Róyal Shakespeare Company (RSC) production of *King Lear* (1962, toured the Continent and the United States in 1963 and 1964). Starring Paul Scofield and clearly displaying the influence of both Brecht and Beckett, this production was arguably the most influential *Lear* since Shakespeare's original script was restored on the stage in the early nineteenth century. Brook created theatrical proof of the critical proposition that the apocalyptic and nihilistic *Lear* was displacing the psychological and individualistic *Hamlet* as the great example of Shakespearean tragedy and as the most meaningful Shakespearean parable for our lives in the second half of the twentieth century.

And still, like Virginia Woolf's painter, Lily Briscoe, Brook was restless for "the thing itself before it has been made anything." From the late 1950s through the 1960s, Brook repeatedly described himself as "searching" and "experimenting." This experimental phase of his career, with its questions about audience and abstraction, eventually led Brook to abandon commercial theatre for the International Centre of Theatre Research (CIRT), the continuing noncommercial workshop he founded in Paris in 1970. One particular period in this phase, during 1963–1964, presents an interesting study. In the first part of this chapter, I describe how Brook's workshop investigations of Antonin Artaud's ideas during that period began a process issuing in his famous production of Peter Weiss's *Marat/Sade*. In the second part I analyze this production.

Sir Barry Jackson called Brook "the youngest earthquake I've known," and many others have described him as a surprisingly forceful person with a style to match.[1] At the beginning of his production of *The Brothers Karamazov* in 1946, the theatre grew dark until even the exit lights went out, and suddenly a gunshot rang out. In his production of *Dark of the Moon* three years later, he made audiences gasp at a young witch hanging upside down from the proscenium arch and staged a revival meeting scene that Kenneth Tynan remembered as "one of the most exciting events I had ever witnessed on the stage."[2]

Surprise endings became a Brook trademark. So did plays with flashy dramaturgy, poetic words, and faraway, fantastic locations. In his formative period, the 1940s, he found British theatre as colorless as wartime and postwar Britain, and he saw there a "great gap between good material and indifferent achievement." Consequently, he elected to direct by "shaping, turning, shifting actors and materials in a certain direction, a new direction."[3] "When I first started work," he has recalled, "what seemed to me most important was that the result should be alive."[4] His reputation for "ingenious" directing grew until, as one actress said, "No one could mention Peter without prefixing the word 'clever' to his name, and in an odd way, it trivialized all his work."[5]

Brook has had a radical effect on the classical drama he has directed so often. "To communicate any one of Shakespeare's plays to a present day audience," he wrote in 1948, a director "must be prepared to set every resource of modern theatre at the disposal of his text."[6] No William Poel bare-boards antiquarianism here, and no phony "tradition" either—that was only "orthodox post-Victorian" style, said Brook. At the Shakespeare Quatercentenary of 1964, he urged the RSC "through bold experiment and the risk of failure, to create a new tradition, to put into question the entire process of interpretation, to revivify Shakespeare's meaning, moment for moment, with today's means for today's spectators."[7] At times he has sounded cavalier on the subject of reviving the Bard: "I do not for one moment question the principle of rewriting Shakespeare—after all, the texts do not get burned."[8] But Brook's basic position, which is both radical and controversial, has always been that finding and conveying "Shakespeare's meaning" is the goal of a production and that such meaning resides less in the text per se than in "the essential living heart of the play—the poetic inner dream." Directors should find that dream's "theatrical correlatives," not merely respect its textual dress.[9] At his best, when Brook has found the inner dream of a play, he has created productions that seem to explode into meaning. After Tom Johnson of New York's *Village Voice* had seen Brook's *Carmen*—four singers, an orchestra of fifteen, one eighty-minute act of heavily rewritten plot—in Paris in 1982, he began his review with words that echo those of dozens of earlier critics: "It was as if I had never seen *Carmen* before. It was almost as if I had never seen an opera before."[10]

Brook's preference for meaning over text may help explain his frequent forays into the fringes of the Shakespearean canon. He made his directing debut at Stratford in 1946 with an unloved and neglected comedy full of high-minded wit, *Love's Labour's Lost,* which he reclaimed for the modern theatre by the single stroke of taking Watteau as his decorative model. A few years later, with John Gielgud as his leading actor, Brook succeeded with *Measure for Measure* (1950), and *The Winter's Tale* (1951), both unpopular works in those years. His ultimate reclamation project was *Titus Andronicus* starring Olivier and Leigh (Stratford, 1955; London, 1956; on tour, 1957), a production characterized by veteran Shakespeareans as "a miracle." Of course Brook gained a reputation; he had achieved a huge intellectual and popular success with Shakespeare's "worst play." Tynan's witty review of the revived *Titus* and Peter Hall's *Cymbeline* featured the following mock advertisement:

Hall & Brook, Ltd., the Home of Lost Theatrical Causes. Collapsing plays shored up, unspeakable lines glossed over, unactable scenes made bearable. Wrecks salvaged, ruins refurbished: unpopular plays at popular prices. Masterpieces dealt with only if neglected. Shakespearean juvenilia and senilia our specialty: if it can walk, we'll make it run. Bad last acts no obstacle: if it peters out, call Peter in. Don't be fobbed off with Glenvilles, Woods, or Zadeks: look for the trademark—Hall & Brook.[11]

Critics have sometimes said that Brook merely makes clever theatre from minor drama, but a look at the record proves otherwise: *Romeo and Juliet* in 1947, *Hamlet* in 1955, *Lear* in 1962, *A Midsummer Night's Dream* in 1970, and, at last count, three productions of *The Tempest.* It is more accurate to say that he has made successes out of major and minor plays and that he makes a success by blowing the dust off the forgotten dream at the heart of a Shakespearean work.

His *Titus Andronicus* exemplifies the qualities that made his early directing famous: critical ingenuity, vivid decoration, and questing experimentalism. For centuries this play had been scorned by critics and neglected by theatres (it had been an outcast even at Stratford), but Brook found *Titus* to be a moving study of madness, social collapse, and apocalyptic pessimism—ideas and subjects that were a good deal more relevant after 1945 than before. Brook cut and reinterpreted the flawed dialogue, ingeniously turning a classroom laughing stock into vaulting poetic theatre. The eye was dazzled by a unit set depicting the Andronici tomb, which then opened to reveal landscapes and Titus's blood-red study. The ear was assaulted by a *musique concrète* sound track, "sounding rather as if it were scored for Malayan nose-flute, deep-sea tuba, and the Gorgon's eyeball," according to Penelope Gilliatt.[12] Brook abstracted the play's grotesque violence: Vivien Leigh, as the raped and mutilated Lavinia, struck pretty poses with pretty red ribbons dripping from her arms and mouth. His interest in primitive societies and ritual led him to view the play as "a dark flowing current out of which surge the horrors, rhythmically and logically related . . . the expression of a powerful and eventually beautiful barbaric ritual."[13] The result was that spectators fainted. Critics called the production "compulsive and incantatory" and said that it communicated the "original foulness of primitive blood sacrifice."[14] He was greatly aided by a classic performance from Laurence Olivier, then at the peak of his stage career. Olivier illuminated the hero's military bearing, his loss of control, his mad destruction of a world that was destroying him, and his wild attempt, in the last three acts, to control his incipient madness by expressing it in eloquent metaphors. But this was "Brook's *Titus Andronicus*" if ever the possessive could be used to indicate a director's influence. This ambitious director also edited the text, designed the sets, designed the costumes, and recorded the show's sound track. As a devotee and friend of the elderly Gordon Craig, Brook understood the ambition necessary to be an "Artist of the Theatre." He began putting "Peter Brook's Production of" on his programs at a tender age.

But lest my reader think that Brook was too much the solipsistic tyrant and master of the *übermarionette,* I should note that he walked into the first rehearsal of his first big production, the Stratford *Love's Labour's Lost,* carrying the carefully prepared *Regiebuch* associated with tyrannical directors. When he saw that his visualizations did not match the flesh and blood in the room, Brook closed his book and began to experiment. He became famous for saying, "I don't know." He encouraged looseness of staging and interpretation until very late in the rehearsal process. Designers and technicians fidgeted while he waited for visual or musical ideas to emerge during rehearsals. He stood by while actors thrashed through their parts on their own and frequently drove them to exhaustion in his relentless search for a breakthrough. Some actors hated Brook's method. Others as various as Gielgud, Alfred Lunt, and Diana Rigg thought him a Svengali. But he would not base his direction on old ideas, neither his own nor a tradition's. Consequently, his best directing has had a freshness virtually without parallel in modern British theatre.

"I don't know." These words might have served as his motto during the late 1950s and early 1960s when his career began to change. He showed other signs of change in his mid-thirties: more interest in film, and a preference for plays by Jean Genet, Friedrich Dürrenmatt, and Rolf Hochhuth, so that his repertory took on a more political flavor. But this period of change was dominated by Brook's doubt, by his radical questioning of theatre. Why and how were words part of theatre? What was the correct relation of actor to audience? Was the theatre progressive enough for its time? Were its troubles ascribable to the economic conservatism of its managements? To the shapes of its theatre houses? To a failure of spirit? Finally, was there any legitimate need for theatre in modern Western culture? On into the 1970s he pursued this question: "How to make theatre absolutely and fundamentally *necessary* to people, as necessary as eating and sex?" He had concluded that "make believe is *necessity*."[15]

Brook's first line of questioning concerned realism. His reaction against it was already evident in his abstract set designs. But his reaction was also literary. He felt that Ibsenite dramaturgy failed to embody modern ideas of time, self, or reality:

> We know that the theatre lags behind the other arts because its continual need for immediate success chains it to the slowest members of its audience. But is there nothing in the revolution that took place in painting fifty years ago that applies to our own crisis today? Do we know where we stand in relation to the real and the unreal, the face of life and its hidden streams, the abstract and the concrete, the story and the ritual? (1960)[16]

Brook knew that his search was in the direction of hidden streams, abstraction, and ritual. Theatre could be "real, dramatic and meaningful" and still abandon the "traditional crutches" of clock time, consistent characterization, and suspenseful plotting. He wanted to show "the true driving forces of our time" rather than superficial "social problems." "And are we sure that in relation to twentieth-century living, the great abstractions—speed, strain, space, frenzy, energy, brutality—aren't more concrete, more immediately likely to affect our lives than the so-called concrete issues?"[17]

The Victorian psychology still in the baggage of realistic "characterization" would no longer serve, even though new writers like John Osborne continued to rely on it. Brook preferred to experiment with "characters behaving out of character," with "the lies, inconsistency, and total confusion of daily life."

> What are we—you and I? Things enclosed in solid, stolid frames? Rather, we are at any instant a flow of mental pictures that stream from us and superimpose themselves on the outside world, sometimes coinciding with it, sometimes contradicting it. We are all at once voices, thoughts, words, half-words, echoes, memories, impulses. We change purpose from instant to instant. . . . I do not recognize myself or my neighbor in those closed and finite dummies that "characterization" gives us. (1960)[18]

Realistic dialogue, even words themselves, seemed terribly problematic when subjected to his questioning. Like other artists and intellectuals in the late 1950s and early 1960s, Brook raised a dread specter before the literary community—"the death of the word," He contrasted the dialogue in classical drama (in which words were the play's primary reality) and non-Western theatre (in which words were aesthetically subsidiary) with contemporary drama's realistic dialogue, whose words were absolutely dominant but empty of content—constituting blather, evasion. "I don't believe in the word much today, because it has outlived its purpose," he said. "Words don't communicate, they don't express much, and most of the time they fail abysmally to refine."[19] To Brook it was "an age of images," and he wondered if "we must go through a period of image-saturation, for the need for language to re-emerge?"[20]

"Outer reality" or some steadily photographic image of it could not be relied on, and Brook recommended showing the world as images "in endless flux, with barriers and boundaries that come and go, people and situations forming, unforming before my eyes." Such expressionism would show reality breaking down into our perception of it. A newer abstractionism, the "inner realism" he was urging on theatre, would show states "of movement and flux" where the abstractions of modern life—"the true forces which impel our false identities"—became "stronger and clearer and more defined."[21] Theatre could abandon behavior, speech, and the materialistic world; he opted on the one hand for psychological revelation and on the other for poetic expression of those social and human forces that were shaping the era.

Brook's line of questioning about theatrical imagery was fundamentally modernist, by which I mean that twentieth-century art attitude in which self-consciousness about both life and art makes formal experimentation not only the normative procedure (thus "the myth of the avant-garde") but also a topic in itself—conception and process thus becoming subjects for art. For a new modernist theatre Brook saw propitious signs, including the art market's enthusiasm about Picasso and abstract expressionism. Film was an even more relevant example—he noted that *Last Year at Marienbad* (1961), a film that evoked the modernist novels of the 1920s, was in international distribution. The *nouvelle vague* directors and the *Cahiers du Cinéma* school of criticism were familiar to Brook, for he frequently lived in Paris, knew the relevant French innovators, and was himself considered a collateral *vaguiste* on the strength of *Moderato Cantabile* (1960), his effort at "photographing the intangible."[22] In the early 1960s, Brook was prescient in prophesying a similarly modernist theatrical wave. Over the next decade, actors, directors, and writers would increasingly reject realistic convention as an artistic stranglehold, choosing instead to experiment with imagism and formal self-consciousness.

Brook's second line of questioning concerned audiences. His directing before 1960 had stressed beautiful pictures—composition and cutting à la film—but pictures implicitly isolated from the audience. In his search for a new theatre, he investigated the transaction between actors and audiences. He placed an actor on a stage facing an audience and asked, Is he interesting? Has he captured our attention? Why or why not? Jerzy Grotowski noticed this emphasis in Brook's work soon after they became acquaintanced and made the following comparison: "My search is based on the director and the actor. You base yours on the director, actor, and audience." Brook agreed, saying that "the only thing that all forms of theatre have in common is the need for an audience."[23] In 1973, after having taken his CIRT troupe to Africa, he said:

What is of total importance is that the theatre phenomenon only exists when the chemical meeting of what has been prepared by a group of people, and is incomplete, comes into relationship with another group, a wider circle which is the people who are there as spectators. When a fusion takes place, then there is a theatre event. When the fusion doesn't take place there is no event.[24]

Brook is not describing good theatre or successful theatre or ideal theatre but the "theatre event," which *"only exists when"* actors and audience move each other to affective and intellectual interaction.

The relation between actor and spectator ultimately becomes the relation between theatre and community. Brook stated this credo when he founded CIRT: "The special virtue of the theatre as an art form is that it is inseparable from the community."[25] This partially explains his lifelong fascination with Shakespeare and the Elizabethan theatrical model. If Grotowski was aiming at "a new Mass," Brook wanted "a new Elizabethan relationship—linking the private and the public, the intimate and the crowded, the secret and the open, the vulgar and the magical."[26] He believed that theatre could still serve as a crucible, or a forum where "this fragmented world comes together and for a certain time it can rediscover the marvel of organic life. The marvel of being one."[27] But, given the social climate of the early 1960s, theatre would have to disturb in order to create the interactive theatrical event. Disturbance, he believed, was theatre's "one precise social function"; anything less was an indication of artistic and intellectual bad faith. His message to a London interviewer at the time of *Marat/Sade* was that:

> violence is the natural artistic language of the times. A play must leave you in a more receptive mood than you were before. It isn't there to "move" people. That's a ghastly idea. You cry, you have a bath of sentiment. You come out saying you've had a lovely time. I prefer the notion of disturbance which leaves you in a greater state of disturbance.[28]

Disturbance and division dominated the headlines in 1963 and 1964. The presidents of the United States and South Vietnam were assassinated within the same month in 1963. Vatican II ended in disharmony, and *The Deputy* created a storm among Catholics both inside and outside theatres on several continents. China and the Soviet Union had a historic falling-out and thus split the international Left. France refused Britain entry into the Common Market, thus intensifying the traditional enmity between them. The streets of the world were centers of disruption during these years: Buddhists burned themselves with frightening regularity, British youths waged war as Mods and Rockers, and, in the United States, blacks were burned, bombed, shocked, and stoned. The ideological camps of American politics prepared for the most divisive election campaign in years, the Johnson-Goldwater contest of 1964. The generation gap was an issue in many fields. Young Cassius Clay bought a life of controversy by defeating the older Sonny Liston for the heavyweight boxing title and announcing that the champ was now a Black Muslim named Muhammad Ali. The Beatles paid their first visit to the United States, creating the beginnings of a youth culture, in which many saw popular music as a vehicle of political and cultural protest. A thousand irrationalities bloomed in this atmosphere. The youthful counterculture promoted a romantic derangement of the senses, in which drug states, prophetic vision, madness, and philosophical borrowings from Oriental religions were often equated. William Blake's literary stock shot up, as did that of the surrealists and the Beats. Two prominent objects of cultural analysis were "The Bomb" (even more threatening after the Cuban missile crisis of 1962) and the concentration camps (a well-publicized 1964 trial of ex-Auschwitz personnel was a reminder of that particular horror). And the fractiousness of 1963/64 was only a beginning, for almost a decade of televised conflict, hatred, and disturbance was still to come. A participant in the disturbed times might well have said, as did the Young Man in Artaud's *Spurt of Blood,* "We are intense. Ah, how well ordered the world is!"[29]

Artists of this period, caught up by the enthusiasm for disruption and irrationality, found an ideal predecessor and prophet in Antonin Artaud (1896–1948). During the 1920s and 1930s, Artaud had achieved a certain notoriety as a surrealist poet and theatre artist in Paris, but his mental instability prevented most of his endeavors from enjoying sustained success. He was an occasional actor, particularly in film, whose work demonstrated questionable skill but startling intensity. He not only wrote for and acted in theatre, but created theatres, including an unsuccessful one named for Alfred Jarry, the great precursor (*Ubu Roi,* 1896) of modernist irrationality in drama. Artaud was more efficient at creating a theatre in his hyperactive imagination, particularly that imaginary construction we call "The Theatre of Cruelty" after his famous manifestos on the subject. In these fervid theatrical writings, he projected an art that would mirror his own madness and, at least ideally, induce madness in its spectators by administering severe theatrical shocks to the nervous system. In his last years, Artaud lost all self-control and was institutionalized, becoming a Poundian madman singing in his cage, terrifying those who encountered him with speech and writing that were a galactic babble. Artaud's madness, rather than his particular activities or achievements, explains his peculiar eminence after his death. His example can be detected in psychological literature of the early 1960s, including Michel Foucault's *Histoire de la folie à l' âge classique* and R. D. Laing's books about schizophrenia as journey. Laing's breathless ending to *The Politics of Experience* is Artaud distilled: "If I could turn you on, if I could drive you out of your wretched mind, if I could tell you I would let you know."[30] Grotowski confirms the importance of Artaud's madness: "Artaud teaches us a great lesson which none of us can refuse. This lesson is his sickness."[31]

During the first decade after his death, Artaud remained a curiosity of the French literary underground, but translation widened his influence in the late 1950s. When M. C. Richards translated Artaud's *The Theatre and Its Double* in 1958, she sent a prepublication copy to the Living Theatre, where Julian Beck "opened it and read one line and quickly read it from start to finish, and then again and again." Beck used nearly identical words to describe his first reading of *The Connection* (1959) and *The Brig* (1963), original plays with which Beck and Judith Malina sought to design an anarchist spectacle worthy of Artaud. They wanted to "so shake people up, so move them, so cause feeling to be felt, there in the body, that the steel world of law and order which civilization had forged to protect itself from barbarism would melt."[32] Artaud was also being translated in Eastern Europe. In 1960, the Polish journal *Dialog* published an Artaud essay that one of Grotowski's actors brought to his attention at the Theatre Laboratory he directed in Opole. Grotowski did not read *The Theatre and Its Double* until 1964, by which time his work was fully developed, but his productions were immediately read in the West as Artaudian. Artaud was also associated with one of the period's most popular experimental playwrights, Jean Genet. Brook began his Artaud workshop in 1964 as a preparation for staging *The Screens*. In the same year, critic Robert Brustein published his study of modern drama entitled *The Theatre of Revolt,* and he included a final chapter on Artaud and Genet.[33] Such prominence given to the ahistorical combination of playwright and poet-theorist could be explained by the general Western interest in social deviance, madness, and things French (new novel, new wave, theatre of the absurd, existentialism). But by the mid-1960s, when *Marat/Sade* had completed its several runs, Artaud had become material for Sunday newspaper supplements, and no theatre student who merited a degree could fail to know the outlines of his thought.

The productions of the Living Theatre between 1959 and 1968 were the most famous example of Artaud's extreme effect on his followers. *The Connection* was an early attempt to capture his visions, but Kenneth Brown's *The Brig,* a documentary about life in a Marine Corps prison, was the first serious opportunity for Beck and Malina to liberate their "madman muse" and to create "a theatre so violent that no man who experienced it would ever stomach violence again." Malina was passionately taken by Artaud's descriptions of a transcendental style of acting—an agonized, convulsive, yet formalized movement that he thought he had seen in the Balinese theatre but could never articulate in the Paris of the 1930s. In an epigraph to her article on directing *The Brig,* Malina quoted him on the "mystic athletic play of bodies and the undulatory use of the stage." In this article she quoted phrases about the "physical obsession of muscles quivering with affectivity," about the director's need to "conduct in the physical domain an exploration of intense movement and precise emotional gesture," and about acting that unleashed "certain blind forces which activate what they must activate and crush and burn on their way what they must crush and burn."[34] Drawing on the actual Marine Corps Brig Regulations for authenticity, and both Erwin Piscator and Meyerhold for additional inspiration, Malina and her troupe created a production so physically shocking that it aroused demands for a congressional investigation. After *The Brig,* when tax evasion charges against Beck and Malina led to the loss of their New York theatre and their brief imprisonment, the Living Theatre moved to Europe, where the influence of Artaud on its productions grew ever stronger. Their all-male version of *The Maids* by Genet, the Artaudian dramatist of the moment, was a repertory staple during 1965 and 1966. They contemplated a production of *The Balcony,* and their failure to mount one was a loss to modern theatre, since Genet's play was appropriate to their program of sexual and political liberation. The second and canonical version of *Mysteries and Smaller Pieces* (1964) ended with a long, beautiful section called "The Plague," an image lifted from Artaud. *Frankenstein* (1965), *Antigone* (1967), and *Paradise Now* (1968), all influenced by Artaud, were the other productions that established the Living Theatre's reputation, during the late 1960s, as the world's premiere experimental group.

Brook became interested in Artaud at approximately the same time as Malina and Beck. I do not know when he first read Artaud, or whether he first read him in French, but Brook began quoting the famous essays in 1960. Late in that year, after finishing his work on the Broadway *Irma La Douce,* he saw *The Connection* and traveled to Mexico, as had Artaud, to investigate a rural Indian culture. A year later, Brook began and ended his article entitled "Search for a Hunger" with quotations from Artaud on theatrical necessity. At the time of *Marat/Sade,* Brook gave a series of lectures on theatre (published as his famous book, *The Empty Space,* in 1968) in which he made Artaud the leading spokesman for "The Holy Theatre," the theatre of invisible-made-visible. When *Marat/Sade* was brought to the United States in 1965/66, Brook was repeatedly interviewed about the Theatre of Cruelty—could audiences feel safe in their seats? He patiently explained that cruelty did not mean bloodshed and torture but rigor and attack on defenses.

Brook viewed Artaud as he would view any serious influence— from a critical distance. Like Grotowski, the English director was convinced that Artaud's value was primarily inspirational rather than practical. His ideas wanted assent rather than study. Brook criticized Artaud's stylistics, all that yearning "for darkness and mystery, for chanting, for unearthly cries . . . for vast shapes, masks, for kings and emperors and popes, for saints and sinners and flagellants, for black tights and writhing naked skins."[35] Even as decorative style this had serious limitations. Brook would turn the lights up full and try to stimulate wakefulness and intelligence in his audiences. He argued strenuously against Artaud's urge to overwhelm audiences, to put them into trances of passive receptivity. That was *proto*fascist, Brook said, and his criticism shows the simultaneous influence of Brecht during this period.

Yet Artaud qualified as teacher because he asked extremely radical questions. He too condemned realism for disguising human nature and human perception. He too desired a passionately disturbing connection with the audience. Like Brook, Artaud was intrigued by the

Orient, inclined to see theatre as ritual, and inclined to make apoca-
lyptic-pessimistic conclusions about human nature and history. Both
believed that texts were secondary in theatre and that "the play, the
event itself, stands in place of a text." Brook increasingly adopted an
Artaudian tone, embodied in this celebrated quotation from *The
Empty Space:*

> Is there another language, just as exacting for the author, as a lan-
> guage of words? Is there a language of actions, a language of sounds —
> a language of word-as-part-of movement, of word-as-lie, word-as-par-
> ody, of word-as-rubbish, of word-as-contradiction, of word-shock or
> word-cry? If we talk of the more-than-literal, if poetry means that
> which crams more and penetrates deeper—is this where it lies?[36]

If this sounds strange coming from the period's most famous Shakespearean director, it is that much more indicative of the crisis in the
theatre of the 1960s.

Peter Hall, the other younger star among British directors, sensed
that crisis too, and when he took over the RSC in the early 1960s, he
asked Brook to join the new organization as chief of exploration. The
first fruit of Brook's leadership was *King Lear* in 1962. His experi-
mention became even more pronounced during the special RSC
workshop he initiated in the autumn of 1963. Brook took the workshop's title and theme, "The Theatre of Cruelty," from Artaud's most
famous writings. His mission was to explore new theatrical language
and form.

Joseph Chaikin, one of the most widely influential experimenta-
lists of the 1960s and 1970s, has explained the need for workshops as
follows:

> Julian Beck said that an actor has to be like Columbus: he has to go out
> and discover something, and come back and report on what he discov-
> ers. Voyages have to be taken, but there has to be a place to come back
> to, and this place has to be different from the established theatre. It is
> not likely to be a business place.[37]

This analysis has been confirmed (especially during the early 1960s)
by theatre artists around the world.

At a Warsaw theatre conference in the summer of 1963, a Grotowski assistant named Eugenio Barba passed around copies of an
essay describing a Theatre Laboratory in Opole and told anyone who

would listen how Grotowski's group, founded in 1959 with eight actors, was changing the face of modern theatre. Barba persuaded a group of conferees—among them, Michael Kustow, who was to become Brook's assistant in the Theatre of Cruelty workshop—to see a performance of Grotowski's *Dr. Faustus*. At this time, very few people in or out of Poland knew about Grotowski's work. Andrzej Wirth, who did, had found his earlier productions quite bad, but this *Dr. Faustus* seemed "an astonishing demonstration of a mature doctrine in practical application."[38] As the productions improved and gained notoriety, Grotowski became internationally known for a revolutionary approach to texts, an extreme acting style, and an instinct for theatre-as-laboratory.

Joseph Chaikin left New York in that summer of 1963 to work at Chicago's Second City Playwrights Unit, but he planned to return East in the fall to rejoin a newly created organization called the Open Theater. This was not a performing unit but a study group founded by ex-students of a New York acting coach named Nola Chilton, one of Chaikin's earliest teachers and influences. Chaikin had just graduated from the Living Theatre with his performance as Galy Gay in *Man Is Man* (late 1962). Tired and distracted by the Becks' constant agitation, he now wanted a calmer atmosphere. He also wanted a chance to extend and explore theatrical technique, beginning with a nonrealistic approach to Method acting that he had learned from Chilton. During his summer in Chicago, Chaikin studied with Viola Spolin, whose continuing experimentation with improvisation was yielding widely various stylistic discoveries, particularly about subtext and nonrepresentation. (Spolin's collection of exercises, *Improvisation for the Theater,* was first published in 1963; her son, Paul Sills, soon made those techniques nationally famous by using them in his "Story Theatre" productions.[39]) Thus when Chaikin returned to New York in the fall and began his first serious workshop, he used games, transformations, sound-and-movement, mirrors, machines, and orchestras. The Open Theater would not become a public performing group for another two years, and when it did, it presented plays and improvisations generated from within its workshops.

During that same summer, Peter Brook was acting most distinctly like a successful commercial director, for 1963 was a year in which he mounted five productions in four cities in two languages. But he was committing his autumn to an experimental workshop for which he already had a collaborator, a bank account, a rehearsal hall, and a sacred text. He did not have a serious performance deadline ahead of him. Brook also had a part in initiating and promoting use of the workshop in the contemporary theatre. A workshop is neither an acting class nor a rehearsal, though it may sometimes resemble both. Historically, its foundations are in the Moscow Art Theatre's Studios, and, like "studio" and "laboratory," the term "workshop" describes a place for experimenting and creating, not a product. Many workshop directors begin without any text. Others introduce one as an aid, reference, or beginning. (Richard Schechner investigated *The Bacchae* and then made *Dionysus in 69,* and Joseph Chaikin began the workshops that issued in *The Serpent* with exercises based on the Bible.) The workshop's only imperative is to explore various aspects of theatre, stylistic options, and actor potentialities. This means that the best workshop leaders are often teachers, inventors, or explorers, not necessarily successful directors. It also means that some freedom from deadlines and financial worry is necessary so that the participants can feel free to examine just those accidents or fundamental questions that are so frequently shunted aside in rehearsal. Personally and institutionally, workshops require a certain openness, a receptivity to internal or interactive moments, a license to guess, develop, discover, grow, and try alternatives. There are possible dangers in the method, including an endless addiction to process, a frustrating directionlessness, and an excessive psychotherapeutic focus. But the advantages may be summarized by noting that a workshop is a form of research; its results are not shows but ideas (hypotheses, even conclusions).

The workshops established during the 1960s and 1970s were a result of a widespread dissatisfaction, similar to Brook's, with realistic acting and dramaturgy. Notwithstanding their local differences, these workshops posed at least four general questions and arrived at some provisional answers that deserve to be called experimental. First, how could Western theatre rediscover an expressive style beyond realistic portrayal of behavior? (Their answers: release the body, explore the subconscious, look to the East, and analyze the implied or hidden meanings of texts.) Second, how could the actor's whole human mechanism be liberated to achieve this new expressivity? (Study mind-body connections and systems of parsing human nature that go beyond traditional mind-body dichotomies.) Third, how could theatre distinguish itself from the more popular and automatic dramatic media? (Become modernist at the risk of becoming obscurantist. Emphasize concept and presence over narrative and spectacle, the areas where theatre feels its handicaps.) Finally, how could actors and directors relate to the audience? (Engage them more directly, with eyes and with body, with the moment's political imperative, with psychologically direct, nonrealistic imagery.)

In the RSC workshop of 1963, Brook's questions and experimental procedures intersected with those of his collaborator, Charles Marowitz, a young American who had emigrated to London in 1957 after Off Broadway experience and Method training in New York. Upon arriving, Marowitz had joined the staff of *Encore*, which would be the most influential theatre magazine in Britain during the next decade, and built a reputation for himself as a theatre reviewer on both sides of the Atlantic. He also became active in London's "fringe" theatre, founding a group called In-Stage and directing plays by Beckett, Murray Schisgal, and Paul Ableman. Marowitz's exposure to Artaud in the late 1950s intensified his reaction against realism and Stanislavskyism. He began directing even stranger plays, by Genet, Fernando Arrabal, and René de Obaldia. In the early 1960s, Brook asked Marowitz to join the RSC experimental wing that Hall was creating. Marowitz and Brook, the latter believed, were "looking in the same direction—even if not actually seeing eye to eye."[40] Marowitz worked first on *King Lear* as assistant director, resident gadfly, and Boswellian recorder. His next major assignment was the Theatre of Cruelty, where his experimental methods dominated the auditions for the workshop.

Marowitz surprised the actors by letting individuals present their familiar audition pieces but then asking for the same speech as spoken by another character (Hamlet giving Romeo's balcony speech, for instance). He subsequently had each actor superimpose a third image on the text and then switched the actor rapidly from one image to another. In discontinuous improvisations, he shifted the reality base as new actors entered the scene. He set them to speaking nonsense texts and gave them objects for free association, and led groups of eight to ten through sets of exercises. Such procedures were highly irregular in the London theatre world of 1963, but Marowitz was searching for an unusual sensitivity. He whittled a group of fifty actors down to twelve (their average age was twenty-four; only one was over thirty). Collectively, they had little experience in the West End or in major repertory theatres. When Marowitz exhibited his dozen for Brook's approval, the senior director objected to only one, a twenty-seven-year-old graduate of the Royal Academy of Dramatic Art who had performed sporadically with regional repertory groups and most recently in London productions of *The Idiot* (1962) and *Alfie* (1963) and in the movie *This Sporting Life* (1963). So unimpressed was Brook with this woman (he wondered if Marowitz had romantic designs) that he needed serious reassurance before accepting Glenda Jackson into the Theatre of Cruelty group.

The leaders of the workshop had a twelve-week limit and a vague intention to produce some kind of final exhibition. For eight hours a day, beginning at 10 A.M., they worked in a bare wooden church hall behind the Royal Court Theatre in Sloane Square. At night, Brook and Marowitz conferred by telephone on the next day's work.

On the first day, before they had completed the introductions, the directors gave each actor an ordinary object and the instruction to explore the object's tonal range—not just the sounds it might yield in normal usage, but any sounds. This exercise was typical of the experimentation in this workshop, for Brook and Marowitz intended to explore vocal sound beyond "grammatical combinations of the alphabet" and physical movement beyond "facsimiles" of social behavior. They believed that by dislodging the familiar and bringing it into the realm of the abstract, actors could "communicate feelings and ideas" in a new way.[41]

An exercise called "similes" began with realism to achieve an effect that was beyond realism. An actor played an ordinary improvised scene realistically—a man arrived home, found a note, and read some shattering news. At this pressure point the directors redirected the actor to another style, making him express the shattered reaction through pure sound or abstract gesture. "The final beat is an externalized expression of the character's inner state and totally non-naturalistic," said Marowitz.[42] Simile, they found, tells us not only that A is like B but that B expresses (aspects of) A. The trope throws an imaginative veil over the subject *(A)*, poeticizes it.

In another exercise, "essentials," the actors played a scene and then labeled each beat with a single sentence describing the vital content. They then repeated the scene playing only these sentences in sequence. Sentences were progressively reduced to key words, which were also played as a scene, and finally each key word was reduced to its most prominent sound. At this point the original scene had been divested of its realism, leaving a short, essentialized, and quite nonmimetic core. It is a technique that Gorchakov described Stanislavsky using, but Marowitz and Brook were interested in the essentialized results not only as pedagogy but as product.

In the search for essentials, Brook placed sometimes "drastic" restrictions on the actor's expressive means. How much could spectators understand from a motionless, silent actor imagining "a dramatic situation that did not involve any physical movement?" (The answer was, of course, very little.) "What was the very least [the actor] needed before understanding could be reached: was it a sound, a movement, a rhythm—and were these interchangeable—or had each its special strengths and limitations?"[43] Thoughts and desires were presented using one finger, a single vocal tone, cries, whistles.

Using another method, inspired by Artaud and Meyerhold, the directors forced the actors to speak while performing difficult physical exertions, so that the voice of the straining body overcame the actor's ordinary vocal habits or tricks. Since Brook found language, especially the language of classical drama, increasingly meaningless, he wondered whether the shock of the "physical" voice might not provide a tonic. "Get thee to a nunnery," if spoken by a man swinging upside down above a woman, might mean something new, or (given the prevailing artistic crisis) it might mean anything at all.

This kind of theatre work has been the subject of various misunderstandings. Some have claimed that such exercises are really calisthentics—designed to improve actors' equivalents of muscle tone, flexibility, and strength—when in fact they were designed to provoke expression for its own sake. Another misconception is that such work is just more improvisation, a method particularly distrusted in the British theatre. (Even Brook, the innovator, could scold improvisers for "lending themselves blindly to their inner impulses.")[44] These sound-and-movement exercises are no more innately improvisatorial than the techniques of modern dance, with which they are frequently confused.

At its best, this nonmimetic technique of abstract sound and movement offered a new kind of poetry to the theatre of the 1960s. Paul Goodman had predicted its outlines in 1955 when he described the "pre-verbal" aspect of his own plays:

> I am well aware that the actors we have are quite unable both by character and training to open their throats to such sounds or loosen their limbs to such motions. But this is also why they simply cannot read

poetic lines. It would be worthwhile, to the renovation of our art, to make a number of plays of just these pre-verbal elements in abstraction, as the painters have returned to the elements of color and form.[45]

Painting and dance had advanced beyond representationalism and had become arts of pure form, subconscious vision, and abstract energy. Romantic verse had long since established poetry as the rendering of consciousness, no matter that it was fragmentary, incoherent, and divorced from materialism. Beckett was already creating a dramatic tradition in which even the most prosaic stories could aspire to the condition of poetry if they included arias of consciousness. A theatre of sound and movement was another way to bury Galsworthy and Dreiser and Soviet realism and all those dreary prose Gradgrinds. Brook called it a new "language."

But he and Marowitz took pains to point out that it was a language—a medium for expression—and not merely a nonverbal "experience." They criticized those who believed that "all the essential action lies" in the subtextual world. Increasingly the heretic Stanislavskian, Marowitz criticized "the Method actor's test for truthfulness . . . the intensity and authenticity of his personal feeling" and considered it better to adopt the attitude of the Artaudian actor: "unless that feeling has been shaped into a communicative image, it is a passionate letter without postage."[46] Brook's summary of the workshop stressed this "most important result": the individual actor "was led inexorably to the conclusion that he needed form. It was not enough to feel passionately—a creative leap was required to mint a new form which could be a container and a reflector for his impulses. That is what is truly called an 'action.'"[47]

The demand for form led them to explore structure as well as isolated images. The modernist in Brook kept challenging the limits and transmutations of traditional narrative. Ritual seemed a provocative solution to the problem of structure, so they experimented with patterned repetitions. They frequently worked on exercises that we can lump together as "discontinuities" (for example, their disrupted audition pieces), which trained actors to respond to changing premises in mid-speech, mid-gesture, and mid-scene. Such exercises closely resembled the Open Theater's techniques of "transformation" and had a similar rationale. A discontinuous acting style, according to Marowitz, "corresponded to the broken and fragmentary way in which most people experience contemporary reality."[48]

As an abstract, modernist grammar began to emerge from the workshop experiments, Brook and Marowitz realized that their next significant step would be to explore the relationship between actor and audience.

In *The Empty Space,* Brook described the experimental atmosphere of the early 1960s:

> At a time when all sands are shifting, the search is automatically a search for form. The destruction of old forms, the experimenting with new ones: new words, new relationships, new places, new buildings; they all belong to the same process, and any individual production is just a separate shot at an unseen target.[49]

When the Theatre of Cruelty workshop presented its experimental forms in public performance on January 12, 1964, the group appeared in a new place, a flexibly designed theatre inside the London Academy of Music and Dramatic Art (LAMDA). The ten actors in the program were Mary Allen, Jonathan Burn, Richard Dare, Freda Dowie, Rob Inglis, Glenda Jackson, Alexis Kanner, Leon Lissek, Robert Lloyd, and Susan Williamson. The performances were conducted on a "theatre club" basis to avoid censorship. In a publicity release, Brook promised not experimental plays but an exploration of "theatre-language." It would be "a collage, a form of surrealist revue composed of shots in the dark, shots at distant targets." "This experiment," he said with characteristic deadpan, "is not primarily a literary one."[50]

They performed Artaud's short, hallucinatory *Spurt of Blood* and then repeated it using nothing but screams, a device Brook would use in 1971 with Handke's *Kaspar* at CIRT. They also played Paul Ableman's nonsense texts, a mime entitled "The Analysis," and a movement version of a Robbe-Grillet story, as well as some orthodox literary pieces, including a short play by John Arden, *Ars Longa Vita Brevis,* and three scenes from Genet's *The Screens.* But the members of the audience, watching without program or explanation, remained totally unaware of authorship. They probably recognized the strains of *Hamlet,* but the workshop's collage version lasted twenty-eight minutes and consisted of images of the play, not its narrative. (Marowitz later extended this seminal experiment in textual reconstruction first to sixty minutes, then to ninety minutes, and produced it as *The Marowitz Hamlet* in various European theatres during the next few years.)

The company organized the shows loosely, staging impromptu debates between Brook and Marowitz or between Arden and a workshop actor who disliked *Ars Longa,* and frequently presenting improvisations, some based on audience suggestions. Performances also featured demonstrations of workshop methods. On opening night Brook rehearsed the scene between Richard III and Lady Anne, essentializing from a normal rendition to a wordless, gestural version and, finally, to a series of facial expressions. The directors adapted this loosely organized format without much concern for sustaining audience attention, for they did not want to produce a play or to "do a show" so much as to display their experiments in public. They came to regret that decision, for spectators and reviewers, however intrigued by individual items, found the evening generally unsatisfying and the program incoherent.

Perhaps the most successful piece was "The Public Bath." In this four-minute imagist playlet created by Brook himself, Glenda Jackson was led forward and stripped of all her clothes while an actor read a *Times* report about the Christine Keeler case, which was then dominating the headlines. The naked Jackson was then put in a tub and bathed in a way suggestive of ritual purification. As the reading of the Keeler report continued, Jackson was dressed in prison clothes. Then, as the report was read again, the other actors picked up the bathtub and paraded around the room with it on their shoulders. Jackson followed them, wrapped in a shapeless raincoat and surrounded by guards. The bathtub now appeared to be a coffin, the actors were pallbearers, and the guards were fellow mourners. Jackson became by imagistic transformation the very likeness of Jacqueline Kennedy, whose husband had been assassinated less than two months earlier. This stunned the audience, as Brook's best work always does. Spectators saw a woman through a complex of imagery that was tensely and provocatively ambiguous at the same time that it was immediate, fresh from the daily news. Brook also shocked his audience with a naked body and then used this shock to evoke and illuminate symbols of sacred and profane femininity.

Reactions were varied and uncertain. Bamber Gascoigne grumbled in *The Observer* that the LAMDA performance was "a public love affair with the mere idea of newness, supported by wooly romantic notions about the crisis in theatre and society." J. C. Trewin, Brook's biographer, remembers the collage *Hamlet* as "pointless," the whole event as "esoteric."[51] The *Times* reviewer had much the same reaction, being most disturbed by the "distrust of language."[52] Martin Esslin disliked the screaming but called the show "a considerable success."[53] Four years after *Marat/Sade,* Marowitz described the LAMDA performance as "something between a surrealist vaudeville show and an end-of-term program at an artistically inclined mental asylum."[54] Brook called the premiere "interesting" (high praise from him) because the opening-night audience, which had been given little advance information and thus had no preconceptions, had reacted naturally and revealingly. These spectators laughed at pieces that the company thought serious, took seriously material intended as humor. They were caught completely unawares by Jackson's nudity and had no idea where the performance might go at this point. But even by the second night, "the fact that there was *nothing* in the papers in itself telegraphed a reassurance," said Brook. "No news was good news."[55] With their reactions preconditioned by chatter and the media, later audiences did not share an experience quite so immediate and perilous.

By running for slightly over a month, longer than had been anticipated, these Theatre of Cruelty "open workshop" sessions marked another step in Brook's progress. The leaders of the group were pleased, for their experiments had increased their knowledge, they had gained access to contemporary anger and madness, and they had moved beyond mere dissatisfaction with prevailing theatre trends. Marowitz came away deeply influenced by Brook's demystifying approach to classical texts, his instinct to pith the narrative and treat the old plays "not as peerless masterworks, but simply as *material* that could be reworked and rethought."[56] (Artaud's battle cry would ring out more loudly with every passing year: "No More Masterpieces!") Brook's summary of their experience as "a groping towards a theatre, more violent, less rational, more extreme, less verbal, more dangerous" is a good characterization of theatre in the 1960s and of Artaud's vision.[57]

Brook was struck by the importance of the actor in such a theatre. If his early directing had been concerned with the making of images, in the workshop "90 per cent of our work was on the actor—the actor in relation to the audience and in relation to each other."[58] With traditional literary-dramatic values in decline, the actor on stage became even more lonely and naked, and the actor's presence became even more vital to the theatrical event. Four years before, Brook had said:

To me, what matters is the difference between the man who stands motionless on the stage and rivets our attention, and the man who fails to do this. What is the difference? Where, chemically, physically, psychically, does it lie? Star quality, personality? No. I don't know what the answer is. But I know that it is just here, in the answer to this question, that we can find the starting point of our whole art.[59]

On the strength of his experience in the workshop, Brook came to believe that "Holy Theatre," which makes the invisible visible, could accomplish its task "through the performer's presence," so long as there was sufficient theatrical form to contain the presence.[60] He also became a devout believer in the value of workshops themselves, and all his later productions were preceded by similar periods of unstructured searching. Eventually, the workshop was the given, and productions became an occasion.

Two of the pieces Brook created for the LAMDA show—"The Public Bath" and "The Guillotine"—presented images that seem to anticipate *Marat/Sade*. Other anticipations include dramatic debates, nudity, madness, ululation, and cruelty of various kinds. But Brook was just beginning to read Weiss's play at the beginning of 1964. His next step was to bring the workshop's stylistic and conceptual discoveries to a production of Genet's *The Screens*.

Brook was a busy man during the spring of 1964, touring with *King Lear* in Eastern Europe and the United States, collecting an honorary degree, flying to West Berlin to see a new play, and celebrating Shakespeare's 400th birthday. In the midst of all this, he rehearsed *The Screens* for six weeks with a company nearly twice the size of the workshop. The play was a monstrous fairy tale about the Algerian revolution. Confrontation between colonialist Europe and incomprehensible, angry Africa was not only one of Genet's best subjects (compare *The Blacks*) but a variation on one of Brook's favorite thematic situations (compare *Lord of the Flies,* his 1963 film).

In the context of my discussion, the most interesting thing about Brook's work on *The Screens* was its Brechtian aspect. The play, like Brecht's plays, was episodic in structure and political in subject. Brook and Marowitz were intrigued by its mixing of complicated psychology, for which the Artaud experience had prepared them, with "political bedrock." (The same mixture was apparent in *Marat/Sade,* of course, and journalists frequently noted the play's political-psychological dichotomy by attaching the label "Brecht/Artaud.") In rehearsing *The Screens,* Brook and Marowitz adopted such standard Brechtian rehearsal techniques as titling scenes and restyling them into factual reports for courtroom or newspaper. Marowitz explained that alienation was at the heart of their preparatory strategy: "As with Shakespeare, one began to test the truthfulness of every moment in terms of the ring of the words in their context. We found that every moment of naturalism, even the most obvious and unquestionable, benefited by being knocked off balance; by being winged by a metaphor, or studded with a stylization."[61]

This territory was familiar to Brook, especially after his revival of *King Lear,* in which he had gone on a Brechtian tear against catharsis. The most famous and debatable moment in that production came at the end of act 3, scene 7, where the newly blinded Gloucester is left to "smell his way to Dover." Brook eliminated the play's last scrap of compassion by doing away with the servants who help Gloucester at this moment. Then the director brought up the house lights for intermission as Gloucester continued to stumble offstage, so that the audience was forced to watch itself watch (and not help) the devastated blind man. Similarly at the end, on Marowitz's suggestion, Brook deemphasized the final emotional catharsis with yet another storm rumbling in from the distance. Brook was so rough on the *Lear* audiences, so strict about not allowing empathy for old men's destructions, that even Marowitz came to believe the production "more cerebral than moving."[62] But the enthusiastic public approval of the production did more to enlarge Brecht's reputation in Britain than any event since the Berlin Ensemble's London tour of 1956.

Brook could criticize Brecht, particularly his fanatical antipsychological stance, but more often Brook admired him and learned from him. Few dramatists had more thematic "clarity." Few directors had done more to further the "idea of the intelligent actor, capable of judging the value of his contribution." Brook called Brecht "the strongest, most influential and the most radical theatre man of our time" and held up Brechtian theory as the alpha and omega for contemporary theatrical thinkers.[63] Brook spoke highly of alienation, "a new device of quite incredible power," and of its poetic consequences: "Alienation is the language open to us today that is as rich in potentiality as verse."[64] He also admired Brecht's artistry, especially his poetic dramaturgy: "His poetic vision was deeply symbolic, he worked in powerful images, in precise but unrealistic gestures, and precise but unnatural tones of voice. . . . powerful forces . . . made vivid to us in a kaleidoscope of concrete patterns. Here is poetic order."[65] Brook also described Brecht's theatre as "a rich compound of images appealing for our belief," which in turn describes the modernist-poetic theatre that Brook aspired to create.[66]

This quotation also describes the theatre of Jean Genet, the contemporary playwright whom Brook most frequently compared to Brecht. Genet, he thought, was the "most prophetic" voice in modern theatre.[67] Like Brecht and Shakespeare, Genet handled political concerns panoramically. He fused sexual allegory with political fable, portrayed abnormal minds in a changing culture, gave dramatic reality the speed and shimmer of hallucination. Brook's appraisal of *The Screens* echoed his praise for Brecht. The play, he said, avoided the surrealist marsh by virtue of its "rigour of construction and richness of detail," and it had "a geometric structure in which words and actions criss-crossed to produce deeper sense."[68] Brook had confirmed his appreciation of Genet's style in 1960, when he directed the first Paris production of *The Balcony*, using brothel improvisations as his workshop base.

That production, and others in Paris, London, and New York, had put Genet on the celebrity circuit in the early 1960s. Sartre's *Saint Genet: Comédien et Martyr* (1952) was translated into English in 1963, giving a boost to Genet's reputation in English-speaking countries.[69] The publication of *Les Paravents* in 1961 and its English translation, *The Screens*, in 1962 was a major event, partly because the play had a headline subject, Algeria. The play was so controversial in France that, as late as 1966, riots broke out when Jean-Louis Barrault and Madeleine Renaud mounted the first French production, directed by Roger Blin. All these events seemed to conspire to make Brook's RSC version in April 1964 a milestone in modern experimental theatre.

But that production was an incomplete version—the play's first twelve scenes only. Moreover, it was presented obscurely, at a rehearsal hall in Seven Dials, with little RSC promotion and no invitation to the *Times*. Marowitz remembers the whole experience as being a bit desultory until Sally Jacobs's arresting costumes were brought in and saved appearances. What was the reason for this? Was Brook too busy? Was "absurdism" passing its apogee of influence? (Ionesco's conservatism was becoming increasingly visible, Beckett's plays were becoming increasingly short, and prominent younger absurdists, such as Arrabal with his theatre of *panique,* were becoming increasingly independent.) Or was it that *The Screens* was not, finally, Genet's best work? At least to those outside France, it has seemed to lack both the sensational qualities of his earlier works and the literary and intellectual solidity that supported the sensationalism.

The one indisputable triumph in Brook's *Screens* came in scene 10, where two colonists sat in front of screens representing an orange grove at night. As the men talked, a band of Arabs stole in behind them and painted flames on the screens. The chatter continued, and so did the image of revolution, each in completely decorous isolation from the other. In the Artaud workshop, the actors had prepared for this scene with a simile: at the critical point of a realistic scene, instead of using movement or sound, the actor rushed immediately to some paints and painted an expression, "action-painting" style. In the LAMDA performances they had used this device in *Spurt of Blood.* (Brook would work another variation in *Antony and Cleopatra* in the late 1970s.) By the time of *The Screens,* the painting technique had reached its intended maturity and had become an unqualified success. The famous Russian film director Grigori Kozintsev, visiting London that spring, came into the Donmar Rehearsal Theatre and felt like he had been transported back into the Russia of the 1920s. He described the actors using red chalk in "rapid-fire tempo" (this was Brook at his best) to scribble "tongues of flame on to the white screens," eventually covering the paper from top to bottom with "whirling, fiery spots" as the colonists continued to talk. The revolutionaries also wrote the graffiti of war on the screens.[70] Martin Esslin described the sequence in performance as having "an almost unbearable excitement"—another sign of Brook's best work. He called it "a magnificent performance . . . some of the greatest moments I personally have ever witnessed in a theater."[71]

But in retrospect, *The Screens,* which led Brook to initiate the workshop, was an anticlimax, eclipsed historically by the workshop itself and by another, unexpected result.

❖

The Persecution and Assassination of Jean-Paul Marat as Performed by the Inmates of the Asylum of Charenton under the Direction of the Marquis de Sade. The title may have occasioned jokes ("I haven't seen the play but I've read the title" was the best) but the play itself was a marvel, for it had everything Brook might have asked from a major contemporary work: highly developed intellectual content combined with strong entertainment values (Shakespeare could serve as Brook's model); the formality of verse coupled with sensational violence (as in *Titus* and *Lear*); a story of subjection, tyranny, and revolution (compare *The Screens* and Dürrenmatt's *The Visit*, which Brook directed twice, in 1958 and 1960); insane asylum as cultural emblem (compare Brook's 1963 RSC production of Dürrenmatt's *The Physicists*); Artaudian sound and movement in the frightening, lunatic ravings and convulsive behavior of the inmates; and Brechtian alienation as not even Brecht had imagined it. It was a play (Corday murders Marat, 1793) within a play (Sade presents his historical drama at Charenton, 1808) whose characters were all alienated from self by their madness and from society because of their social deviance and the effects of long-term institutionalization. Scenes from different plot levels were juxtaposed, and the whole was peppered with songs, mimes, announcements, dizzying tonal shifts, intellectual gymnastics, and dances. Horrifying eighteenth-century atrocities were described with patently modern epithets like "the final solution." *Marat/Sade* was a play with the potential to change modern theatre. It was also a piece with such a complex structure that it could sink most directors without a trace.

Brook studied the piece in early 1964 during the LAMDA run and the rerehearsals of *King Lear*. In May of that year he and Marowitz flew to Berlin for a look at the first production of *Marat/Sade*, which had opened April 29 at the Schiller Theater. The premiere's director, Konrad Swinarski, was a Polish Marxist who saw the play as a tract about naive democracy being a prelude to dictatorship. Marowitz found the production "an indictment of revolutionary fascism."[72] This first production was tame by comparison with Brook's, but it sustained its quite proper interpretation with a final *coup de théâtre.* As Swinarski's massed inmates sang the closing song, marching downstage in their revolutionary advance, a figure marched out from their ranks with his back to the house. The hat, coat, and posture revealed the figure of Napoleon. Downstage, he faced the advancing crowd as its leader. Then he turned to face the audience. A skull was under the tricorn—it was Death wearing the Napoleonic overcoat! Tableau and curtain!

In Berlin Brook also met Peter Weiss (1916–1982). Weiss was enigmatic and multitalented, a childhood refugee from fascism who was still a refugee living in Sweden and writing in a German he thought culturally neutral. His art had been rather more French than anything else until the early 1960s. He had written a number of novels, some autobiographical and some on the subject of contemporary blankness, all determinedly experimental in the mode of the "new novel." Weiss was also a painter and a film maker in the surrealist vein. He had designed the set for Swinarski's *Marat/Sade*. That his art generally had both a social and a psychological vision was attributable to influences both early (Franz Kafka and Henry Miller) and late (Brecht and Artaud). But Weiss was hardly known at that time and had served virtually no apprenticeship in the theatre.

In late June Brook began two months of rehearsal, this time without Charles Marowitz, who had left the RSC to pursue his own directing. Brook did have some actors from the Theatre of Cruelty workshops, however. Glenda Jackson received the most important assignment as Charlotte Corday and would become an international star as a result of her performance. Robert Lloyd, who would follow Brook to CIRT in 1970, created a famous Jacques Roux, the madman-priest-revolutionary. The one actor with asylum experience, Susan Williamson, used a real case as her model for Simonne Evrard, the unforgettable squinting, twisted, ministering angel. Jonathan Burn was cast as Polpoch, one of the four singers. Mary Allen was cast as one of the inmates, and so was Leon Lissek, the dark, brooding creature who played Lavoisier in scene 26, "Marat's Nightmare," with a retort on his head.

In addition to this group, Brook had the basic RSC–Aldwych Theatre company of that year, the repertory regulars. One such actor was Clifford Rose, who portrayed Coulmier, the asylum director, grandly but precisely and without strident political emphasis. Another was Michael Williams, who played Kokol in London and the Herald in the United States. Like his wife, Judy Dench, Williams was a rising figure in the English theatre—he had been Puck in Peter Hall's *A Midsummer Night's Dream* (1962/63), Eichmann in Brook's version of *The Deputy* (*The Representative*, 1963), and Oswald in Brook's revived *Lear*. The most estimable of the regulars was Ian Richardson, who played the Herald in London and a deservedly famous Marat later in New York. Born and trained in Scotland, Richardson joined the Birmingham Repertory Theatre in 1958 and in 1960 moved to the Shakespeare Memorial Theatre (which in 1961 became the RSC). He played mostly walking gentleman parts until 1962, when his career gained momentum: he portrayed Oberon in Hall's *Dream,* Antiphon of Ephesus in a hit production of *Comedy of Errors* (1962/63), the Doctor in *The Representative,* and Edmund in the touring *Lear.* The experience of *Marat/Sade,* particularly the months spent playing Marat, created serious personal strains for Richardson, but it also reversed his acting technique from outside-in to inside-out. He remained a leading actor of the RSC for many years.

The original Marat was Clive Revill, a strange choice. Revill had come from New Zealand to join the Old Vic School in 1950 at the age of twenty and quickly developed a facility for music and comedy that led to his first substantial notice for playing Sam Weller in *Mr. Pickwyck* (New York, 1952). He played repertory in Ipswich (1953–1955) and acted with the Shakespeare Memorial Theatre (1955–1957), notably as Trinculo, part of a Laurel and Hardy team with Stephano in Brook's *The Tempest.* For three years Revill acted in Brook's productions of *Irma La Douce* in London, New York, and Las Vegas, then returned to London in 1962 to play in Gilbert and Sullivan, and received his second Tony Award nomination for his portrayal of Fagin in *Oliver!* (January 1963). These credits obviously describe an actor who was not terribly well prepared for playing Weiss's Marat, a shrill demagogue and paranoid. Revill's acting style was lighter and brisker than the part required, and his Marat has not been remembered as a particular triumph.

But Patrick Magee's Sade was one of the era's great acting achievements. An Irishman of the school of Anew McMaster, Magee had been a West End actor in the late 1950s when he happened into a very close acquaintance with Samuel Beckett. Hearing Magee in a 1957 BBC radio production of *All That Fall,* Beckett thought he heard the voice inside his own head that had haunted him through a trilogy of novels, so within a short time he wrote a play for Magee, *Krapp's Last Tape.* By 1963 Magee was in Paris reviving the role of Hamm in *Endgame.* This performance brought him to the RSC a year later to take four parts during the experimental Aldwych season (later known as "the season of dirty plays"): Sade, Hamm, Roche in David Rudkin's *Afore Night Come,* and McCann in Harold Pinter's production of *The Birthday Party,* a performance that Brook, among others, judged a classic. Magee went on to achieve success in films, appearing in everything from *Die, Monster, Die!* to *Young Winston* to *King Lear* to *A Clockwork Orange* to *Chariots of Fire.* He was an extraordinary actor with a haunting face and voice who possessed that wealth of inner mystery necessary to make Sade a plausible character. Was Sade saint or debauchee? Or was he both? Magee looked both, and in moments like the Damiens speech (scene 12), he showed the kinship of opposites.

Brook did not distribute the text among his group at first, but used the early rehearsals as a workshop on madness. To begin with an exploration of subject matter rather than with more orthodox play preparation was still a highly unusual procedure, though Grotowski, the Living Theatre, and Brook himself had experimented with it. But in the next decade, scores of directors around the world would build productions in this new manner. Brook created *US* in 1966 on the basis of a workshop's collective views on the Vietnam War. In 1968, he guided the sedate cast of the National Theatre through simulated pagan orgies in order to prepare for *Seneca's Oedipus*. His production of *The Tempest* at the Round House, also in 1968, was an outgrowth of his first experimental workshop in Paris early in that year. If, as he told Marowitz while directing *King Lear,* rehearsals had two parts ("looking for meaning and then making it meaningful"), beginning the rehearsal process with workshops was a fruitful method of "looking for meaning."[73] Brook has frequently stated his distaste for the "lifeless" and "schematic" early rehearsals that are traditional in the theatre and his preference for starting, like an abstract painter, with "an instinct and a vague sense of direction."[74] "What matters in the early stages is the energy, not the result," he has said. "As you clear away the debris, the process gets hotter."[75]

Madness was the topic at these sessions. "My first approach was to have the actor do anything he could think of, in a wild way," Brook explained.[76] That no doubt cleared away debris. He described the next step at these "harrowing" early rehearsals as follows:

By conversation and by improvisation each person began to remember—but of course, he had seen, he had lived with, he had had in his family one, two, three very close, intimate cases of madness, and as he began to talk about them he began to illustrate them. And so, in fact, he was then, as an actor, beginning to live them with his body; and in talking about four or five different cases, and then showing it, and then perhaps playing it out, he began to find that one of them corresponded more to himself than another. And in this way he began to discover something of his own possible madness.

Brook was searching for "kinetic images of insanity."[77] Glenda Jackson later remarked that "we were all convinced that we were going loony."[78] Brook, I suppose, could have quoted the line spoken by Jimmy Cagney, the harried Broadway director in *Footlight Parade:* "How do you suppose an insane asylum number might go? I could do the lead myself!"

Other research was intended to give perspective to the actor's personal exploration. Brook's knowledge was increased and his imagery made more accurate as a result of information supplied by his psychologist brother, as well as visits to French and English asylums. He did not take his cast on any organized field trip of the Stanislavskian kind. But he brought them powerful literary examples to study — Sade himself, Ezra Pound, and Artaud. Brook also distributed articles on madness and pictures of paintings by Hogarth, Brueghel, and Goya. When they were six weeks into the process, he showed two films that left strong impressions. *Regard sur la Folie* depicted an annual party at a provincial French asylum. Jean Rouch's *Les Maîtres Fous,* shot in Nigeria, showed "a unique and savage ritual played out in a state of extreme madness."[79]

But as in the past, the actors felt stranded as the director rejected one solution after another. Brook's long silences could intimidate. (Peter Hall remarked that "his actual presence makes one think, Where am I going, and what am I doing in life? . . . He's the greatest lie-detector there is in theatre."[80]) But dictatorial he most assuredly was not, as Jackson pointed out: "What I can never understand . . . is when people cite him as an example of an autocratic dictator of productions when, in fact, the reverse is the case, for he just sits and says nothing for weeks and months, and you have to find it yourself. Then he will suddenly come in and orchestrate it."[81] Most directors used rehearsal as a means of realizing their productions, but Brook used it to see whether a production would discover itself. (A few years later, Jacques Derrida quoted Edmond Jabès to the effect that "the art of the writer consists in little by little making words interest themselves in his book."[82])

Brook's collaborators had their usual problems with his method. Richard Peaslee, a composer who had worked with him at the Theatre of Cruelty workshop and on *The Screens,* recalls an afternoon in May 1964 when he met with Brook, translator Adrian Mitchell, and a few others in an RSC office. Sharing a single "battered" copy of the rough English translation—"no verse, no lyrics, no music, with rehearsals starting in a fortnight" —they discussed their options. Educated at Yale and Juilliard, and later by Nadia Boulanger and Bill Russo, Peaslee needed trained singers and a flexible instrumentation. He came away with actors and a band consisting of tuba, harmonium, flute, trumpet, and drums. When rehearsals started, he had drafted only a few melodies, among them the "Copulation Round." Soon he was struggling to compose as fast as Brook and the actors could learn the songs. Peaslee also had to do a great deal of rewriting, since Brook could not help but experiment in rehearsal. He transformed "Don't Soil Your Pretty Little Shoes," originally a "simple folk-like ditty," into a wild, roaring song depicting a trip to the guillotine.[83] Peaslee kept trying to find a proper revival hymn to use for "Marat's Liturgy," but Brook finally discarded the idea. "Marat We're Poor," the show's basic choral refrain, went through a half-dozen changes before being returned to its original form. Soon it would be a hit tune on Top-40 radio.

The actors' difficulties intensified and multiplied as the date of the opening approached. Having already articulated mad characters and mad images in the workshop phase, they now had to learn how these deranged and overinstitutionalized characters would react in dramatic situations. How, for instance, does a catatonic rebel? And why would a paranoid act a part in a play—in public? These inmate characters had to take parts in Sade's drama about Marat, had to speak, dance, and sing. So all the actors, and particularly the principals, were offered a complex technical situation. What would the inmate do here? What would the historical character do here? How much does the inmate know? How thoroughly can the inmate's behavior be controlled for a theatrical performance? How does this inmate dance? These were not the members of the Living Theatre in blue jeans; this was not just Artaudian nightmare vision, and not just crazy Uncle Harry, either—but a play about an historical asylum whose real-life director, Coulmier, did in fact believe in art therapy, particularly for his esteemed guest, the Marquis de Sade. History presented its own stern test for the actor. Brook describes it:

> He may have used an image from observation, from life, but the play is about madness as it was in 1808—before drugs, before treatment, when a different social attitude to the insane made them behave differently, and so on. For this, the actor had no outside model—he

looked at faces in Goya not as models to imitate but as prods to encourage his confidence in following the stronger and more worrying of his inner impulses. He had to allow himself to serve these voices completely; and in parting from outside models, he was taking greater risks. He had to cultivate an act of possession.[84]

When producing *The Brig* in 1963, Judith Malina had realized the same thing—that the actor's internal imagery needed the objective balance provided by those Brig regulations for the full horror of Brown's vision to emerge. Brook found form through history as well as through personal exploration.

The final restraint on the actor's necessary frenzy was the text of *Marat/Sade*, which contains short rhymes, long rhetorical flights, screams, songs, and stabbing free verse. This idea of the text as check is fundamental to Brook's work, and his reputation for exploration and free handling of texts should not cause the reader to overlook what any auditor at a Brook production knows—that he has a brilliant ear and demands crisp diction, strong inflection, and remorseless pace. He can cut lines or change words to screams or reduce a text to its images, but when he has settled on a script, he demands clarity as few other directors do. "Here is the actor; here is the line; here is the director," he summarized ten years later while criticizing the Performance Group's *Makbeth*. "That line exists, and it helps you; it doesn't change, you change."[85] Surrendering to the text could lead to self-discovery. Speaking at a New York forum about *Marat/Sade* in January 1966, he said that the actor "must let the speech itself strike with its own force the portion of him that's resisting."[86]

In the final fortnight of preparation, Brook sifted the "bewildering" mass of material that he and his actors had generated during weeks of rehearsal and months of workshop sessions. This was the phase of making the meaning "meaningful," the phase in which he brought out "the true shapes, the true lines [of the play], that were there all the time."[87] For Brook's taste, this formative moment when the group discovered the play's shape could "never happen too late."[88] The orchestrator described by Jackson was suddenly at the actors' sides as they launched themselves into their parts.

On August 20, 1964, the actors were onstage at the Aldwych, where they opened to immediate acclaim and continuing debate. *Marat/Sade* ran for sixty-eight performances that season, a very respectable run in a repertory house. The RSC production opened on

December 27, 1965, with a slightly changed cast, at New York's Martin Beck Theatre under David Merrick's sponsorship. This wildly controversial run lasted nearly three months, after which the actors returned to Britain and reassembled at Pinewood Studios for two and a half frantic weeks to shoot the movie that made the production available around the world.

Product: Images of Marat /Sade

A theater event should burn into time as a movement cuts into space.   —Joseph Chaikin, *The Presence of the Actor*

Brook's *Marat/Sade* was a production that most audiences experienced as powerful. Viewers showed that they were strongly affected by its magnitude, whether they walked out in anger or stayed seated, shaking, at the end. The show usually had a similar impact on critics, other theatre workers, and the actors themselves.

Brook's *Marat/Sade* was also generally experienced as complex. The play's many scenes, many parts, many angles of vision, many styles, many characters might have created merely a plurality of experience, but Brook's work with Weiss's script produced a complexity—collisions and frictions, weights and leverages, interactions of ideas and characters and sounds and pictures.

These two basic conclusions about the "experience of *Marat/Sade*" provide a simple yet comprehensive explanation for the production's enormous success. The combination of power and complexity can be found in much of the world's greatest theatrical art.

Scene 1: Assembly

As in most of his productions since the late 1950s, Brook began by attacking the illusionism of the normal theatrical situation—the curtain provocatively hiding the set, the half-lit house, and other implicit separations of audience and stage. The audience entered the theater and found itself immediately confronted with Sally Jacobs's set—the bathhouse of Charenton, with its hard, white lights already turned up high. The gray and white stage was an uninviting construction of brick and pipe and wood with heavy doors and bare floors, with grates and traps (three downstage and a ring of a dozen in the middle, the latter covered by heavy wooden grills). In the middle, draped across some raised trap lids, was the single soft item and the source of the production's few color accents: the French tricolor. The inmate-musicians were over at the side (in the New York production, they were in boxes above both sides of the stage), so no pit intervened between the bathhouse and the audience. There were no bars across the downstage area, as in Brook's movie; rather, the stage was so open to the house that they seemed like parts of a single room. This sense of interconnectedness became stronger when the Coulmier family rustled, murmuring, through the house. They spoke to spectators while heading toward the stage and the dais from which the director, his wife, and their daughter watched the program. Many in the audience worried about this openness and continuity between acting area and viewing area, because recent theatrical news had featured a number of experimental productions in which actors had made conversational and even physical contact with members of the audience.

A large contingent of actors then straggled into the bathhouse. For many spectators, this entrance was one of the production's most electrifying moments, because as the inmates came in, it became immediately apparent that Brook's Charenton was patterned after fifteenth-century England's Bedlam. These actors drooled, muttered, and played with themselves obscenely. Sharp giggles mixed with moans and bizarre cries. A harmonium faded in a low smear and then built tone over tone as the entrances continued. Two guards in butcher aprons stomped about. Two nuns in wide-winged headdresses fluttered ominously in the background. One inmate sucked her thumb. Another played with an imaginary child. Others seemed catatonic or betrayed manic confusion. One in particular peered out at the audience with distinct hostility. In addition to their behavior, what made these inmates shocking was their facial pallor, ratted hair, deteriorating scalps, and syphilitic degeneration of skin and muscular control—all achieved by extraordinary makeup techniques. Costumer Gunilla Palmstierna-Weiss swathed them in rough, stained uniforms of white, off-white, and light gray. Nuns and guards wore gray and white. Among the principals, white and black predominated: Marat's sheet and bandages, Corday's dress and hat, and Sade's shirt were white; Sade's dirty pants, Coulmier's uniform, his ladies' dresses, and the Herald's hat were black. So was Marat's bath, a garb of another kind. The use of black, white, and gray, which would dominate the postmodern palette of the 1970s, made the overall picture of *Marat/Sade* harsh, unornamented, and sharply delineated.

What the audience was drawn into in these opening moments was no Grotowskian "poor" theatre (though the play portrayed such a theatre within Charenton), but a strikingly realistic rendition of an early nineteenth-century asylum. Beyond the visually mimetic instincts in the design and direction, an important reason for the success of this realistic illusion was the production's immediate implication of the audience. Spectators were not protected here—neither from the hostile looks of that singer who, throughout the performance, spent extra energy isolating two spectators down left and projecting hatred in their direction, nor from that grotesque creature who advanced menacingly downstage at the end of the assembly until he was stopped by the guards at the very edge of the stage. The audience had been warned to remain alert. A trumpet fanfare signaled the beginning of the action.

Scenes 2–4: Presentations

As Coulmier stepped forward to welcome the audience to his asylum-theatre, the production shifted to a frankly presentational mode. It faced front, like the theatre of Brecht and the theatre of 1808. Coulmier's introduction of the general situation indicated to the spectators of the mid-1960s their fictional roles as his guests in 1808. The Herald's introduction of the players developed the alienation of inmates from their theatrical roles, the distance between 1808 and 1793. He moved around the ring of traps where the principals were all posed: Marat and Simonne down left, Corday down right, Duperret and Roux upstage, and Sade, sitting off right of the circle, detached as usual. When the Herald banged his staff a bit too long and too forcefully for attention, he gave a hint that everything was not right with the inmate playing this role in Sade's dramatic presentation.

Both introductory speeches are written in couplets, strongly rhymed but unevenly stressed (four to five stresses per line, as a rule). After the shocking realism of the inmates' assembly, the sound of rhyming verse was surprising to audiences. The verse changed as the production continued: the Herald kept returning to heavily accented tetrameter couplets but Marat and Sade tended to speak in free verse. Weiss's German verse is compellingly dramatic speech, and Adrian Mitchell had transformed Geoffrey Skelton's prose translation into English poetry that equals (some think it surpasses) its original. The text displays a modernist flexibility that is both metrical and psychological, but periodic tightening of its meter and rhyme achieves a more traditional, musical effect. Because standard poetic ornamentation is almost entirely absent from the script, occasional readers find the verse flat. But those who heard it in Brook's production believed that the poetry of *Marat/Sade*, like most great Anglo-Saxon theatrical poetry, captured the speaking voice. It is no wonder that the poetry was one of this production's great successes, when we consider that it was being spoken by a company considered the world's best at theatricalizing the world's best dramatic verse (Shakespeare's), under the supervision of a director famous for reanimating Shakespeare with clever, striking inflections.[89]

Brook's two rules about verse were: (1) "A line should have no more than one or two stresses. If it is given all the stresses inherent in its rhythm, it becomes metrically correct and dramatically meaningless." Thus Clifford Rose spoke Coulmier's opening lines as follows: "I a*gree* with our *au*thor Monsieur de Sade / that his play . . . set in our . . . *mod*ern *bath* house . . . won't be *marred* / by, uh, . . . all these instruments for mental and physical *hygiene*. / Quite on the contrary . . . they *set* the *scene*." (2) "In verse which is properly spoken, each character plays his own rhythm—as personal as his own handwriting, but what often happens in Shakespeare is that everyone shares a generalized rhythm that passes impersonally from one to the other."[90] Ian Richardson's Marat spoke Weiss's words in a flat, fast, hard voice, emphasizing that Marat's voice itself was an instrument of revolutionary foment and passion. Patrick Magee's Sade, by contrast, lingered over his speech as over some delicious concoction he could not bear to finish. Although his tempo was mostly brisk, Magee brought out with great clarity how Sade identifies speech with imagination and luxuriates in both.

Scenes 5–9: The Beginning of Sade's Play

Scenes 5–9 contain the opening production number, "Homage to Marat," and the first dramatic interchanges featuring Corday, Marat, and Simonne. These scenes are just as formal as the introductions and they emphasize again the alienation of levels.

In scene 5, "Homage to Marat," the four singers described the condition of France "Four years after the revolution / and the old king's execution." On cue, some inmates stepped forward to speak or yell their lines about the needs of the people. Others pledged allegiance to Marat by waving sympathetically worded picket signs when so directed by the nuns. The entire chorus paraded around the stage with Marat on their shoulders as the four singers sang verses about corruption. This large and colorful scene had the potential to be tumultuous, but Brook took it at a measured pace. Even during its noisiest, busiest sections, Corday remained sleeping on the floor and the Coulmier family munched on bonbons. The direction was similarly restrained in the scene's memorable chorus ("Marat we're poor and the poor stay poor") and during the staged discontent that threatened to become real discontent in scene 6. After Coulmier brought the action to a complete stop with his stern warning against disorder, scenes 7 through 9, in which Corday and Marat are introduced and have their first encounter, proceeded in the same unhurried manner. Brook was clear and sober in his directing during this part of the play, and by avoiding the dynamic extremes, he gave his cast an opportunity for subsequent theatrical expansion.

Another result of the measured rendition of these scenes was that the audience could discover some of the distance and interplay between the inmates' characters and their theatrical roles. Scene 8 gave hints of the paranoid playing Marat. "Everywhere you look / everywhere," he said, his voice accelerating in fear, "There they are / Behind the walls / Up on the rooftops / Down in the cellars / Hypocrites / . . . There is a rioting mob inside me." At the end of his speech, Ian Richardson stopped, called on Simonne, was framed by her with a gesture, and issued his mad summary: "I am the Revolution." More inmate-character tension became evident when Glenda Jackson's Corday began speaking, singing, and dancing for Marat in a strange mixture of eroticism and hostility. Here and later, her Corday combined intense passion with irony and distance, the distance based on the inmate's disturbed somnambulism, the irony a permanent feature of Jackson's voice. Jackson indicated the inmate-role tension and the conflicts within Corday herself in a superb vocal performance full of abrupt shifts in tempo, rhythm, intonation, and imagery.

At the end of scene 9, internal tension between inmate and theatrical character shattered dramatic decorum when Corday nearly stabbed Marat. Sade's double role was also becoming apparent. When giving Corday the wooden prop knife during her song's second verse in scene 7, he moved it back and forth before her eyes as if he were hypnotizing her into an assassin's frenzy. But in scene 9, as she walked toward Marat in a clearly disturbed fashion, Sade was forced to check her. At the climax, Corday stood above Marat in his tub, her attacking gesture frozen by an inmate's scream, while Sade strolled across the stage to take the knife from her upraised hand. The director of the asylum theatrical needed to delay the killing for dramatic effect, though the Marquis de Sade lusted after violence.

Scenes 10–11: Vision of the Terror

The Herald announced the title of scene 10, "Song and Mime of Corday's Arrival in Paris," and the inmates arranged themselves for a new presentation. Standing still, the singers raced through three verses in $\frac{5}{8}$ time describing Corday's arrival. Positioned around them, other inmates enacted scenes representative of Parisian street life. The song then slowed for two darker verses in $\frac{6}{8}$ time about Charlotte's buying the dagger. During these, Brook focused the singers and the mime sequence on Sade acting the street-side knife-seller, seductively opening a handsome case to reveal a real knife with a shiny blade and a pearly white handle. With this real weapon in her hand, both Corday and the inmate playing her became fascinated and girlishly sexual. Then the scene exploded with the tumbrel driver's song, "Don't soil your pretty little shoes / The gutter's deep and red," and the mime of the tumbrels frightened Corday. Brook rapidly contracted the stage focus again as Jackson began Corday's speech about Paris during the Terror ("What kind of town is this"). As she built the speech from question to question, her inflections jolted word after word loose from context: "slaughterhouse," "hop," "racked," "hacked," "buttocks." Near the end of this description Jackson climbed a bathhouse ladder and precipitously increased Corday's fear and vocal pitch. At the ladder's top, she described the faces of the bloodthirsty mod and the "eyes and mouths" of the guilllotined corpses, all calling her to—and at this point Jackson swooned off the ladder into the singers' arms, shrieking— "JOIN, THEM!!" Trapdoors were slammed down onto the floor and inmates cried excitedly. Marat's "Now it's happening and you can't stop it happening" (the beginning of scene 11) climaxed in frenzy, for Richardson delivered this passionate outburst about the Terror at breakneck speed amid the increasing inmate noise. The situation cooled considerably when Coulmier remonstrated with the inmates and the Herald protested ironically that "we are more civilised." For the third time in five scenes, disturbances in the asylum threatened the continuation of Sade's play. Following the ups and downs of Weiss's play, Brook directed by rapidly and repeatedly varying the tempo, volume, and size of his imagery. Such theatre has the capacity (and is intended) to disturb the perceptual equipment of its spectators.

To end scene 11, Brook created one of his most powerful images, a sound-and-movement depiction of the executions at the height of the Terror. Exemplifying his boast that "I've never observed a stage direction in my life," Brook considerably altered the intentions of his playwright.[91] Weiss had imagined an execution mime that would bridge all of scene 11, but the director allowed Marat's "Now it's happening," the interlude with Coulmier and the Herald, and Corday's "Up there on the scaffold" to proceed unaccompanied by any organized theatricality from the inmates. By the end of Corday's speech, the stage had become completely still and the atmosphere was charged. This was the moment Brook chose for the mime sequence, which lasted two minutes.

At the beginning of the execution scene, the Herald cried, "The Execution of the Aristocrats!" Accompanied by loud raspings of broomhandle and trapdoor against the central grate, a group of inmates came forward. As these "aristocrats" approached the down center trap, each in turn sharply jerked his head down and descended into the pit. Sade gave his speech about the perverse pleasure the aristocrats found in death. By the time he finished, the pit was full of severed heads with protruding tongues, goggling eyes, and twisted attitudes (see Plate 4). In the stillness, the focus moved to Polpoch, one of the four singers, as he poured red paint (blood) from one bucket to another. A delicate run on the glockenspiel accompanied his symbolic action. (45 seconds had elapsed since the announcement.) During an elaborate fanfare (lasting 35 seconds), the aristocrats dispersed from the pit and introduced a dummy made from broomhandles and bits of clothing, with a cabbage head and a carrot nose. The Herald then announced "The Execution of the King!" and the royal dummy was rudely pushed into the pit. Another bucket of blood was poured out, to the same accompaniment. But this blood was blue. (The scene was now 105 seconds old.) The inmates suddenly began to fight over the cabbage and carrot (Brecht to the res-

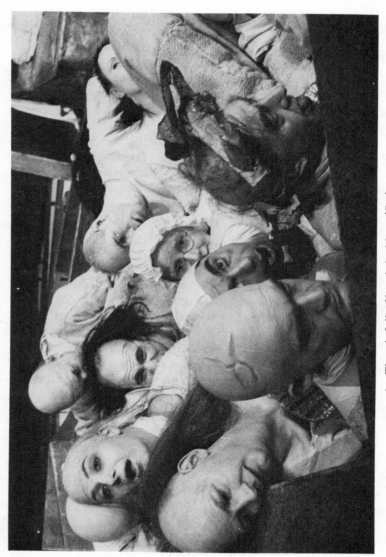

4. The pit full of heads in *Marat/Sade*.

cue), until the guards subdued them and stuffed them down into the ring of traps.

The execution scene sounds simple enough, but it astonished the audiences. Everyone reviewing the play wrote about it, and everyone recalling the production mentions it. The pit full of heads and the pouring of blood (the latter descended from the paint tropes of the Theatre of Cruelty workshop) were unforgettable pictures. The English critic Bamber Gascoigne called this sequence "probably the most stunning scene of all" eight months after condemning the pointless innovations of the LAMDA shows.[92] On the other side of the Atlantic, Theophilus Lewis testified to seeing "gallons" of blood poured down the drain.[93] Four years after the premiere, Irving Wardle described Brook's direction generally as having an "unrivalled capacity for directing the audience's eye to single chosen details in the midst of elaborate spectacle, and for creating potent imagery."[94]

Scene 12: "Conversation Concerning Life and Death"

The ideological debate between Marat and Sade begins in scene 12 with a discussion of the tendencies of Nature and the self's involvement with the world. As the play proceeds, the debate widens to cover the injustices of the world, the nature of revolution, the character of revolutionaries, the efficacy of writing in a revolutionary situation, and fundamental conceptions of human nature. Stated most simply, the discussion between the two principals reveals two conflicting views of liberation: Marat's belief that political revolution will right the world's wrongs and Sade's conviction that the true revolution must be interior and psychosexual in nature. But the debate is not often simple. Nor is it peripheral to the action, for as the play proceeds after scene 12, the discussion between Marat and Sade becomes increasingly prominent, and it led some reviewers to question the literary or theatrical success of Weiss's piece.

The London critics in 1964 were not enthusiastic about these long debate sections. The first-night reviewer for the *Times* avoided full-scale intellectual analysis of the play due to deadline pressures but commented that "on a first showing one is far less impressed by the intellectual line of the play than its [tremendous] impact on the visceral level."[95] John Gross complained that Revill's and Magee's speeches were "swamped by the general turbulence" and that their arguments were finally less impressive than the set.[96] Frank Kermode later recalled the debates as moments when "the brilliantly sustained succession of theatrical *coups* lapsed, with awful doctrinaire deliberation, into the boring conversations of the principals, and tedium became almost a novel theatrical effect."[97] Reviewers convinced that Brook's successes always came with second-rate plays repeated this charge in attempting to dismiss the discussions between Marat and Sade.

But in New York in 1965/66, the more mature production with a new Marat met a very different reception. A few reviewers objected on approximately the same grounds as their English counterparts, but most were caught up in the debates. Political involvement was the question of the moment among American intellectuals and artists, and a critical position was forming around the example of Brecht and the proposition that revolutionary didacticism was important in contemporary drama. Jack Richardson asked what intellectuals formerly would have considered a rhetorical question: "Isn't it spurious to stage, in effect, a Roman circus to pump some life into a dry argument?" He answered, surprisingly, in the negative: "I would not object to a playwright arranging automobile accidents on stage if he could get his audience to listen to him."[98] *Marat/Sade,* with its long set pieces on political and sexual change, not only concerned the questions being debated by Americans in the mid-1960s, but made it possible for those debates to be put on stage.

The central question about the debates was, Who wins? Was Marat correct when he said that society must be changed before humanity can change? Or was it more important, as Sade believed, to change the self before changing society? Over the years, audiences, reviewers, and academic critics have reached no agreement on this issue. Weiss wrote his play at the beginning of his own political conversion to Marxism and revised it repeatedly throughout that conversion, so his own position on the debate changed from version to version and month to month. This apparent confusion in his views was both understandable and pertinent, at least in Peter Brook's opinion. For Brook, the play's force resided in its questions rather than its answers, and the play's debates existed to be staged, not won. At a New York forum on the production held in 1966, with more than a year of the journalistic wars behind him, Brook insisted that ambiguity, no matter how irritating, was Weiss's basic intention. Brook's metaphor was that Weiss boldly opened a head full of unresolved contradictions

and served up its contents to the audience. The director also remarked: "I think the action of the play is that Sade honestly gives rein
to an opponent whom he respects only if he can feed him the best
possible material."[99] I assume that Brook used "action" in the Aris-
totelian sense, meaning that the play is an enactment and a concreti-
zation of the searching of a dialectical mind.

In Brook's interpretation, Sade stated one side of the central problem in scene 15:

> Before deciding what is wrong and what is right
> first we must find out what we are
> I
> do not know myself

Marat stated the other side most succinctly in the conclusion to scene
12:

> The important thing
> is to pull yourself up by your own hair
> to turn yourself inside out
> and see the whole world with fresh eyes

(In the recorded version, Brook also inserted these lines in the play's
epilogue as Marat's summary position after his death.) One man circles endlessly in the attempt to answer his own questions and is drawn
inevitably and without hope of rescue into the vortex of his own
moral nature. The other man changes, painfully and destructively, in
order to engage the outside world. Brook's production made these
the gravitational poles of *Marat/Sade*'s thought.

In the RSC production, many of the most exciting moments occurred during the long speeches of the debates: Sade on Damiens,
the tailor, and the Carmelite Convent (scenes 12, 15, 20); Marat's
remarkable tirade beginning, "These lies they tell about the ideal
state" (scene 23); and Sade's response to Simonne, "That's how it is
Marat / That's how she sees your Revolution" (scene 25). Brook intensified these scenes in a variety of ways. He sometimes kept the
stage very quiet, as when he crowded the chorus of inmates into the
traps during scene 12, an equivalent to Weiss's idea of drawing a back
curtain to conceal them. At other times, Brook emphasized points
with Brechtian wake-up devices. An example of this technique is the
following interpolation at the end of Marat's "These lies they tell" in
scene 23:

MARAT: Watch out
     for as soon as it pleases them
     they'll send you out
     to protect their gold
     in wars

DUPERRET: [Still loose after his second Corday scene]: FREEDOM!

MARAT: whose weapons rapidly developed
     by servile scientists
     will become more and more deadly
     until they can with a flick of a finger
     tear a million of you to pieces

DUPERRET: FREEDOM!!

At the end of the debate in scene 12, as Marat answered Sade's speech about extremism, the Herald mistakenly rushed forward, ringing his bell for the liturgy in the next scene. Marat restrained the man and his bell and, kneeling, turned downstage to finish with the lines, "The important thing / is to pull yourself up by your own hair," and so on. Then the Herald leaned down, encircled Marat's neck with his arms, arranged his own hands as if in prayer, and ironically announced, "Marat's Liturgy." Using the Herald and his bell, Brook framed and underlined this speech that he believed to be thematically central to the play.

Scenes 13–20: The Problem of Pace

Marat/Sade is an extremely difficult play to direct well, and its most challenging feature is its lack of apparent organization. Like a big Broadway musical or a panoramic Shakespeare play, Weiss's script contains a wide variety of dramatic components strung together without a simple, obvious through-action. For example, scenes 13–20 include Marat's angry anticlerical outburst, an inmate's prayer to Satan, three beatings, three interruptions from Coulmier, two debates between Marat and Sade, the "mad animal" diatribe, a major production number called "The People's Reaction," the Herald's lengthy introduction of the Caen scene, the hilarious yet shocking duet between Duperret and Corday, a song about fat capitalist monkeys, two rousing outbreaks from Roux, and a long, agonizing confessional scene in which Corday whips Sade. Scenes 21–26 are also a mixture of polemics, mimes, rhymes, and violence, and again their arrangement seems more erratic than elliptical. Another difficulty of *Marat/Sade* is the disproportion, by conventional standards, between its two acts; the first is three times the length of the second. Act 2 (scenes 27–33) ran barely over thirty minutes, but act 1 took Brook eighty-five minutes in production, and he had to race through some sections. (I have seen act 1 take an additional ten or fifteen minutes without losing its momentum or its audience.) Direction of this farraginous and misshapen play requires a masterful control of pace.

For Brook, the problems of variety and pace were great opportunities. He has always preferred contrasts to similarities and jangles to chords, and he has theorized that variety is a necessary or structural element in modernist theatre. In his preface to the American edition of *Marat/Sade,* he spoke glowingly of the contrasts in this play's affect: "Starting with its title, everything about this play is designed to crack the spectator on the jaw, then douse him with ice-cold water, then force him to assess intelligently what has happened to him, then give him a kick in the balls, then bring him back to his senses again."[100] As for "that marvelous thing called pace," Brook's career offers many proofs of his contention that pace is the "one god whom we all serve—whether in musicals or in melodramas or in the classics."[101] Much of the most extravagant critical praise of Brook's directing has emphasized his mastery of pace. Many reviewers of *Marat/Sade* called him a "ringmaster."

"Pace" is a confusing term in theatrical jargon because it means at least three things in everyday usage: (1) the tempo (also mood) of a particular scene or speech, (2) the overall tempo of a production, and (3) the changing of tempo from one bit to another, which is also known as "change of pace." In the narrowest sense, pace is measured in the audience's ears, for the term's most limited meaning is the speed at which characters speak. But, since theatre combines stimuli for ear and eye and understanding, a better definition of pace includes the rate at which characters move and events transpire. Directors may even be said to "pace" a production for the eye, in which case the word "tempo," in the three meanings just given, should be replaced by "picture" or "visual focus."

In directing *Marat/Sade,* Brook vigorously moved the audience's eyes around the stage. In the overall stage picture, he established a basic visual balance between the focus on Marat's tub and the Coulmiers' dias (left) and a focus on Sade sitting in his chair and the singers lounging between assignments (right). More importantly, Brook repeatedly expanded and contracted the stage picture, leading Stanley Kauffmann to say that "the production surges, opens and narrows like the iris of a camera, using its members in mad, stuttering but carefully composed movement."[102] Brook emptied the stage by putting the inmates in the traps (scene 12) or onto the benches around the three walls. For contrast, he spread the entire cast around the stage in bizarre attitudes (as at the end of scene 15 and in scene 19, with Roux). He sometimes forced the audience's eyes to zoom in on particular moments within the bigger picture: the Coulmiers eating their bonbons during a song, Simonne stealing the director's cane during "The People's Reaction." At other times, he emphasized events that occupied the whole stage, such as the production numbers and rebellious disturbances.

Brook also paced the production by alternating moments of violent movement with moments of intense stillness. During scenes 13–20, violence erupted repeatedly. The "abbot" of scene 14, played by Mark Jones, threw himself across the stage at the Coulmier family, then was drenched with water and beaten by the guards who held him upside down by the legs over the central drain. In the next scene, the inmate who gave the "mad animal" speech (Morgan Sheppard) nearly choked the life from Coulmier before being restrained. Marat heaved his papers into the air to punctuate a point later in the same scene, and the inmates scurried around the stage after them. Duperret (John Steiner) chased Corday in the second half of scene 17, and the guards chased Roux around the stage two scenes later. During the same scenes, Brook repeatedly tightened the stage focus and isolated the audience's attention. Sade sat quietly on a bench to deliver "Before deciding what is wrong and what is right" (scene 15) in two clean beats. Morgan Sheppard began the "mad animal" diatribe with eerie deliberation. At the beginning of the dialogue in scene 17, Duperret stood behind Corday like a statue, slowly cracking. Brook interpolated some funny moments in scene 18 by collapsing the focus onto Coulmier's daughter, who could not stifle an inopportune cry of "Long live the Revolution!" She found herself suddenly "onstage" between Marat and Sade and had to stand very still during the second verse of the "Those fat monkeys" song as the singer Polpoch rested his hands on her breasts. With everyone awaiting her reaction, she giggled uncontrollably during the song's final line, which the singers elongated: "we are the ones who get . . . screwwwed!" A final and famous example of Brook's ability to isolate attention in a small and still picture was the ending of Jacques Roux's rant in scene 19. During most of his first, exhortatory speech ("Pick up your arms") and during the exchange between Coulmier and the Herald, Roux (Robert Lloyd) moved around the stage above the bodies of the prostrate inmates. He began his second diatribe, the list of demands, standing behind Marat's bathtub (left), then, excoriating the war, he moved slowly downstage until he was kneeling, facing the audience, and pleading for the "frightened men" who "all want the same thing / Not to lie under the earth / but to walk upon it / without crutches."

The ear of the audience was entertained by pace as well. Since in this play the long speech, rather than interactive dialogue, bears almost all the dramaturgical weight, the play's director must be able to handle operatic skeins of language. In Brook's handling, the rhythm and tempo of the long speeches constantly changed. Marat's liturgy (scene 13) began slowly and deliberately and accelerated until it was a driving, ringing cry. Replying to "The People's Reaction," the Herald appealed for allegiance to the rich and strong, shifting slowly from loud-and-fast to soft-and-slow. Brook also made marked shifts in tempo within sequences of speeches. Late in scene 18, Marat responded to Sade's denunciation of idealists, mass movements, and patriotism with a slow, intense speech. The four singers sang the first two verses of "Those fat monkeys" at an aggressive tempo, but gradually decreased the tempo of the final verse right up to the last line ("screwwwed!"). This was followed by Roux's first diatribe (scene 19), which Robert Lloyd raced through, shouting above the accompaniment of blows against a bucket. After Roux was restrained, Coulmier spoke quickly and insistently, but the Herald restrained the proceedings again with a slow, wordy speech delivered in a calming tone. Roux began his second speech in this same deliberate tempo. As he quietly listed his demands, walking downstage from Marat's tub, his voice increased in volume and his speech became rhythmically agitated but Lloyd maintained the deliberate pace he had picked up from the Herald. His vocal tempo seemed to symbolize his physical confinement, and reacting against both tempo and confinement, he exploded into violence at the scene's end.

The explosiveness that characterized life in Charenton, evidenced by the inmates' voices and movements during scenes 13–20, facilitated Brook's changes of pace. Marat, the abbot, the mad animal, Roux—the list of specific dangerous inmates gradually lengthened. Corday's Girondist lover, Duperret, was one of the most obviously explosive characters. One of this role's two principal values is its comedy, and John Steiner was very comic in his stiff poses, his failed hairdo and his bulging, stained crotch belying his fussy aristocratic manner. Yet the part has Caliban in it, and although Duperret's erotomania was rigorously contained, it repeatedly reached a boiling point (as in scenes 17 and 23), and when it did, Duperret would suddenly jump after Corday. Because he was comic, these jumps usually ended with him falling on his face, but he joined the list of patients about whom the audience could never be entirely certain. By the middle of act 1, the audience had associated the constant threat of a breakout with individual inmates, with the inmates collectively, and with the dispossessed class that the inmates portrayed in Sade's drama about the revolution.

Scenes 19–20: Two Arguments with Brook

As with the inmates' entry and the mime of Corday's arrival in Paris, Brook created strong and memorable images in the rabble-rousing of Roux and the whipping of Sade. But I think both scenes are open to criticism.

Robert Lloyd's Jacques Roux was an aggressive, energetic revolutionary. I have already discussed one reason he was remembered—the startling rhythmic delivery of his speeches. Another is his photogenic quality in that straightjacket. (Max Waldman took a vastly overrated sequence of photographs of Brook's *Marat/Sade* that became icons of the revolutionary movement, and several of Roux were among the most powerful.) Roux's appeals for popular resistance to tyranny and for conversion of capitalist holdings to general use were expressions of sentiments that were widely popular in the mid-1960s. What American at that time could fail to be struck by his demand to stop the war ("This damned war / which is run for the benefit of profiteers / and leads only to more wars")? Most audiences applauded passionately. Many people thought his lines in scene 33 were the thematic conclusion of play and production alike: "When will you learn to see / When will you learn to take sides / When will you show them."

And yet the rudimentary fact is that Lloyd showed almost no distance between the political passion of the historical Roux and the passion—whatever it may have been—that drove the inmate to speak his lines with such force. It was as if both Brook and Lloyd thought they were realizing the actual, historical Roux on stage. Most spectators certainly interpreted it that way. As a result (in some ways, a positive result), Lloyd's Roux sharply intensified the play's political line and became Marat's left wing, but he lost his humanity, specifically the humanity of the inmate presenting the political arguments. Considering that in the mid-1960s, the prevailing tendency was to judge people by their ideology rather than by their personality, this approach to the character is understandable. But there are other and better approaches to playing the role.

Brook's treatment of scene 20, "Monsieur De Sade Is Whipped," was even more questionable, since the scene is a vital one, a climax of sorts. The Marquis tells the revolutionary "what I think of this Revolution / which I helped to make," and in the middle of his explanation, Corday is brought to center stage, given a whip, and invited to whip his bare back as he proceeds. While being whipped, Sade recalls the period in which he was a revolutionary judge with the power to kill, and he confesses his failure to enact the spectacular "outburst of revenge" and "orgy" that he had originally imagined the French Revolution might be. He also attacks the revolution for turning execution into meaningless sensationalism: "all the meaning drained out of this revenge / It had become mechanical / It was inhuman it was dull / and curiously technocratic." Corday keeps whipping until she is exhausted and he has crumpled to his knees, the position from which he ends his speech about "the withering of the individual man" and the death of subjectivity. Weiss's speech is powerful and his scene— intelligence flourishing under the lash—is truly provocative. A hostile reviewer said that Sade, here and in the Damiens speech of scene 12, was "sick, sick, sick, . . . using the theatre less to advance an argument than to excite himself."[103] Well, of course—he was the Marquis de Sade, for whom self-excitation was a matter of the highest importance, rather than a reviewer for a tony quarterly worried about "arguments." By arranging to be whipped in front of Marat and Coulmier, his philosophic opponent and his immediate antagonist, Sade is also trying to teach both men a lesson: that personal experience is important for its subjectivity, immediacy, and reality, not for its relation to abstractions, institutions, or societies.

In Brook's production, Magee spoke Sade's preparatory lines about the revolution and the Bastille vigorously, but with gradually decreasing speed. The atmosphere was filled with expectation as Corday was ushered to the center of the arena, Sade knelt before her, and the other inmates drew up in a semicircle behind her. When the whipping began, Jackson used her hair, sometimes holding it in her hand and sometimes letting it hang free, sometimes slowly and provocatively caressing Sade's shoulders, and sometimes lashing him, simultaneously snapping her neck. The well-orchestrated whistling and buzzing of the inmates accompanied her strokes. With his characteristically brilliant musical phrasing, Brook brought the excitement to a climax in the Carmelite Convent passage. The chorus whistled faster and faster, higher and higher, as Corday's strokes became more frequent, building toward the (fictionally) punishing blow she delivered on "the severed genitals of men." Brook kept up the intensity through Sade's next lines ("as the tumbrels ran regularly to the scaffolds / and the blade dropped and was winched up and dropped again"). Like a winch, the whistles pulled the tension up into a knot, to be released surprisingly after "It had become mechanical."

My objection is not that Corday's whipping deflected interest from Sade's speech, for that was inevitable given Weiss's conception, but that Brook aestheticized the whipping. The chorus even did Sade's groaning for him. The entire apparatus of Brook's modernist treatment—the noises, the symbolic whipping, the distanced suffering—strikes me as arty, even phony, given the circumstances. By "circumstances," I do not mean the unavailability of the Open Theater style to the inmates of Charenton in 1808, though this argument from historical stylistics could be made about much of the sound-and-movement imagery in Brook's production. I mean that Brook's image conflicted with the scene's point, which I have already stated as a demand to make life personal and real, not aestheticized, abstracted, or distanced. I hope I will not seem a simplistic advocate of "cruelty" if I propose an alternative whose plausibility has been confirmed by experience of other productions. Let the director put a real whip into the actress's hand and let her whip Sade, making whatever allowances are necessary for personal safety. Played realistically, the scene can be traumatic—unquestionably the play's most gripping scene—and an experience that literally embodies Sade's beliefs.

Scenes 21—26: The End of Act 1

I have already said that the greatest problem at the end of act 1 was to maintain momentum by controlling pace. Throughout the soliloquies, arguments, songs, mimes, and hallucinations, Brook maintained a surprisingly leisurely tempo and a surprisingly low volume. But he kept inserting contrasts and punctuations. One of the singers dressed like Marat and mimicked his writing during "Poor Old Marat" (scene 21), giving Marat the opportunity to watch himself. Duperret was chained for his second conversation with Corday (scene 22), but while he sang, another inmate drooled on the Coulmier women in counterpoint. At the scene's conclusion, John Steiner managed to free himself and took off after Jackson, only to be stopped and thrown down by Ian Richardson as the latter turned and began Marat's speech, "These lies they tell about the ideal state" (scene 23).

In this portion of the play, the production number was "Marat's Nightmare" (scene 26, "The Faces of Marat" in the published translation). It began with a flood of steam and a dance of white linen but quickly turned into a triumphant display of Brook's musical talent. Weird vocal and instrumental sounds created an atmosphere of auditory hallucination. As the men playing figures from Marat's past itemized his failings, they were accompanied by squeaks, groans, and whines. Each speech was set to a distinctive accompaniment, of scraped violin strings, rubbed balloons, moans and jibberings, or trumpets played underwater. Each speech was spoken in a distinctively distorted voice—Voltaire's high and piping, Lavoisier's dark and low. And the volume rose and fell with the stage action, cresting twice when Marat called "Bas." All of this was projected down to the horrified and paranoid Marat, who had been dumped naked into a downstage trap at the scene's beginning.

One of the show's most touching moments came at the scene's end: the nude Marat climbing up out of the trap as Roux delivered an extremely restrained yet urgent speech about Marat's heroism, beginning "Woe to the man who is different / who tries to break down all the barriers." After shifting to the second person, Roux concludes:

And you came one day to the Revolution
because you saw the most important vision

> That our circumstances must be changed fundamentally
> and without these changes
> everything we try to do must fail

To the audiences of the mid-1960s, few theatrical speeches were as telling as this one. The words defined the age's radicalism and were matched by a stunning visual image (not used until late in the London run): Marat's naked backside as he made his way upstage across the silent and still bathhouse toward the bath. The final chorus ("Marat We're Poor") had never been sung more quietly and hauntingly. Its tone was meant to reflect what Marat's body expressed visually—that radicalism is hard work, and the human constitution is frail. As is more apparent in act 2, Sade may write scenes that expose Marat's failings and may defeat him in debate, but the playwright honors his subject with a certain sentimental sympathy.

Dismissing the spectators for the interval, the Herald reinforced the quiet, depressed ending of act 1.

Scene 27: The National Assembly

Marat's address to the National Assembly provokes a large, colorful, and noisy debate—a perfect beginning for the second act in a commercial theatre. The scene illustrates how the passionate insights of a political prophet can be distorted by the endless wrangling typical of partisan politics. At first Marat quietly and gradually wins the crowd to him, but then loses it. He reestablishes a sober focus on the topics of leadership, dictatorship, and "a man / who will rule for you." This raises the question of his own ambition, but Weiss evades that issue with the frenzy of the crowd. Brook added a near breakdown by the inmate playing Marat, beginning with "We are fighting / for our lives." By the end of the scene, the audience realized that political confusion can lead to fanaticism and that a reluctant and increasingly confused leader can lose control over a crowd.

A grace note. The Herald introduced this scene downstage with the tricolor over his shoulder. With the ominous "It is almost night," he turned upstage toward Marat, quickly unfurling the flag and whipping the staff up over his head and then down onto the floor beside him. This was Brook directing in the style of Tyrone Guthrie—using assertive, colorful banner movements to introduce and focus the action.

An irony. When Marat started to list the revolutionary traitors, "those powdered chimpanzees / Necker Lafayette Talleyrand," Coulmier intervened, protesting that if any more such lines were resurrected from his cuts, "I will stop your play." While everyone watched silently, Sade took up his script, read down the long page, and tore a very thin strip off the bottom. He handed this strip to the Herald, who carried it upstage to Marat, who—everyone still waiting—read it silently, checked visually with Sade, and finished: "and all the rest of them." The wait made the expurgated list seem longer still.

A quibble. Brook altered Weiss's stage directions about seating the inmates. Marat's tub stood up center where it was at the end of act 1, but his audience was not divided into clearly defined groups but dispersed generally downstage of the tub. The effect was to blur the Assembly's factionalism, its most obvious subject.

Brook steadily and carefully accelerated and intensified this scene up to Coulmier's threat to stop the play and the final confusion. Both the Herald and Marat began their speeches slowly enough, but Marat quickly sped up his delivery. By the climax ("We do not murder / we kill in self-defence / We are fighting / for our lives"), he was hysterical, throwing the flag staff javelin-style toward Duperret and nearly missing the Coulmiers. Duperret broke in, pleading for an end to "hysteria and fanaticism," but was toppled by Roux who, running like a battering ram, lurched downstage in his straightjacket to exhort the crowd to collective action. Chanting, they became a surging, shouting mass of people: "Ma-rat. Ma-rat. Ma-rat."

This was a paradigm of scene and play, a movement from speech to violence, from order to revolution. It was subdued —again —this time by Sade's intervention and the delicately formal singing of "Poor Marat in your bathtub seat" to accompany the tableau at the end of scene 27. In such stillness, it was easy to notice the Coulmiers, who had been drinking tea throughout the scene, now nodding sympathetically with the new rhythm.

Scenes 28–32: The Experience of Act 2

Anyone primarily interested in the ideas debated by Marat and Sade may think that Sade had already defeated Marat in scenes 23–26, leaving act 2 with no serious substance. Seen from that point of view, act 2 is short and anticlimactic, a brief excuse for some further preaching before the final riot. But the thematic development of the play is not completely finished, for the final scenes of Sade's play contain some of his strongest statements on the subjective nature of reality and on the superiority of experience to dogma and other "ideas about" experience. Brook's reinforcing production strategy was to draw the audience into a fascination with the personalities of Corday, Duperret, Marat, and Sade.

The final formal debate between Marat and Sade (scene 28) illustrated how a director can transform a discussion of ideas into an interpersonal meeting between remarkable men. In the script, Sade attacks Marat's literary labors and draws two admissions from Marat: that his writing has indeed proved futile, and that he suffers from "doubt," the subjective condition that revolutionaries traditionally regard as defeat. In the RSC production, the scene became more emotional, and the polemical debate became a conversation about shared experience. Magee took care not to gloat in reciting Marat's errors. Richardson, in Marat's defense, acknowledged Magee-Sade as a person —it was one of the few times in the play that he had done so. Although consumed by paranoia and doubt, haunted by the false ring of his own rhetoric, Marat was now more than ever personalized by Sade, which was one of his hidden homages to his opponent. At the end, when Richardson admitted doubt, Magee sighed in relief rather than crowing in triumph. He pushed Richardson's head onto the writing table on the singers' line that ends "you lie prostrate," but the push was gentle and Magee's face was full of sorrow. The moment argued that any self-respecting revolutionary hates to defeat any other, no matter how necessary their struggle.

The next major sequence, scenes 29–30, focuses on Corday, who speaks movingly about the guillotine, puts off Duperret, and approaches Marat's door. What is notable about the sequence is that her words and actions are all repetitions of bits from earlier scenes, and one of her major speeches, which begins "What kind of town is this," is actually a reprise of a prominent speech made upon her arrival in Paris (scene 10). Lacking novelties of plot or thematic developments, Brook put his directorial stress on Corday-Jackson and the personal eccentricities she revealed in performance. When Jackson delivered the guillotine speech that begins "Now I know what it is like / when the head is cut off the body," she spoke the first sixteen lines of verse with sustained momentum, ending with a loud, plosive rendition of "split us in two" and a fake suicidal stab at her own midsection with the real, sharp knife that the Herald had given her earlier. During the speech's final lines, her voice trailed off, and she gazed at the knife with eerie playfulness. Jackson delivered the second of Corday's great solos in scene 29 ("Look at this city") as if utterly absorbed in a vision, and she ended with a shriek indicative of fearful anticipation while waiting "for our own names to be called." In the third of these solos, the reprise of "What kind of town is this," Jackson demonstrated the inmate's depressive drowsiness, for she spoke while being supported on each side by the nuns. As in her other speeches, her self-absorbed intensity was mesmerizing, and the audience could neither avoid her nor resist sharing her estranged vision. In arranging his play thus, Sade is using Corday to prepare the audience for his last big point.

As a playwright, Sade is at his most seductive in scene 30, and so was Patrick Magee as a speaker. Describing Corday's girlhood, Magee lingered provocatively over certain phrases: "pure girls," "hard floors," "rough shifts," "barred windows," "moist thighs and breasts," "the outside world." He had placed Jackson on the central grate of the bathhouse, focusing pornographic and philosophic attention on her person, just as the real Sade would have done. Attention on persons was also the theme of his memories of imprisonment and his discovery of the analogy between psychological and social "cells." In Sade's last substantial argument to Marat, Patrick Magee was at his most candid while stating the conclusion toward which Sade has driven his play:

> Marat
> these cells of the inner self
> are worse than the deepest stone dungeon
> and as long as they are locked
> all your Revolution remains
> only a prison mutiny
> to be put down
> by corrupted fellow-prisoners

The primary liberation is the personal, psychological one, runs Sade's argument, and without that revolution, the kind of social upheaval that Marat envisions is futile. One of the production's most whistleable melodies supported this ironic restatement of Sade's point: "And what's the point of a revolution / without general — / general copulation copulation cop-u-la-tion." Since the song was a round, it went on: "*And* what's the point . . . "

Scene 30 climaxes with the thrilling yet alienated assassination sequence. During the "Copulation Round," Marat's tub was brought down center, facing left, and Corday walked off down left. After miming her way through the door, she approached Marat straight across the front of the stage, from down left to down center, saying, "I will tell you the names of my heroes," fearlessly now because she was "speaking to a dead man." Marat protested that he could not understand her —night was falling fast —though he was facing her and was close enough to reach her when he said, "Who are you / Come closer." The inmates watched raptly. Richardson and Jackson touched, and she moved upstage of his tub, then said, "I name you names / Marat" and began her long list of the rebels. Weiss imagines Corday's face at this moment being "distorted increasingly by an expression of hate and lust." In her performance, Glenda Jackson ignored these obvious sources of tension and concentrated on the inmate's difficulty in speaking the names: "and Brissot / and Vergniaud / and Gaudet / and Gensonné." The audience had to hang on her every syllable, on her every consonant, as she confusedly went through the list. Then Richardson cried, "Bas / Take this down," and Jackson drew up behind him, to the right of the tub, her knife raised for the kill.

Scene 31 and the song "Fifteen Glorious Years" interrupted with breathtaking swiftness. Sade's "dramatic plan" is as boldly dialectical as anything Brecht ever wrote. The singers were mocking and sassy as they casually recounted the horrors and hypocrisies of the years 1793–1808.

Scene 33: The Riot

When *Marat/Sade* opened in London, Weiss confessed, "I learnt most from Brecht."[104] In *The Empty Space,* Brook said that "the *Marat/Sade* could not have existed before Brecht."[105] There are many points of comparison between Weiss's drama and Brecht's theory and practice, but I wish to show that *Marat/Sade* illustrates Brecht's dictum about *The Threepenny Opera:* "the whole power of this kind of drama comes from the accumulation of resistances."[106]

Weiss's first act establishes resistances and frictions between inmates, between inmates and keepers, between intellectual positions, between sides of the stage, and between theatrical styles. The second act provides a series of moments in which inmate restlessness and resistance reach higher and higher peaks of intensity. At the end of the play, the energy accumulated by all these resistances is unleashed in rebellion. Sade's dramaturgical triumph is to write a play that can pass the censor and then, by virtue of its internal dynamic, nearly destroy the censor and the order he supports.

In the second act, the inmates' resistance increases in the following moments of unified sound and movement: the chant "Ma-rat Ma-rat" at the end of scene 27, the "Copulation Round" in scene 30, the song about "Fifteen Glorious Years" in scene 31, and the ending of the epilogue —the song that begins when the evening is apparently over. Directing these scenes, Brook emphasized that the inmates' violence and unity increased until, during the epilogue song, they marched in a mass, like an attack force, and headed directly for the audience. Like a dutiful Brechtian, Brook also restrained each of these threatening moments, first by following each with a scene of quiet intensity, second by providing a kind of formal restraint within each moment. For example, Magee formalized the "Ma-rat Ma-rat" chant by directing it with his hand. The copulation song was formally sung, since it was a round, and formally staged, with pairs of inmates performing coordinated, obviously rehearsed mimes of copulatory movements. "Fifteen Glorious Years" required intense concentration on the part of the singers, because its lyrical density and musical speed ($\sJ$ = 124–28, with many eighth and sixteenth notes) could render obscure the points it had to make. Brook's productions are usually famous for being energetic, but not for being unruly, and in these scenes of *Marat/Sade* he strongly contained, without squelching, the rising energy on the stage. Only at the end did he completely release it.

Unlike many plays that move from question to answer, *Marat/Sade* provides many answers in its beginning and middle but ends with an overriding question. The strategy is reminiscent of Brecht and characteristic of Brook, especially the Brook of this period. The final question demonstrates Weiss's unresolved contradictions at a certain point in his political development. Of course, the play's question is also that of the fictional playwright, Sade.

In Brook's stage version (in both London and New York), the Herald addressed Sade immediately after the death of Marat:

> Tell us Monsieur de Sade for our instruction
> just what you have achieved with your production.
> Who won? Who lost? We'd like to know
> the meaning of your bath-house show[107]

In answering, Magee lingered over Sade's ironies:

> Of course you'd like to take away
> a meaning or a moral from my play.
> Well so you shall, for one of you will see
> a sensual interpretation of history.
> Another one undoubtedly will say,
> "It wasn't about Marat, but about today."
> Husband and wife most certainly will quarrel.
> He'll say it's filthy, she'll insist it's moral.
> Well, you may all create your varying theses —

(Hear the scatological rhyme coming?) Slowly, and disgustedly, he added:

> and keep them on your mantlepieces

All Sade would say was that the play was meant to work deeply serious but unconscious changes on the audience's spirits. This was Artaud's method:

> A word of useless warning in your ear:
> everything that we see or hear
> can add to or increase us in some way.
> And so it might be with this play.
> Some seeds have drifted from our stage. A few
> may have entered and taken root in you.
> But what these seeds are, even though
> in your darkest places they feed and grow,
> whatever these seeds are, you will never know[108]

In the spring of 1966, when making the movie, Magee had another epilogue speech. It began:

> Our play's chief aim has been —to take to bits
> great propositions and their opposites,
> see how they work, then let them fight it out.

> The point? Some light on our eternal doubt.
> I have twisted and turned them every way
> and find no ending to our play.

He continued by analyzing his and Marat's differences over the question of power. Finally, he looked away and said:

> So for me the last word cannot ever be spoken.
> I am left with a question that's always open.[109]

A question that is always open —a perfect summary of Brook's production. "In the twentieth century you can't teach anyone anything in the form of a proclamation, a declaration," Brook has said. "You can only ask people questions, and open your ears to their questions."[110]

The textual changes just noted constitute only a few of many variant versions of Weiss's epilogue. In fact, nearly every *Marat/Sade* seems to conclude with a slightly different epilogue: Weiss's two German editions (1964 and 1965); Atheneum's English translation; Brook's scripts for the stage production, the movie, and the phonograph record; and the German productions about which I know. In the briefest version, the finale consists of Coulmier's short summary speech and the inmates' song. In the longest version, the Herald, Marat, Corday, Roux, Sade, and Coulmier all have a chance to comment before the song begins. Variations may stem from political orientation, production needs, or literary taste. But an open textual conclusion is appropriate to the play's open intellectual conclusion.

The final song began quietly ("And if most have a little and few have a lot / you can see how much nearer our goal we have got") and, ironically affirming the unity of Napoleon's France, built quickly and steadily in volume. The inmates marched vigorously in a group at center stage. Over to one side, Jacques Roux began to yell. The song ended with unison chants: "Chá-rén-tón, Chá-rén-tón, Napó-lé-ón, Napó-lé-ón." As they continued chanting—"Ná-tión, Ná-tión, Rév-o-lú-tion-rév-o-lú-tion"—the inmates abandoned their unison and their tight physical grouping. Suddenly bodies were flying through the air, along with the portrait of Napoleon that the Herald had held on the ladder. Inmates attacked the guards and the nuns and the bathhouse itself, wildly banging buckets against the grates and traps. Duperret and another inmate viciously assaulted Coulmier's women, at last releasing the sexual tension that had been accumulating. Clothes and props were thrown about the room and the improvised mayhem sometimes resulted in the shedding of real blood and the breaking of real teeth, as well as truly unconscious actors. Ever the repertory professional mindful of his next night's duties, Ian Richardson tried to find a way to participate in the riot while avoiding the worst. Patrick Magee stood to one side laughing wildly at the results of Sade's infernal work. Clifford Rose (Coulmier) rushed about the room exhorting the asylum forces to attempt more vigorously to subdue the inmates. "Nothing, we feel, could ever stop this riot," wrote Brook. "Nothing, we conclude, can ever stop the madness of the world."[111]

The final seconds of Brook's production were among his most brilliant. In his research, he had been deeply concerned about how theatre—its artists and its art—could or should relate to the audiences that were so vital to the theatrical event. In *Marat/Sade,* he followed this line of questioning in deciding on an appropriate conclusion. He rejected the conventional relief and relaxation implicit in the conventional curtain call and searched instead for a mode of provocation. In a "stable and harmonious society," Brook said, productions might end with goodwill and declarations of community between stage and house, but the world of 1964 was a "shifting, chaotic world" forced to choose between "a playhouse that offers a spurious 'yes' or a provocation so strong that it splinters its audience into fragments of vivid 'nos'."[112] This perception led him to impose a final theatrical alienation that stopped the proceedings with a jolt and left the play's questions for the audience to resolve.

The riot was interrupted at its peak by a loud whistle, similar to the sound emitted by the whistle of a modern athletic coach. The actors abruptly stopped what they were doing. Onto the stage came the RSC stage manager, dressed in contemporary clothing, still blowing her whistle to end the riot. Some actors removed their wigs. Others straightened their clothes and looked up. The lights remained up and no curtain closed over the scene. The off-balance audience, realizing that this was apparently the ending, began clapping, first tentatively and then more assuredly. At this point the actors moved to the front of the stage (further down than they had been during the play), looked out at the audience, and clapped back at them, sometimes in rhythmic unison. This was not the return of applause seen particularly in revolutionary theatres—the "we love you too" variety. This applause conveyed alienation and hostility. The audience, wondering whether the actors were still in character or whether there would be more "play," stopped applauding. Some individuals were put off by Brook's tactic, and many of them left the theatre hurriedly. The rest waited, talking or thinking or watching the actors. Gradually the actors straggled off. The production was over. But it still had to face "the acid test."

The Acid Test

I know of one acid test in the theatre. It is literally an acid test. When a performance is over, what remains? Fun can be forgotten, but powerful emotion also disappears and good arguments lose their thread. When emotion and argument are harnessed to a wish from the audience to see more clearly into itself—then something in the mind burns. The event scorches on to the memory an outline, a taste, a trace, a smell—a picture. It is the play's central image that remains, its silhouette, and if the elements are rightly blended this silhouette will be its meaning, this shape will be the essence of what it has to say.[113]

As examples of central images, Brook recalled two tramps under a tree, a woman pulling a wagon, and a trio of people in a hotel room. The last image, of course, was from *No Exit*, which was called *Vicious Circle* when Brook directed it in 1946. Fifteen years after directing that Sartre play, Brook could bring back not "one word of the dialogue, not one detail of the philosophy," only a very clear picture of those "three people locked in an eternal hotel room."[114] That image, the product of imagination rather than of journalistic or philosophic intelligence, so commanded the imaginations of a generation that many, like Brook, always saw that hotel room whenever anyone mentioned hell.

Those who viewed Brook's *Marat/Sade* remembered a central image of the Charenton madhouse—not its bricks, boards, and traps but its microcosmic humanity. It was a complex and powerful image of obscure passions and unfathomable vehemence, and it was fraught with echoes of the strangely insistent voices of Roux, Duperret, Marat, Simonne, and Sade and of the unpredictably nervous voice of Glenda Jackson as she described Judith, who "entered the tent of the enemy / and with a single blow / SLEW HIM!!!" Spectators also remembered the inmates' bodies and physical expressions, all somehow out of kilter, and their frantic attempts at dance. (They banged their feet on the raked wooden stage and rushed to make the downbeat). The inmates, by their very insistence, forced the audience to acknowledge their presence and to realize that the mad men and women of Charenton might have something to tell about social conditions and human identity. Most often, audiences left *Marat/Sade* with memories of faces, especially the faces of members of the inmate chorus: the androgynous drooler with the wispy hair; the man whose face seemed cut from stone; the timid, bespectacled old woman wearing a cap; the man with the cracked skull; and Leon Lissek, with his dark and threatening eyes. Whether catatonic or hostile, the inmates were all obsessed by some vision, urge, or idea. As we say of such people in real life, they presented a challenge by virtue of their extraordinary presence.

But it is not enough to say that the central image of Brook's *Marat/Sade* was the madhouse and its inhabitants. Brook used Charenton as both Sade and Weiss did, to make contact with the madhouse that is the world. His image was not a remote artistic construction framed by a proscenium or enclosed within theatre walls, except during the play's two hours' traffic. His art had reality and meaning only as an event involving the audience. During the New York run, Brook said that the production's two "protagonists" were "the play" and "the audience." My inference from that remark is that dramatic conflict, suffering, and catharsis were experienced far more intensely by the audience than by Marat, Sade, or anyone else on the stage.[115] Audience involvement had negative side effects: spectators stormed out in mid-performance, spectators became ill, and at least one spectator, the German actress Ruth Yorick, died in the auditorium during a performance. The positive effect, predictable from Brook's research, was that he disturbed his audiences politically, morally, and emotionally. Their being disturbed depended on two factors: (1) what Brook called the "wish from the audience to see more clearly into itself," a fervent wish among audiences during the company's New York engagement; and (2) Brook's desire to disturb and provoke in order to achieve his highest artistic and personal goals. In 1973 he summarized his intention for an interviewer:

> The *Marat/Sade* production in New York was possible on that scale because it wasn't affirming what was good and glorious in life, but something that most spectators could relate to very directly, violence and madness. And that whole wave of dark plays came out of a sense, perhaps, of this being the only area where an affirmation was possible, even if the response was through disturbance. In fact, disturbance is one of the lifelines in large-scale performances.[116]

Notes

Introduction

1. Bertolt Brecht, *Collected Plays,* vol. 5, ed. Ralph Manheim and John Willett (New York: Vintage Books, 1972), p. 355.
2. W. B. Yeats, *Explorations* (New York: Macmillan, 1962), pp. 94, 107.
3. Ezra Pound and T. E. Hulme are quoted from William Pratt, ed., *The Imagist Poem* (New York: Dutton, 1963), pp. 18, 28.
4. Andrew Sarris, "Notes on the Auteur Theory in 1962," in Gerald Mast and Marshall Cohen, eds., *Film Theory and Criticism: Introductory Readings,* 2d ed. (New York: Oxford Univ. Press, 1979), p. 660.
5. David Cole, *The Theatrical Event: A Mythos, A Vocabulary, A Perspective* (Middletown, Conn.: Wesleyan Univ. Press, 1975), p. 5.
6. Meyerhold quoted by Harold Clurman, *On Directing* (New York: Macmillan, 1972), p. 84.
7. J. Robert Wills, *The Director in a Changing Theatre* (Palo Alto, Calif.: Mayfield, 1976), p. 3.
8. Clurman, *On Directing,* p. 14.
9. Interview of Stella Adler in *Theater* (New Haven) 8, nos. 2–3 (Spring 1977): 36.
10. Edward Gordon Craig, *The Art of the Theatre: First Dialogue,* reprinted in Eric Bentley, ed., *The Theory of the Modern Stage* (Baltimore: Penguin Books, 1968), p. 137.
11. Jerzy Grotowski, *Towards a Poor Theatre* (New York: Simon & Schuster, 1968), p. 48.

1. Konstantin Stanislavsky and *The Seagull:* The Paper Stage

1. S. D. Balukhaty, ed., and David Magarshack, trans., *The Seagull Produced by Stanislavsky* (New York: Theatre Arts Books, 1952), p. 57.
2. Vladimir Nemirovitch-Dantchenko, *My Life in the Russian Theatre,* trans. John Cournos (London: Geoffrey Bles, 1937), pp. 150–51.

3. David Magarshack, *Stanislavsky: A Life* (London: MacGibbon & Kee, 1950), p. 173.

4. Konstantin Stanislavsky, *My Life in Art*, trans. J. J. Robbins (1924; reprint, New York: Meridian, 1956), p. 321.

5. Nemirovitch-Dantchenko, *My Life in the Russian Theatre*, p. 149.

6. Magarshack, *Stanislavsky: A Life*, p. 168.

7. Konstantin Stanislavsky, *Stanislavsky on the Art of the Stage*, trans. David Magarshack (New York: Hill & Wang, 1961), p. 95.

8. Nemirovitch-Dantchenko, *My Life in the Russian Theatre*, pp. 153–54.

9. Balukhaty, *The Seagull Produced by Stanislavsky*. Throughout the text, I have quoted from play text and mise-en-scène notes without page citation.

10. Nemirovitch-Dantchenko, *My Life in the Russian Theatre*, p. 165.

11. Stanislavsky, *My Life in Art*, p. 355.

12. *The Letters of Anton Chekhov*, ed. Avrahm Yarmolinsky (New York: Viking Press, 1973), p. 261.

13. Balukhaty, *The Seagull Produced by Stanislavsky*, p. 55.

14. Stanislavsky, *My Life in Art*, p. 356.

15. Stanislavsky, *My Life in Art*, p. 279. References are to act and scene.

16. Konstantin Stanislavsky, *Stanislavsky's Legacy*, rev. ed., trans. and ed. E. R. Hapgood (New York: Theatre Arts Books, 1968), p. 20.

17. Konstantin Stanislavsky, *An Actor Prepares*, trans. E. R. Hapgood (New York: Theatre Arts Books, 1936), p. 14.

18. Stanislavsky, *An Actor Prepares*, p. 122. In the original, "belief" is twice italicized.

19. Stanislavsky, *My Life in Art*, pp. 465–66.

20. *Konstantin Stanislavsky, 1863–1963*, ed. Sergei Malik-Zakharov and Shoel Bogatyrev, trans. Vic Schneierson (Moscow: Progress Publishers, 1965), p. 130. The writer is Yuri Olesha.

21. Stanislavsky, *My Life in Art*, p. 383.

22. Stanislavsky, *My Life in Art*, p. 270.

23. Konstantin Stanislavsky, *Stanislavsky Produces Othello*, trans. Helen Nowack (New York: Theatre Arts Books, 1948), p. 79.

24. Stanislavsky, *Stanislavsky Produces Othello*, pp. 203, 190, 151.

25. Stanislavsky, *An Actor Prepares*, p. 14.

26. Nikolai M. Gorchakov, *Stanislavsky Directs*, trans. Miriam Goldina (n.p.: Minerva Press, 1954, 1968), p. 63.

27. *Konstantin Stanislavsky, 1863–1963*, p. 198.

28. Stanislavsky, *An Actor Prepares*, p. 136.

29. Magarshack, *Stanislavsky: A Life*, p. 184.

30. Balukhaty, *The Seagull Produced by Stanislavsky*, p. 130.

31. Stanislavsky, *My Life in Art*, p. 322.

32. Stanislavsky, *My Life in Art*, pp. 210, 207, 229.

33. Stanislavsky, *My Life in Art*, p. 210.

34. Stanislavsky, *My Life in Art*, pp. 197–98, 201.

35. Stanislavsky, *My Life in Art*, p. 281.

36. Stanislavsky, *Stanislavsky's Legacy*, pp. 131–32.

37. *Konstantin Stanislavsky, 1863–1963*, pp. 114, 116.

38. Gorchakov, *Stanislavsky Directs*, pp. 250–51.

39. J. B. Priestley, *Anton Chekhov* (London: International Profiles, 1970), p. 78.

40. Magarshack, *Stanislavsky: A Life*, p. 303.

41. Balukhaty, *The Seagull Produced by Stanislavsky*, p. 65.

42. *Meyerhold on Theatre*, ed. Edward Braun (New York: Hill & Wang, 1969), p. 30.

43. Stanislavsky, *My Life in Art*, p. 420.

44. *The Letters of Anton Chekhov*, ed. M. H. Heim and Simon Karlinsky (New York: Harper & Row, 1973), p. 357.

45. Balukhaty, *The Seagull Produced by Stanislavsky*, p. 72.

46. Stanislavsky, *My Life in Art*, p. 358; and Stanislavsky, *Stanislavsky on the Art of the Stage*, p. 13.

47. *Letters of Anton Chekhov*, ed. Heim and Karlinsky, p. 357.

48. Stanislavsky, *Stanislavsky on the Art of the Stage*, p. 85.

49. *Letters of Anton Chekhov*, ed. Heim and Karlinsky, p. 357.

50. Balukhaty, *The Seagull Produced by Stanislavsky*, p. 81.

51. David Magarshack, *Chekhov: A Life* (London: Faber & Faber, 1952), p. 339.

52. Stanislavsky, *Stanislavsky Produces Othello*, p. 199.

53. Harvey Pitcher, *The Chekhov Play: A New Interpretation* (London: Chatto & Windus, 1973), p. 64.

54. Nemirovitch-Dantchenko, *My Life in the Russian Theatre*, p. 58.

55. Gorchakov, *Stanislavsky Directs*, p. 310.

56. Henrik Ibsen, *Hedda Gabler and Three Other Plays*, trans. Michael Meyer (Garden City, N.Y.: Anchor Books, 1961), p. 370.

57. Nemirovitch-Dantchenko, *My Life in the Russian Theatre*, p. 259.

58. Stanislavsky, *Stanislavsky's Legacy*, p. 79.

59. Nemirovitch-Dantchenko, *My Life in the Russian Theatre*, p. 162.

60. Balukhaty, *The Seagull Produced by Stanislavsky*, p. 72.

61. Stanislavsky, *My Life in Art*, p. 353.

62. Theodore Komisarjevsky, *Myself and the Theatre* (New York: Dutton, 1930), p. 136.

63. Komisarjevsky, *Myself and the Theatre*, p. 136.

64. Stanislavsky, *My Life in Art*, p. 353.

65. Komisarjevsky, *Myself and the Theatre*, p. 137.

66. Konstantin Stanislavsky, *Building a Character*, trans. E. R. Hapgood (New York: Theatre Arts Books, 1949), p. 108.

67. Komisarjevsky, *Myself and the Theatre*, p. 137.

2. Bertolt Brecht and *Couragemodell 1949:* Meaning in Detail

1. The volume's cover reads, "Brecht, *Couragemodell 1949*"; its inside cover reads "Brecht, *Mutter Courage und ihre Kinder: Text, Aufführung, Anmerkungen*" (Berlin: Henschelverlag, 1958). I quote without page citation from this volume and from the translation of play and notes in Brecht, *Collected Plays*, vol. 5, ed. Ralph Manheim and John Willett (New York: Vintage, 1972). Since Manheim and Willett do not include all the notes of the original, I have supplemented their translations with my own and with those of Eric Bentley and Hugo Schmidt published in Toby Cole and Helen Krich Chinoy, eds., *Directors on Directing* rev. ed. (Indianapolis: Bobbs-Merrill, 1963), pp. 333–46.

2. Klaus Volker, *Brecht Chronicle*, trans. Fred Wieck (New York: Seabury Press, 1975), p. 167.

3. Bertolt Brecht, *Brecht on Theatre*, trans. John Willett (New York: Hill & Wang, 1964), p. 209.

4. Volker, *Brecht Chronicle*, p. 169.

5. Brecht, *Brecht on Theatre*, p. 211.

6. Ruth Berlau et al., eds., *Theaterarbeit: 6 Aufführungen des Berliner Ensembles* (Dresden: Dresdner Verlag, 1952), pp. 296–302.

7. Brecht, *Brecht on Theatre*, p. 211.

8. Brecht, *Brecht on Theatre*, p. 224.

9. Brecht, *Brecht on Theatre*, pp. 224, 211.

10. *Collected Poems of William Butler Yeats* (New York: Macmillan, 1956), p. 91.

11. Brecht, *Brecht on Theatre*, p. 65.

12. Quoted by Wolfgang Roth in "Working with B. B.," *Brecht Heute/ Brecht Today* 2 (1972): 133.

13. Brecht, *Brecht on Theatre*, p. 248.

14. John Heilpern, *Conference of the Birds* (Indianapolis: Bobbs-Merrill, 1977), p. 57.

15. Egon Monk quoted from Bertolt Brecht, *Collected Plays*, vol. 9, ed. Ralph Manheim and John Willett (New York: Vintage Books, 1972), p. 370.

16. Carl Weber, "Brecht as Director," *The Drama Review* 12 (Fall 1967): 102–3.

17. Weber, "Brecht as Director," p. 104.

18. Quoted from "Dialogue: Berliner Ensemble," *The Drama Review* 12 (Fall 1967): 114.

19. Brecht, *Brecht on Theatre*, p. 213.
20. Weber, "Brecht as Director," p. 103.
21. Brecht, *Brecht on Theatre*, p. 42.
22. Brecht, *Brecht on Theatre*, p. 198.
23. Brecht, *Brecht on Theatre*, p. 236.
24. Roland Barthes, "Seven Photo Models of *Mother Courage,*" *The Drama Review* 12 (Fall 1967): 44
25. Brecht, *Collected Plays*, vol. 9, p. 346.
26. Brecht, *Brecht on Theatre*, pp. 14–15.
27. Walter Benjamin, *Understanding Brecht*, trans. Anna Bostock (London: NLB, 1973), pp. 106–7.
28. Bernhard Reich, "Erinnerungen an den jungen Brecht," *Sinn und Form* 9 (1957): 431–36.
29. Benjamin, *Understanding Brecht*, pp. 106–7.
30. Roth, "Working with B. B." p. 131.
31. Brecht, *Brecht on Theatre*, pp. 127, 135.
32. Benjamin, *Understanding Brecht*, pp. 119–20.
33. Brecht, *Brecht on Theatre*, p. 173.
34. Brecht, *Brecht on Theatre*, pp. 180–81.
35. Brecht, *Brecht on Theatre*, p. 243.
36. John Fuegi, "*The Caucasian Chalk Circle* in Performance," *Brecht Heute/Brecht Today* 1 (1971): 149.
37. Volker, *Brecht Chronicle*, p. 152.
38. The Teo Otto model is in *Theaterarbeit*, p. 282.
39. Roth, "Working with B. B.," p. 133.
40. Brecht, *Collected Plays*, vol. 9, p. 339.
41. *Major Barbara* quoted from *Bernard Shaw: Complete Plays with Prefaces*, 6 vols. (New York: Dodd, Mead, 1962), 1: 341.
42. *Juno and the Paycock* quoted from *Three Plays by Sean O'Casey* (New York: St. Martin's Press, 1967), p. 6.
43. *Desire Under the Elms,* quoted from *Nine Plays of Eugene O'Neill* (New York: Modern Library, 1941), p. 155.
44. Quoted by Manfred Wekwerth in "From *Brecht Today,*" *The Drama Review* 12 (Fall 1967): 119.
45. Eric Bentley, "Introduction: Homage to B. B.," *Seven Plays by Bertolt Brecht* (New York: Grove Press, 1961), p. xxiii.
46. Kenneth Tynan, *Tynan Right and Left* (New York: Atheneum, 1967), p. 63.
47. Wekwerth, "From *Brecht Today,*" p. 120.
48. Bentley, "Introduction: Homage to B. B.," p. xlviii.
49. Brecht, *Collected Plays*, vol. 9, pp. 361, 392.
50. Darko Suvin, "The Mirror and the Dynamo," *The Drama Review* 12 (Fall 1967): 64.

51. Bentley's translation is from *Seven Plays by Bertolt Brecht,* p. 330.

52. Roth, "Working with B. B.," p. 134.

53. Bertolt Brecht, *Collected Plays,* vol. 7, ed. Ralph Manheim and John Willett (New York: Vintage Books, 1974), p. 299.

54. Paul Dessau, "Composing for BB: Some Comments," *The Drama Review* 12 (Winter 1968): 153.

55. The timings appear in *Theaterarbeit,* p. 302.

56. Brecht, *Brecht on Theatre,* p. 37.

57. Bentley, *Seven Plays by Bertolt Brecht,* p. 330.

58. Volker, *Brecht Chronicle,* p. 176.

59. Brecht, *Brecht on Theatre,* p. 181.

3. Elia Kazan and *A Streetcar Named Desire:* A Director at Work

1. James Poling, "Handy 'Gadget,'" *Collier's,* May 31, 1952, p. 58.

2. Frederic Morton, "Gadg," *Esquire,* February 1957, p. 123.

3. Poling, "Handy 'Gadget,'" p. 58.

4. Michel Ciment, *Kazan on Kazan* (London: Secker & Warburg, 1973), p. 42.

5. Ciment, *Kazan on Kazan,* pp. 41–42.

6. Ciment, *Kazan on Kazan,* p. 175.

7. I have quoted from the following sources without page citation: *A Streetcar Named Desire: Acting Edition* (New York: Dramatists Play Service, 1953); *A Streetcar Named Desire* (New York: New Directions, 1947); Williams's filmscript for the Warner Bros. movie, *A Streetcar Named Desire,* in G. P. Garrett, O. B. Hardison, and J. R. Gelfman, eds., *Film Scripts One* (New York: Appleton-Century-Crofts, 1971), pp. 330–484; and Kazan's notes in Toby Cole and Helen Krich Chinoy, eds., *Directors on Directing,* rev. ed. (Indianapolis: Bobbs-Merrill, 1963), pp. 364–79.

I have also made extensive use of information available in the Robert Downing Collection at the Humanities Research Center, Univ. of Texas (Austin). Downing was both *Streetcar*'s production stage manager and a meticulous collector, so this material includes telegrams from the callboard, cue sheets, early promptbooks, and extensive books of newspaper clippings. I have a few times quoted from the latter without page citations.

8. Francis Fergusson, "The Notion of 'Action,'" *Tulane Drama Review* 9 (Fall 1964): 85–87.

9. Richard Schechner and Theodore Hoffman, "'Look, There's an American Theatre': An Interview with Elia Kazan," *Tulane Drama Review* 9 (Winter 1964): 73.

10. Ciment, *Kazan on Kazan,* p. 41.

11. Schechner and Hoffman, "'Look, There's an American Theatre,'" p. 73.

12. Hermine Rich Isaacs, "First Rehearsals: Elia Kazan Directs a Modern Legend," *Theatre Arts* 28 (March 1944): 147.

13. Schechner and Hoffman, "'Look, There's an American Theatre,'" p. 74.

14. Schechner and Hoffman, "'Look, There's an American Theatre,'" p. 73.

15. Morton, "Gadg," pp. 118–19.

16. Rosamund Gilder, "The Playwright Takes Over: Broadway in Review," *Theatre Arts* 32 (January 1948): 10.

17. Ciment, *Kazan on Kazan,* p. 105.

18. Tony Thomas, *The Films of Marlon Brando* (Secaucus, N.J.: Citadel Press, 1973), p. 15.

19. Ciment, *Kazan on Kazan,* pp. 106–7.

20. Tony Thomas, *The Films of Marlon Brando,* p. 2; and Elia Kazan, "What Makes a Woman Interesting?" *Vogue,* January 15, 1962, p. 27.

21. Tony Thomas, *The Films of Marlon Brando,* p. 15.

22. Ciment, *Kazan on Kazan,* pp. 105–7.

23. Bob Thomas, *Marlon: Portrait of the Rebel as an Artist* (New York: Random House, 1973), p. 40.

24. Bob Thomas, *Marlon,* p. 41.

25. Tony Thomas, *The Films of Marlon Brando,* p. 14.

26. Truman Capote, "The Duke in His Domain," *The New Yorker,* November 9, 1957, p. 65.

27. Tony Thomas, *The Films of Marlon Brando,* p. 43.

28. Bob Thomas, *Marlon,* p. 49.

29. Eric Bentley, *In Search of Theater* (New York: Knopf, 1953), pp. 87–89.

30. Elsa Maxwell, "Party Line," *New York Post,* November 28, 1947, p. 12.

31. Robert Garland, "Williams' New Play Exciting Theatre," *New York Journal-American,* December 4, 1947, reprinted in *New York Theatre Critics' Reviews* 8 (1947): 251.

32. Wolcott Gibbs, "Lower Depths, Southern Style," *New Yorker,* December 13, 1947, p. 55.

33. John Chapman, "*Streetcar Named Desire* Sets Season's High in Acting, Writing," *Daily News* (New York), December 4, 1947, reprinted in *New York Theatre Critics' Reviews* 8 (1947): 249.

34. William Beyer, "The State of the Theater: Late Season," *School and Society,* March 27, 1948, p. 242.

35. John Mason Brown, "Southern Discomfort," *Saturday Review,* December 17, 1947, p. 24.

36. Irwin Shaw, "Theater: Masterpiece," *New Republic,* December 22, 1947, pp. 34–35.

37. Tony Thomas, *The Films of Marlon Brando,* p. 15.

38. Gilder, "The Playwright Takes Over," p. 11.

39. Murray Schumach, "A Director Named Gadge," *New York Times Magazine,* November 9, 1947, p. 18.

40. Ciment, *Kazan on Kazan,* p. 12.

41. Poling, "Handy 'Gadget,'" p. 60.

42. James F. Fixx, "Who Cares What the Boss Thinks?" *Saturday Review,* December 28, 1963, p. 14; and Kazan's interview with Dick Cavett (PBS, July 1978).

43. Schumach, "A Director Named Gadge," p. 18.

44. Tennessee Williams, *Memoirs* (New York: Bantam Books, 1976), p. 140.

45. *Tennessee Williams' Letters to Donald Windham, 1940–1965,* ed. Donald Windham (New York: Holt, Rinehart & Winston, 1977), p. 198.

46. Joshua Logan, *Josh: My Up and Down, In and Out Life* (New York: Delacorte Press, 1976), p. 238.

47. Williams, *Memoirs,* p. 163.

48. Ward Morehouse, "Keeping Up with Kazan," *Theatre Arts* 41 (June 1956): 88; and Ciment, *Kazan on Kazan,* pp. 30–31.

49. "Helpful," *New Yorker,* November 29, 1947, p. 34.

50. Jessica Tandy, "One Year of Blanche Dubois," *New York Times,* November 28, 1948, sec. 2, p. 3.

51. Kazan's interview with Dick Cavett (PBS, July 1978).

52. Williams, *Memoirs,* p. 164.

53. Williams, *Memoirs,* pp. 169, 209, 163.

54. Gilbert Maxwell, *Tennessee Williams and Friends* (Cleveland: World, 1965), p. 116.

55. Williams, *Memoirs,* p. 169.

56. Mike Steen, *A Look at Tennessee Williams* (New York: Hawthorn Books, 1969), pp. 171–72.

57. Theodore Strauss, "The Brilliant Brat," *Life,* July 31, 1950, p. 50.

58. Gary Carey, *Brando!* (New York: Pocket Books, 1973), p. 60.

59. Jo Mielziner, *Designing for the Theatre: A Memoir and a Portfolio* (New York: Bramhall, 1965), p. 141.

60. "Bone," "Plays Out of Town: *Streetcar Named Desire,*" *Variety,* November 5, 1947.

61. Williams, *Memoirs,* p. 170.

62. Review by Elinor Hughes in *Boston Herald,* reprinted in Jordan Y. Miller, ed., *Twentieth Century Interpretations of A Streetcar Named Desire* (Englewood Cliffs, N.J.: Prentice-Hall, 1971), pp. 27–28.

63. Elliot Norton, "Tennessee Williams Play Opens," *Boston Post,* November 4, 1947.

64. Linton Martin, "*Streetcar Named Desire* Is Strong Dramatic Meat," *Philadelphia Inquirer,* November 23, 1947.

65. R. E. P. Sensenderfer, "Living Theater," *Evening Bulletin* (Philadelphia), November 18, 1947.

66. Another change, made on the road, was the change in the epigraph to the play, which appeared in the programs. In New Haven and Boston, Williams used T. S. Eliot's translation of St. John Perse's *Anabasis* (London: Faber & Faber, 1930, pp. 35, 37): " . . . and the dustmen at dawn bearing away huge pieces of dead palm trees, fragments of giant wings. . . . Tomorrow the festivals." From Philadelphia onward, he used instead the Hart Crane lines that accompany the published text.

67. Mielziner, *Designing for the Theatre,* p. 41. The cue sheets survive in the Downing Collection.

68. "Plays on Broadway: *A Streetcar Named Desire,*" *Variety,* December 10, 1947.

69. Williams, *Memoirs,* p. 172.

70. Williams, *Memoirs,* p. 172.

71. Brooks Atkinson, "First Night at the Theatre," *New York Times,* December 4, 1947, p. 42; and Atkinson, "*Streetcar* Tragedy," *New York Times,* December 14, 1947, sec. 2, p. 3.

72. Chapman, "*Streetcar Named Desire* Sets Season's High," p. 249.

73. Richard Watts, Jr., "*Streetcar Named Desire* Is Striking Drama," *New York Post,* December 4, 1947, reprinted in *New York Theatre Critics' Reviews* 8 (1947): 249.

74. MacArthur quoted in *Variety,* December 10, 1947.

75. Lincoln Barnett, "Tennessee Williams," *Life,* February 16, 1948, p. 127.

76. Steen, *A Look at Tennessee Williams,* p. 291.

77. Kenneth Tynan, *Tynan Right and Left* (New York: Atheneum, 1967), p. 14.

78. George Jean Nathan, "The Streetcar Isn't Drawn by Pegasus," *New York Journal-American,* December 15, 1947, reprinted in Miller, *Twentieth Century Interpretations,* pp. 36–37.

79. Bentley, *In Search of Theater,* p. 33.

80. "Streetcar on Broadway," *Newsweek,* December 15, 1947, pp. 82–83.

81. Capote, "The Duke in His Domain," p. 56.

82. "Tall Grass," *Newsweek,* October 16, 1961, p. 112.

83. Williams, *Memoirs,* p. 104.

84. Tony Thomas, *The Films of Marlon Brando,* p. 2.

85. Ciment, *Kazan on Kazan,* p. 28.

86. Kazan's letter to the editor, *Theatre Arts* 31 (June 1947): 10.

87. "A Quiz for Kazan," *Theatre Arts* 40 (November 1956): 89.

88. Ciment, *Kazan on Kazan*, p. 155.

89. Ciment, *Kazan on Kazan*, p. 176.

90. Williams, *Memoirs*, pp. 169, 129.

91. Robert Anderson, "Walk a Ways with Me," *Theatre Arts* 38 (January 1954): 31.

92. Ciment, *Kazan on Kazan*, p. 35.

93. John F. Baker, "Elia Kazan," *Publishers Weekly,* January 13, 1975, p. 10.

94. Kappo Phelan, "Stage and Screen," *Commonweal,* December 19, 1947, p. 255.

95. Brown, "Southern Discomfort," p. 23.

96. Ciment, *Kazan on Kazan*, pp. 32, 68; and "A Quiz for Kazan," *Theatre Arts* 40 (November 1956): 30–31.

97. Ciment, *Kazan on Kazan*, p. 71.

98. Gibbs, "Lower Depths, Southern Style," p. 50.

99. Gilder, "The Playwright Takes Over," p. 10.

100. Elsa Maxwell, "Party Line," p. 12.

101. Robert Brustein, *The Third Theatre* (New York: Clarion Books, 1970), p. 207.

102. Steen, *A Look at Tennessee Williams*, pp. 181, 179.

103. Ciment, *Kazan on Kazan*, p. 42.

104. Kazan, "What Makes a Woman Interesting?" p. 28.

105. Gordon Rogoff, "A Streetcar Named Kazan," *Reporter,* December 17, 1964, p. 40.

106. Amy Porter, "Tandy Arrives on a Streetcar," *Collier's,* April 17, 1948.

107. J. W. Krutch, "Drama," *Nation,* December 20, 1947, p. 686.

108. Brooks Atkinson, "First Night at the Theatre," p. 42; and "Streetcar Tragedy," p. 3.

109. Brooks Atkinson, "Streetcar Passenger," *New York Times,* June 12, 1949, sec. 2, p. 1.

110. Bentley, *In Search of Theater*, pp. 87–88.

111. Helen Ormsbee, "The Girl on That New Orleans Streetcar," *New York Herald Tribune,* December 7, 1947.

112. Bentley, *In Search of Theater*, p. 88.

113. Watts, "*Streetcar Named Desire* Is Striking Drama," p. 249.

114. Morehouse, "Keeping Up with Kazan," p. 22.

115. Norton, "Tennessee Williams Play Opens."

116. Shaw, "Theater: Masterpiece," p. 34.

117. Cheryl Crawford, *One Naked Individual: My 50 Years in the Theatre* (Indianapolis: Bobbs-Merrill, 1977), p. 129.

118. Irving Drutman, "Malden Owes Streetcar Role to His 'Poor but Honest Face,'" *New York Herald Tribune,* February 29, 1948.

119. Steen, *A Look at Tennessee Williams,* p. 175.

120. "Streetcar on Broadway," *Newsweek,* December 15, 1947, p. 82; and Atkinson, "*Streetcar* Tragedy," p. 3.

121. Brown, "Southern Discomfort," p. 23; and Shaw, "Theater: Masterpiece," p. 34.

122. Steen, *A Look at Tennessee Williams,* pp. 180–81. A politer version of these thoughts appeared in *Look* on February 1, 1949, illustrated by the Benton painting and by a small photograph of a later incident, the poker night brawl.

123. Bob Thomas, *Marlon,* p. 58.

124. Tennessee Williams, *The Glass Menagerie* (1945; reprint, New York: New Directions, 1970), p. 7.

125. Bentley, *In Search of Theater,* p. 89.

126. Ciment, *Kazan on Kazan,* pp. 47–48.

127. Mielziner, *Designing for the Theatre,* p. 38.

128. Drutman, "Malden Owes Streetcar Role."

129. Schumach, "A Director Named Gadge," p. 54.

130. Richard Schechner and C. L. Mee, Jr., "The Bottomless Cup: An interview with Geraldine Page," *Tulane Drama Review* 9 (Winter 1964): 115.

131. Bentley, *In Search of Theater,* p. 86.

132. Beyer, "The State of the Theater," p. 242.

133. Shaw, "Theater: Masterpiece," p. 34.

134. Brown, "Southern Discomfort," p. 23.

135. Virginia Stevens, "Elia Kazan: Actor and Director of Stage and Screen," *Theatre Arts* 31 (December 1947): 22.

136. Ciment, *Kazan on Kazan,* p. 73.

137. Elliot Norton, "Plot But No Pity in *A Streetcar Named Desire,*" *Boston Post,* November 9, 1947.

138. Morehouse, "Keeping Up with Kazan," p. 91.

139. "Tall Grass," p. 112.

140. Morton, "Gadg," p. 122.

141. Elia Kazan, *The Understudy* (New York: Stein & Day, 1975), p. 339.

142. Fixx, "Who Cares What the Boss Thinks?" p. 114.

4. Peter Brook and *Marat/Sade:* Workshop and Production

1. J. C. Trewin, *Peter Brook: A Biography* (London: MacDonald, 1971), p. 24.

2. Kenneth Tynan, "Director as Misanthropist: On the Moral Neutrality of Peter Brook," *Theatre Quarterly* 7, no. 25 (Spring 1977): 20.

3. Stephen R. Lawson, "The Old Vic to Vincennes: Interviews with Michael Kustow and Peter Brook," *Yale/Theatre* 7, no. 1 (Fall 1975): 91.

4. Lawson, "The Old Vic to Vincennes," p. 91.

5. Charles Marowitz, "From Prodigy to Professional, as Written, Directed, and Acted by Peter Brook," *New York Times Magazine,* November 24, 1968, p. 94.

6. Peter Brook, "Style in Shakespeare Productions," in John Lehmann, ed., *Orpheus: A Symposium of the Arts* (New York: New Directions, 1948), p. 144.

7. Trewin, *Peter Brook,* p. 142.

8. Peter Brook, *The Empty Space* (New York: Avon Books, 1968), p. 74.

9. Brook, "Style in Shakespeare Productions," p. 144.

10. Tom Johnson, "Carmen in the Dirt," *Village Voice,* April 27, 1982, p. 78.

11. Kenneth Tynan, *Tynan Right and Left* (New York: Atheneum, 1967), p. 3.

12. Trewin, *Peter Brook,* p. 100.

13. Brook, *The Empty Space,* p. 86.

14. Richard David, "Drams of Eale," *Shakespeare Survey* 10 (1957): 126; and Muriel St. Claire Byrne, "The Shakespeare Season," *Shakespeare Quarterly* 8 (1957): 462.

15. John Heilpern, *Conference of the Birds* (Indianapolis: Bobbs-Merrill, 1977), p. 16.

16. Peter Brook, "From Zero to the Infinite: A Letter from Peter Brook," in Charles Marowitz, Tom Milne, and Owen Hale, eds., *The Encore Reader: A Chronicle of the New Drama* (London: Methuen, 1965), p. 251.

17. Peter Brook, "*Happy Days* and *Marienbad,*" in Marowitz, Milne, and Hale, *The Encore Reader,* pp. 169, 165, 251.

18. Peter Brook, "Search for a Hunger," *Mademoiselle,* November 1961, pp. 50, 95.

19. Brook, "Search for a Hunger," p. 50.

20. Brook, *The Empty Space,* p. 44.

21. Brook, "Search for a Hunger," p. 50.

22. Brook, "Search for a Hunger," p. 38.

23. Brook, *The Empty Space,* pp. 55, 115.

24. "Brook's Africa: An Interview with Michael Gibson," *The Drama Review* 17 (September 1973): 47.

25. Trewin, *Peter Brook,* p. 191.

26. Peter Brook, Preface to Jerzy Grotowski's *Towards a Poor Theatre* (New York: Simon & Schuster, 1968), p. 14.

27. A. C. H. Smith, *Orghast at Persepolis* (New York: Viking Press, 1973), p. 52.

28. Trewin, *Peter Brook,* p. 148.

29. Antonin Artaud, "The Spurt of Blood," in *Antonin Artaud: Selected Writings,* ed. Susan Sontag, trans. Helen Weaver (New York: Farrar, Straus & Giroux, 1976), p. 73. In Weaver's translation the world is "well made."

30. R. D. Laing, *The Politics of Experience* (New York: Pantheon Books, 1967), p. 138. See also Michel Foucault, *Madness and Civilization: A History of Insanity in the Age of Reason,* trans. Richard Howard (New York: Pantheon Books, 1965); and R. D. Laing, *The Divided Self: A Study of Sanity and Madness* (London: Tavistock, 1960).

31. Grotowski, *Towards a Poor Theatre,* p. 123.

32. Julian Beck, "Storming the Barricades," in Kenneth Brown, *The Brig* (New York: Hill & Wang, 1965), p. 24.

33. Robert Brustein, *The Theatre of Revolt: An Approach to the Modern Drama* (Boston: Little, Brown & Co., 1964), pp. 361–411.

34. Judith Malina, "Directing *The Brig,*" in Brown, *The Brig,* pp. 83, 86, 90.

35. Brook, *The Empty Space,* p. 55.

36. Brook, *The Empty Space,* p. 44.

37. Joseph Chaikin, *The Presence of the Actor* (New York: Atheneum, 1972), p. 54.

38. Andrzej Wirth, "Brecht and Grotowski," *Brecht Heute/Brecht Today* 1 (1971): 189–90.

39. Viola Spolin, *Improvisation for the Theater: A Handbook of Teaching and Directing Techniques* (Evanston, Ill.: Northwestern University Press, 1963).

40. Charles Marowitz, *Confessions of a Counterfeit Critic: A London Theatre Notebook, 1958–1971* (London: Eyre Methuen, 1973), p. 102.

41. Charles Marowitz, "Notes on the Theatre of Cruelty," *The Drama Review* 11 (Winter 1966): 155.

42. Marowitz, "Notes on the Theatre of Cruelty," p. 155.

43. Brook, *The Empty Space,* p. 45.

44. Brook, *The Empty Space,* p. 47.

45. Goodman quoted in Brown, *The Brig,* p. 23.

46. Marowitz, "Notes on the Theatre of Cruelty," pp. 160–61.

47. Brook, *The Empty Space,* p. 46.

48. Marowitz, "Notes on the Theatre of Cruelty," p. 156.

49. Brook, *The Empty Space,* pp. 122–23.

50. *Times* (London), January 1, 1964, p. 13.

51. Trewin, *Peter Brook,* p. 141.

52. "Audience Inside the Workshop," *Times* (London), January 13, 1964, p. 12.

53. Martin Esslin, "The Theater of Cruelty," *New York Times Magazine,* March 6, 1966, p. 72.

54. Marowitz, "From Prodigy to Professional," p. 108.

55. Brook, *The Empty Space*, p. 118.

56. Marowitz, "Notes on the Theatre of Cruelty," p. 172.

57. Brook, *The Empty Space*, p. 49.

58. Marowitz, "From Prodigy to Professional," p. 108.

59. Brook, "Search for a Hunger," p. 40.

60. Brook, *The Empty Space*, p. 47.

61. Marowitz, "Notes on the Theatre of Cruelty," p. 169.

62. Charles Marowitz, "Lear Log," in Charles Marowitz and Simon Trussler, eds., *Theatre at Work: Playwrights and Productions in the Modern British Theatre* (London: Methuen, 1967), p. 146.

63. Brook, *The Empty Space*, pp. 68–69, 65.

64. Brook, *The Empty Space*, p. 66; and Brook, Introduction to the U.S. publication of *Marat/Sade* (New York: Pocket Books, 1966), p. 6.

65. Brook, "Search for a Hunger," p. 50.

66. Brook, *The Empty Space*, p. 71.

67. Brook, "Search for a Hunger," p. 50.

68. Trewin, *Peter Brook*, p. 143.

69. Jean-Paul Sartre, *Saint Genet: Actor and Martyr*, trans. Bernard Frechtman (New York: George Braziller, 1963).

70. Grigori Kozintsev, *Shakespeare: Time and Conscience*, trans. Joyce Vining (New York: Hill & Wang, 1966), p. 33.

71. Esslin, "The Theater of Cruelty," pp. 73, 72.

72. Marowitz, "Notes on the Theatre of Cruelty," p. 171.

73. Marowitz, "Lear Log," p. 135.

74. Marowitz, "From Prodigy to Professional," pp. 105–6.

75. Smith, *Orghast at Persepolis*, p. 109.

76. Irving Drutman, "Was Peter Brook Its Brain?" *New York Times*, January 9, 1966, sec. 2, p. 20.

77. Smith, *Orghast at Persepolis*, p. 17.

78. Trewin, *Peter Brook*, p. 145.

79. Drutman, "Was Peter Brook Its Brain?" p. 20.

80. Heilpern, *Conference of the Birds*, p. 9.

81. Charles Marowitz, "The Honesty of a Suburban Superstar," *New York Times Magazine*, January 19, 1975, p. 52.

82. Jacques Derrida, *Writing and Difference*, trans. Alan Bass (Chicago: Univ. of Chicago Press, 1978), p. 65.

83. Richard Peaslee, "Notes by the Composer," on *Marat/Sade* (Caedmon Records, TRS-312, 1966).

84. Brook, *The Empty Space*, p. 113.

85. Lawson, "The Old Vic to Vincennes," p. 90.

86. "*Marat/Sade* Forum," *The Drama Review* 10 (Summer 1966): p. 236.

87. Smith, *Orghast at Persepolis*, p. 109.

88. Lawson, "The Old Vic to Vincennes," p. 90.

89. I have quoted without page citation from Peter Weiss, *The Persecution and Assassination of Jean-Paul Marat as Performed by the Inmates of the Asylum of Charenton under the Direction of the Marquis de Sade*, trans. Geoffrey Skelton and Adrian Mitchell (New York: Atheneum, 1966).

90. Marowitz, "Lear Log," p. 137.

91. Smith, *Orghast at Persepolis*, p. 124.

92. Trewin, *Peter Brook*, p. 147.

93. Theophilus Lewis, "Marat/DeSade," *America*, January 29, 1966, p. 182.

94. Irving Wardle, "Actors at Their New Exercise," *Times* (London), July 19, 1968, p. 13.

95. "Ambitious Example of Theatre of Cruelty," *Times* (London), August 21, 1964, p. 11.

96. John Gross, "1793 and All That," *Encounter* 23 (November 1964): 59.

97. Frank Kermode, "Tell Me Lies about Viet Nam," *Encounter* 28 (January 1967): 62.

98. Jack Richardson, "The Best of Broadway," *Commentary* 41 (March 1966): 76.

99. "*Marat/Sade* Forum," p. 225.

100. Brook, Introduction to *Marat/Sade*, p. 6.

101. Brook, "From Zero to the Infinite," p. 248.

102. Stanley Kauffmann, "The Provocative *Marat/Sade*," *New York Times*, January 9, 1966, sec. 2, p. 1.

103. Gross, "1793 and All That," p. 59.

104. "Playwright of Many Interests," *Times* (London), August 19, 1964, p. 5.

105. Brook, *The Empty Space*, p. 67.

106. Bertolt Brecht, *The Threepenny Opera*, trans. Desmond Vesey and Eric Bentley (New York: Grove Press, 1964), p. 108.

107. These lines (as punctuated) are quoted from *The Persecution and Assassination of Jean-Paul Marat as Performed by the Inmates of the Asylum of Charenton under the Direction of the Marquis de Sade* (Chicago: The Dramatic Publishing Company, n.d.), p. 109.

108. These lines (with my own punctuation) are quoted from the phonograph version of *Marat/Sade* (Caedmon, TRS-312, 1966).

109. These lines are quoted from the Dramatic Publishing Company's playbook version of *Marat/Sade*, pp. 109-10. In the movie, Magee uses a slightly different and more speakable version of the final couplet: "So for me the last word never can be spoken. / I'm left with a question that is always open."

110. "Peter Brook Interviewed by A. J. Liehm," *Theatre Quarterly* 3, no. 10 (April–June 1973): 15.

111. Brook, *The Empty Space,* p. 68.

112. Brook, *The Empty Space,* p. 36.

113. Brook, *The Empty Space,* pp. 123–24.

114. Brook, "*Happy Days* and *Marienbad,*" p. 165.

115. "*Marat/Sade* Forum," p. 228.

116. "Brook's Africa: An Interview with Michael Gibson," p. 49.

Index

Compositor: Innovative Media
Text: 10/12 Times Roman
Display: Goudy Bold & Times Roman
Printer: Edwards Brothers
Binder: Edwards Brothers